Mindfulness

FOR

DUMMIES®

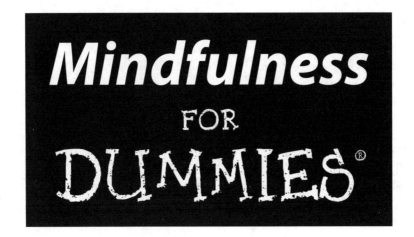

by Shamash Alidina

Foreword by Steven D. Hickman, Psy.D.
Clinical Psychologist, Assistant Clinical Professor, University of California at San Diego, Department of Psychiatry, Director, UCSD Center for Mindfulness

A John Wiley and Sons, Ltd, Publication

Mindfulness For Dummies®

Published by
John Wiley & Sons, Ltd
The Atrium
Southern Gate
Chichester
West Sussex
PO19 8SQ
England

E-mail (for orders and customer service enquires): cs-books@wiley.co.uk

Visit our Home Page on www.wiley.com

For general information on our other products and services, please contact our Customer Care Department within the U.S. at 877-762-2974, outside the U.S. at 317-572-3993, or fax 317-572-4002.

For technical support, please visit www.wiley.com/techsupport.

Wiley also publishes its books in a variety of electronic formats. Some content that appears in print may not be available in electronic books.

British Library Cataloguing in Publication Data: A catalogue record for this book is available from the British Library

ISBN: 978-0-470-66086-7 (hardback), ISBN 978-0-470-66515-2 (ebk),

ISBN 978-0-470-66374-5 (ebk), ISBN 978-0-470-66375-2 (ebk)

Printed and bound in Great Britain by Bell & Bain Ltd, Glasgow

10 9 8 7 6 5 4

WILEY

About the Author

Shamash Alidina has been practising mindfulness since 1998. He was invited to experiment with a short mindfulness exercise whilst studying in an Eastern philosophy evening class, and caught the mindfulness bug! He was amazed at the power of mindfulness meditation to transform his state of mind, both during the meditation itself, and through exercises in day to day life. He decided to dedicate his time to learn and teach mindfulness to others. He taught mindfulness to groups of adults, and then additionally taught in a children's school in London for eight years which integrated meditation into the curriculum.

Shamash formally trained at Bangor University's Centre for Mindfulness in Wales. He runs his own successful training organisation, *Learn-Mindfulness. com*, to teach mindfulness professionally to the general public, as well as to coaches, therapists, clinicians and business organisations, both in-person and through distance learning. He has trained in managing workplace health with the Health and Safety Executive and regularly coaches executives in stress reduction. He has taught mindfulness all over the world, including the Middle East, the USA and Europe.

Shamash has been interviewed by several national newspapers in the UK, including the *Sunday Times Magazine*, has featured in mindfulness campaigns, and regularly blogs on his two main passions, mindfulness and advaita philosophy. He currently lives in London next to the delightful Bushey Park.

Dedication

This book is dedicated to you, the reader. May the practice of mindfulness be of benefit to you, and those close to you.

Author's Acknowledgements

I would like to personally thank Jennifer Prytherch and Nicole Hermitage from Wiley for commissioning me to write this book on such a topical and important subject, and for coming to visit me personally! I would also like to say a special thank you to Jo Theedom who has been so tolerant and patient of my many questions, and hugely supportive of the book throughout production. I would like to wholeheartedly extend my thanks to the whole production team at Wiley, especially Rachel Chilvers, Anne O'Rorke and Zoe Wykes for their incredible attention to detail - I must say, I've honestly been very impressed by the *For Dummies* team.

Special thanks go to Sandra, for sharing my excitement of the project, and providing the many cups of tea while I spent evenings and weekends either practising mindfulness exercises, or staring intently at my laptop looking confused. Thanks to my brother, Aneesh, who first suggested the idea of *Mindfulness For Dummies*, and my parents Manju and Fateh, who supported me throughout. Thanks to Sarah Silverton of Bangor University's Centre of Mindfulness, who commented on some of the chapters, and Jon Kabat-Zinn for his comments and positive support. Thanks to my wonderful friends Maneesh Juneja, for his encouragement, comments and advice on some chapters and Garry Boon, whose wisdom and humor continue to be a source of joy.

I would like to thank Steven Hickman, Director of the UCSD Center for Mindfulness, for his positive comments about the quotes I post on-line, and for writing a beautiful foreword to this book.

Finally I'd like to thank Ramana Maharshi, Nisargadatta and 'Sailor' Bob Adamson for their lifetime of dedication in inspiring others to look deep within themselves and discover who they truly are.

Publisher's Acknowledgements

We're proud of this book; please send us your comments through our Dummies online registration form located at www.dummies.com/register/.

Some of the people who helped bring this book to market include the following:

Commissioning, Editorial, and Media Development

Project Editor: Jo Theedom

Commissioning Editor: Nicole Hermitage

Assistant Editor: Ben Kemble

Development Editor: Rachael Chilvers

Copy Editor: Anne O'Rorke

Proofreader: David Price

Production Manager: Daniel Mersey

Cover Photos: © Okea/Fotolia

Cartoons: Rich Tennant
(www.the5thwave.com)

CD Recording and Production:
Heavy Entertainment, with special thanks to Davy Nougarède and David Roper

Composition Services

Project Coordinator: Lynsey Stanford

Layout and Graphics: Ashley Chamberlain, Joyce Haughey

Proofreader: Lauren Mandelbaum

Indexer: Christine Karpeles

Special Help

Brand Reviewer: Zoe Wykes

Contents at a Glance

Table of Contents

Part IV: Reaping the Rewards of Mindfulness 181

Chapter 11: Discovering Greater Happiness 183

Chapter 12: Reducing Stress, Anger and Fatigue 199

Foreword

Sitting down to start a book has many similarities to sitting down to a great meal. There is a warm felt sense of anticipation (in body and mind) of a pleasant experience. There is curiosity in the mind. There is an awareness of a certain "hunger" for what is about to be taken in. And there we are, fully present to what we encounter before us: whether it is the visual experience of the design of the book or the plate presentation of the meal, whether it is the aroma of a desired food or the fresh smell of a newly-printed and opened book. Perhaps this captures something of your experience as you read these words, but on the other hand, as they say, "your mileage may vary." Take a moment to stop and notice what your experience ACTUALLY is right now in this very moment. What is the quality of your mind? What do you notice in your body? Are you aware of your breath moving in and out of your body, essentially "breathing itself"?

Few things are more elementally basic and simple, yet so hard to convey in words and instructions, than mindfulness. At its essence it is simply being present, to our experience, our whole experience, and nothing but our experience. Yet you can read that previous sentence dozens, even millions of times, and still not know (at a level well below words) how to systematically practice it and bring it into your life with all its stresses and challenges. The only way to truly know mindfulness and cultivate it in one's life is to practice it like your life depends on it. Because in many ways it does. The degree to which you can be fully present to your experience, letting go of judgment when it is not useful and truly seeing things as they are, really determines the degree of suffering and stress you will experience in this crazy life of ours.

So the biggest difference between sitting down to this book and sitting down to a fine meal in a gourmet restaurant is that this book, as wonderful, instructional and inspirational as it is, is simply the menu and not the meal itself. We've all seen many beautiful menus in amazing restaurants the world over, but not one of them would have tasted anything like the meals they described! Those menus, like *Mindfulness for Dummies*, simply (but elegantly) point to the **real** heart of the matter: the *practice* of mindfulness. A practice that has the potential to nourish and fulfill us in ways that nothing else truly can, and bring equanimity, kindness and balance into every corner of our busy, full lives.

So, the invitation is to approach this book as Derek Wolcott (in his poem *Love After Love*) suggests we approach our very existence: "Sit. Feast on your life."

Steven D. Hickman, Psy.D., Clinical Psychologist, Assistant Clinical Professor, University of California at San Diego, Department of Psychiatry, Director, UCSD Center for Mindfulness

Introduction

· ·

*W*hen I was about eight years old, I discovered an amazing fact – I'm actually alive, on this planet, in this universe! And so is everyone else. The fact that there's a universe at all is amazing, but that I'm in it too . . . that was mind blowing. I started going round telling everyone, but they didn't share my excitement. I saw adults mechanically going to work and doing the shopping, and friends playing games, but I was conscious of an incredible sense of existence happening that they weren't able to share. It was like an amazing set of fireworks was exploding, but everyone was looking the wrong way.

As I grew up, I began to lose my grip on this sense of wonder until I stumbled upon mindfulness and a range of philosophies. I was relieved to find others who'd contemplated questions similar to mine, and to learn a way of managing my stress at the same time. I continue to enjoy asking the big questions, and find that mindfulness beautifully compliments my natural tendency to be philosophical.

In this book you can discover how to re-ignite your perception of this mystery called life, so you aren't just existing to complete to-do lists, but are actually living. You find out how to practise mindfulness, so you can integrate a new way of being into your everyday life, helping you to cope with managing stress, challenging emotions, and increasing your general sense of wellbeing in a rich variety of different ways.

About This Book

Mindfulness For Dummies provides you with the tools to practise mindfulness on your own. Each chapter is brimming with insights about what mindfulness is, how to practise mindfulness quickly and easily, and how to deepen your experience. I wrote this book with the beginner in mind, but the knowledge goes far deeper, and experienced mindfulness practitioners will find lots of new aspects to ponder. As the research on mindfulness continues to develop rapidly, I've chosen to explain in detail the core mindfulness practices and approaches that have been tested many times before and found to be effective.

Conventions Used in This Book

To help you get the most from this book, I follow a few conventions:

- *Italic* emphasises and highlights new words or terms that I define.
- **Boldfaced** text indicates the action part of numbered steps.
- `Monofont` text displays web addresses.

What You're Not to Read

You don't have to read everything in this book. From time to time you'll see grey boxes – sidebars – which contain interesting bits of info and stories which may amuse or inform, but aren't crucial to your understanding of the fundamentals. Read them, or not – whatever you want.

I hope you'll get something from the 'Wise Words' icon next to some of the text, but again, feel free to ignore them to your heart's content.

Foolish Assumptions

In writing this book, I made a few assumptions about who you are:

- You're keen to learn more about mindfulness, but don't know exactly what it is, and how to practise it.
- You are willing to have a good go at trying out the various mindfulness exercises before judging if they'll work for you.
- You're interested in the many different applications of mindfulness.
- You're not afraid of a bit of mindfulness meditation.

Beyond those, I've not assumed too much, I hope. This book is for you whether you're male or female, 18 or 88.

How This Book Is Organised

I've organised *Mindfulness For Dummies* into five parts. Each part covers a range of subjects to help you to discover and practise mindfulness, and is further divided into chapters containing all the information you need.

Part 1: Introducing Mindfulness

I know you're keen to dive in and begin practising mindfulness, but you probably need to pick up a few basics from this part. Here you find out what on earth mindfulness is, and how mindfulness can help you. This is also the place to find out what you can hope to achieve if you get into this whole mindfulness thing, and practise over the long term.

Part II: Preparing the Ground for Mindful Living

Everyone knows that if you want to grow a decent plant, you need to prepare the soil, and ensure it's suitable. Well, guess what – it's the same with mindfulness. If you prepare yourself with the right attitudes and motivation, your ability to be mindful will grow big and strong. Check out this part for the lowdown on all this info, and get your mindfulness soil extremely nutritious, so you're all set to be a mindfulness superstar!

Part III: Practising Mindfulness

This is where you get down to some serious mindfulness practice and discover the core mindfulness meditations that have been tested and found to be effective for thousands of people all over the world. Also, you learn how to use mindfulness to look after yourself and enhance your relationships with others, as well as lots of clever little ways of being mindful in your daily activities, to keep you cool, calm and collected no matter what you need to deal with.

Part IV: Reaping the Rewards of Mindfulness

Mindfulness has some powerful benefits for people with a range of different issues. In these chapters you find out how you can use mindfulness to reduce stress, anxiety, depression, anger, chronic pain and other ailments. But mindfulness isn't just for reducing the bad stuff. You also discover the wonderful charm of mindfulness in helping you to feel happier, and use mindfulness with other techniques to boost your wellbeing. You can also find a chapter on how to teach mindfulness to children, as well as tips on parenting in a mindful way.

Part V: The Part of Tens

Every *For Dummies* book has one of these parts. The Part of Tens offers four fun-sized chapters covering top tips for mindful living, how mindfulness helps you, some common unhelpful ideas about mindfulness that often get people stuck, and lots of exciting sources for further study that I personally love, including books, CDs, websites and retreats.

Icons Used in This Book

Sprinkled throughout the book you'll see various icons to guide you on your way. Icons are a *For Dummies* way of drawing your attention to important stuff, interesting stuff, and stuff you really need to know how to do.

This is information you need to know: whatever else you carry away from this book, note these bits with care.

Have a go at different mindfulness exercises and tips with this icon.

Take careful note of the advice beside this icon, and you'll avoid unnecessary problems – ignore at your peril.

Find some precious pearls of wisdom and meaningful stories next to this icon.

The audio CD that comes with this book includes a selection of guided mindfulness meditations. This icon marks some of the exercises that you can find on the CD.

Where to Go from Here

I put this book together so that you can dip in and out as you please. I invite you to make good use of the Table of Contents – or the index – and jump straight into the section you fancy. You're in charge and it's up to you of course. If you're a total beginner, or not sure where to start, take a traditional approach and begin with Part I.

I wish you all the best in your mindfulness quest and hope you find something of use within these pages. Happy mindfulness!

Part I
Introducing Mindfulness

The 5th Wave   By Rich Tennant

In this part . . .

You are introduced to the star of the show, Mindfulness. You learn what it is, explore it's meaning and are taken on a mindfulness journey. You'll discover why mindfulness is so popular as you read about the benefits of mindful living for your body, thoughts, emotions and even for self-discovery.

Chapter 1

Discovering Mindfulness

· ·

· ·

Mindfulness means paying attention on purpose, in the present moment, with qualities like compassion, curiosity and acceptance.

Through being mindful, you discover how to live in the present moment in an enjoyable way rather than worrying about the past or being concerned about the future. The past has already gone and can't be changed. The future is yet to arrive and is completely unknown. The present moment, this very moment now, is ultimately the only moment you have. Mindfulness shows you how to live in this moment in a harmonious way. You find out how to make the present moment a more wonderful moment to be in – the only place you can create, decide, listen, think, smile, act or live.

You can develop and deepen mindfulness through doing mindfulness meditation on a daily basis, from a few minutes to as long as you want. This chapter introduces you to mindfulness and mindfulness meditation and welcomes you aboard a fascinating journey.

Understanding the Meaning of Mindfulness

Mindfulness was originally developed in ancient times, and can be found in Eastern and Western cultures. Mindfulness is a translation of the ancient Indian word *Sati* that means awareness, attention and remembering:

- ✔ **Awareness.** This is an aspect of being human that makes you conscious of your experiences. Without awareness, nothing would exist for you.

- ✔ **Attention.** Attention is a focused awareness; mindfulness training develops your ability to move and sustain your attention wherever and however you choose.

- ✔ **Remembering.** This aspect of mindfulness is about remembering to pay attention to your experience from moment to moment. Being mindful is easy to forget. The word *remember* originally comes from the Latin *re* 'again' and *memorari* 'be mindful of'.

Say that you want to practise mindfulness to help you cope with stress. At work, you think about your forthcoming presentation and begin to feel stressed and nervous. By becoming *aware* of this, you *remember* to focus your mindful *attention* to your own breathing rather than constantly worrying. Feeling your breath with a sense of warmth and gentleness helps slowly to calm you down. See Chapter 6 for more about mindful breathing.

Awareness from the heart

The Japanese character for mindfulness is this:

This Japanese character combines the words for 'mind' and 'heart' and beautifully captures the essence of mindfulness as not just awareness, but awareness from the heart.

Dr Jon Kabat-Zinn, who first developed mindfulness in a therapeutic setting, says: 'Mindfulness can be cultivated by paying attention in a specific way, that is, in the present moment, and as non-reactively, non-judgementally and openheartedly as possible'.

You can break down the meaning even further:

✔ **Paying attention.** To be mindful, you need to pay attention, whatever you choose to attend to.

✔ **Present moment.** The reality of being in the here and now means you just need to be aware of the way things are, *as they are now.* Your experience is valid and correct just as it is.

✔ **Non-reactively.** Normally, when you experience something, you automatically react to that experience according to your past conditioning. For example, if you think, 'I still haven't finished my work', you react with thoughts, words and actions in some shape or form. Mindfulness encourages you to *respond* to your experience rather than *react* to thoughts. A reaction is automatic and gives you no choice; a response is deliberate and considered action. (Chapter 12 delves deeper into mindful responses.)

✔ **Non-judgementally.** The temptation is to judge experience as good or bad, something you like or dislike. I want to feel bliss; I don't like feeling afraid. Letting go of judgements helps you to see things as they are rather than through the filter of your personal judgements based on past conditioning.

✔ **Openheartedly.** Mindfulness isn't just an aspect of mind. Mindfulness is of the heart as well. To be open-hearted is to bring a quality of kindness, compassion, warmth and friendliness to your experience. For example, if you notice yourself thinking 'I'm useless at meditation', you discover how to let go of this critical thought and gently turn your attention back to the focus of your meditation, whatever that may be. For more on attitudes to cultivate for mindfulness, see Chapter 4.

Looking at Mindfulness Meditation

Mindfulness meditation is a particular type of meditation that's been well-researched and tested in clinical settings.

Meditation isn't thinking about nothing. Meditation is paying attention in a systematic way to whatever you decide to focus on, which can include awareness of your thoughts. By listening to your thoughts, you discover their habitual patterns. Your thoughts have a massive impact on your emotions and the decisions you make, so being more aware of them is helpful.

In mindfulness meditation, you typically focus on one, or a combination, of the following:

- ✔ The feeling of your own breathing
- ✔ Any one of your senses
- ✔ Your body
- ✔ Your thoughts or emotions
- ✔ Whatever is most predominant in your awareness

This book and CD include guided meditations.

Mindfulness meditation comes in two distinct types:

- ✔ **Formal meditation.** This is a meditation where you intentionally take time out in your day to embark on a meditative practice. Time out gives you an opportunity to deepen your mindfulness practice, and understand more about your mind, its habitual tendencies and how to be mindful for a sustained period of time, with a sense of kindness and curiosity towards yourself and your experience. Formal meditation is mind training. Chapter 6 contains more about formal meditation.

- ✔ **Informal meditation.** This is where you go into a focused and meditative state of mind as you go about your daily activities such as cooking, cleaning, walking to work, talking to a friend, driving – anything at all. In this way, you continue to deepen your ability to be mindful, and train your mind to stay in the present moment rather than habitually straying into the past or future. Informal mindfulness meditation means you can rest in a mindful awareness at any time of day, whatever you're doing. See Chapter 8 for more ways to be mindful informally.

When I say 'practise' with regard to meditation, I don't mean a rehearsal. To practise meditation means to engage in the meditation exercise – not practising in the sense of aiming one day to get the meditation perfect. You don't need to judge your meditation or perfect it in any way. Your experience is your experience.

Using Mindfulness to Help You

You know how you get lost in thoughts? Most of the day, as you go about your daily activities, your mind is left to think whatever it wants. You're operating on 'automatic pilot mode' (explained more fully in Chapter 5). But some of your automatic thoughts may be unhelpful to you, or perhaps you're so stuck in those thoughts, you don't actually experience the world around you. For example, you go for a walk in the park to relax, but your mind is lost in thoughts about your next project. First, you're not really living in the present moment, and second, you're making yourself more stressed, anxious, or depressed if your thoughts are unhelpful. (Chapters 12 and 13 explore overcoming unhelpful thoughts.)

Mindfulness isn't focused on fixing problems. Mindfulness emphasises acceptance first, and change may or may not come later. So, if you suffer from anxiety, mindfulness shows you how to accept the feeling of anxiety rather than denying or fighting the feeling, and through this approach, change naturally comes about. As an old saying goes, 'What we resist, persists'. Mindfulness says, 'What you accept, transforms'.

This section explores the many ways in which mindfulness can help you.

In mindfulness, acceptance means to *acknowledge* your present moment experience. Acceptance doesn't mean resignation, or giving up.

Allowing space to heal

Physical illness can be a distressing time. Your condition may be painful, or even life-threatening. Perhaps your illness means you're no longer able to do the simple things in life you took for granted before, like run up the stairs or look after yourself in an independent way. Illness can shake you to your very core. How can you cope with this? How can you build your inner strength to manage the changes that take place, without being overwhelmed and losing all hope?

High levels of stress, particularly over a long period of time, have been clearly shown to reduce the strength of your immune system. Perhaps you went down with flu after a period of high stress. Research on care-givers who experience high levels of stress for long periods of time shows that they have a weaker immune system in responses to diseases like flu.

Mindfulness reduces stress and for this reason is one way of managing illness. By reducing your stress you improve the effectiveness of your immune system, and this may help increase the rate of healing from the illness you suffer, especially if the illness is stress-related.

Mindfulness can reduce stress, anxiety, pain and depression, and boost energy, creativity, the quality of relationships and your overall sense of wellbeing. The more you do mindfulness, the better – monks who've practised mindfulness all their lives have levels of wellbeing measured in their brains way above anything scientists thought was possible.

Chapter 14 is all about how mindfulness can help to heal the body.

Enjoying greater relaxation

Mindfulness can lead to relaxation but remember that *the aim of mindfulness is not relaxation.*

Mindfulness is the development of awareness of your inner and outer experiences, whatever they are, with a sense of kindness, curiosity and acceptance. However, relaxation is a possible by-product of mindfulness. You may experience very deep states of relaxation when practising mindfulness, or you may not. If you don't, this doesn't mean you're practising mindfulness incorrectly.

Why is relaxation not the aim? Try being totally relaxed for the next few minutes. Can you 'do' relaxation? If you aim for relaxation, you're going to succeed, or fail. If you feel you're failing, you're just going to become more tense and stressed, which is exactly what you don't want. In mindfulness, you can't fail because you don't have some experience you have to achieve. You simply practise paying attention to whatever your experience is, as best you can, and whatever happens, happens. You gain an understanding from your experience.

Table 1-1 shows the difference between relaxation and mindfulness exercises.

Table 1-1	Relaxation versus Mindfulness	
Exercise	*Aim*	*Method*
Mindfulness	To pay attention to your experience from moment to moment, as best you can, with kindness, curiosity and acknowledgment	To observe your experience and shift your attention back to its focus if you drift into thought, without self-criticism if you can
Relaxation	To become more relaxed	Various, such as tightening and letting go of muscles

Improving productivity

To be mindful, you usually need to do one thing at a time. When walking, you just walk. When listening, you just listen. When writing, you just write. By practising formal and informal mindfulness meditation, you're training your brain. You're training it to pay attention with mindful attitudes like kindness, curiosity and acknowledgement.

So, if you're writing a report, you focus on that activity as much as you can, without overly straining. Each time your mind wanders off to another thought, you notice what you were thinking about (curiosity), and then without criticising (remember you're being kind to yourself), you guide your attention back to the writing. So, you finish your report sooner (less time spent thinking about other stuff), and the work is probably of better quality (because you gave the report your full attention). The more you can focus on what you're doing, the more you can get done. Wow – with mindfulness you can improve your productivity!

You can't suddenly decide to focus on your work and then become focused. The power of attention isn't just a snap decision you make. You can train attention, just as you can train your biceps in a gym. Meditation is gym for the mind. However, you don't need to make a huge effort as you do when working out. When training the mind to be attentive, you need to be gentle, or the mind becomes less attentive. This is why mindfulness requires a kindness about it. If you're too harsh, your mind rebels.

Awareness also means that you notice where energy is being wasted. If you have a habit of worrying or thinking negatively, you can become aware of such thoughts and try to stop them.

Stress is the biggest cause of absenteeism (not turning up to work). Mindfulness is one way of managing your stress levels and therefore increasing productivity, as you're more likely to stay healthy and be able to work in the first place. (Perhaps that's not a benefit after all!)

Your work also becomes more enjoyable if you're mindful, and when you're enjoying something you're more creative and productive. If you're training your mind to be curious about experience rather than bored, you can be curious about whatever you engage in.

Eventually, through experience, you begin to notice that work flows through you, rather than you doing the work. You find yourself feeding the children or making that presentation. You lose the sense of 'me' doing this and become more relaxed and at ease. When this happens, the work is totally effortless, often of very high quality and thoroughly enjoyable – sounds like a nice kind of productivity, doesn't it?

Exploring for personal discovery

Many people begin coming to mindfulness meditation to reduce their levels of stress but as their stress levels reduce they continue to practise in order to help regulate their other emotions, and discover a greater emotional balance. Eventually, meditation becomes a quest for personal discovery.

The word *person* comes from the Latin word *persona*, originally meaning character in a drama, or mask. The word *discovery* means to dis-cover or to uncover. So in this sense, personal discovery is about uncovering your mask.

You probably wear all sorts of different masks for different roles that you play. You may be a parent, daughter or son, partner, employee. Each of these roles asks you to fulfil certain obligations. But who are you behind all these masks?

Mindfulness is an opportunity to discover your true self. In meditation you sometimes have clear experiences of being who you are. You may feel a deep, undivided sense of peace, of stillness and calm. Your physical body, that feels so solid and real, sometimes fades into the background of your awareness, and you have a sense of being more than yourself.

Some people become very attached to these experiences and try hard to repeat them, as if they're 'getting closer' to something. However, over time you come to realise that even these seemingly blissful experiences also come and go. Your true nature, who you truly are, isn't just a feeling. You are that witness, that observer, that which is aware of all that arises and passes away in your mind. This isn't so much an experience to be gained, but something very simple that everyone can observe. In fact, being naturally yourself is so simple, you easily overlook it.

According to Eastern philosophy, as a witness you are perfect, whole and complete just as you are. You don't feel as if you are because you identify with your thoughts and emotions, which are always changing. Ultimately you don't need to do anything to attain this natural state, because you are this natural state all the time – right here and right now.

As Shakespeare said, 'All the world's a stage, and all the men and women merely players'. In this way, you begin to see your roles, your persona or mask(s), as part of the game of life. You still do everything you did before; you can keep helping people or making money or whatever you like doing, but know that this is only one way of seeing things, one dimension of your true nature.

Self-knowledge leads to a freedom from suffering as pointed at by an Indian sage, Ramana Maharshi:

'Wanting to reform the world without discovering one's true self is like trying to cover the world with leather to avoid the pain of walking on stones and thorns. It is much simpler to wear shoes.'

Once you see that you're the witness of all experience, you're no longer disturbed by the ups and downs of life. This understanding offers you the freedom from suffering. You go with the flow and enjoy the play of creation.

Starting the Mindfulness Adventure

Mindfulness isn't a quick fix but the adventure of a lifetime. Imagine mindfulness as being like a journey on a boat. You're an explorer looking for new and undiscovered land. Along the way I'll explain how mindfulness mirrors such a journey.

Beginning the voyage

The journey begins and you set sail. You're not sure what you're going to find, and you may not be too sure why you're going in the first place, but that's part of the excitement and adventure. You may think that you're finally doing something you really enjoy and can gain from. This is what you wanted to do and you're on the boat now. At the same time, you're a bit anxious about what may happen – what if things don't work out?

The beginning of the mindfulness journey may feel like this for you. You may be thinking, 'Finally, I've found what I need to do', and you're keen to find out how to do it, being curious and in anticipation. At the same time, you may feel unsure that you can 'do' mindfulness – you suspect you don't have the patience/focus/discipline/inner strength. You have *ideas* about the journey of mindfulness. At the moment you may suffer from x and y, and after reading this book, you want to have reduced those painful feelings. You may have clear goals you want to achieve and hope mindfulness is going to help you to achieve those goals.

 Having a long-term vision as to what you hope to achieve from mindfulness is helpful, but concentrating too much on goals is unhelpful. Mindfulness is ultimately a goal-less activity. Mindfulness is process-oriented rather than goal-oriented. You're not actually going anywhere. This is the paradox of meditation. If you get overly obsessed with the goals, you focus on the goal rather than the process. However, meditation is the journey itself. You aren't going to reach the present moment sometime in the future – you can only be in the present moment *now*. More important than anything else is how you meet this moment. If you can train yourself to be open, curious, accepting, kind and aware of this moment, the future takes care of itself. So, as you steer your boat, keep aware and awake. See Chapter 3 for more about vision in mindfulness.

Overcoming challenges

As you continue your mindfulness journey, before long the initial excitement begins to wear off. You experience rough seas and pirates! Some days, you wish you weren't on this journey in the first place. Perhaps you should have just stayed at home.

Regularly practising mindfulness can be challenging. What was new and exciting to begin with no longer feels fresh. You may sense a resistance to sit down and meditate, even for a short period, but without knowing why. Don't worry – this is very common. When you overcome the initial resistance, you may discover the practice isn't as bad as you imagined meditating to be. As soon as you start, you feel okay and even enjoy it. You also feel great after-wards, because you managed to overcome the initial resistance of your mind to do something for your own health and wellbeing.

Each time you struggle with the thoughts and feelings in your meditation, you're generally not accepting or acknowledging them as the natural state of your mind. Lack of acknowledgement usually means criticism of yourself or of the whole process of meditation. If you persevere, you discover slowly and surely the importance of accepting your thoughts and emotions and the situation you're in and not blaming anyone for that situation, including yourself. In mindfulness, acceptance always comes first, change comes after.

Another common challenge is understanding the right attitude to bring to your meditation. Unhelpful but common attitudes include:

- ✔ I'm going do this and must get it right.
- ✔ I should focus 100 per cent.
- ✔ I'm going to try extremely hard.

Having done a bit of meditation, you get thoughts like 'I can't focus at all' or 'My mind was all over the place. I can't do it' or 'That was a bad meditation'. However, as you continue your journey of mindfulness, your attitudes begin to shift towards thoughts such as:

- ✔ I'm going to bring an attitude of kindness and curiosity and acknowledge whatever my experience is, as best I can.
- ✔ I won't try too hard, nor will I give up. I'll stay somewhere in the middle.
- ✔ My mind is bound to wander off. That's okay and part of meditation.

As your attitudes change, meditation becomes easier as you're bombarded by fewer judgemental thoughts during and after the meditation. And even if you are, you treat them like all the other thoughts you experience, and let them go as best you can.

Reaching the other side

One day, a young man was going for a walk when he reached a wide river. He spent a long time wondering how he would cross such a gushing current. Just when he was about to give up his journey, he saw his teacher on the other side. The young man shouted from the bank, 'Can you tell me how to get to the other side of this river?'

The teacher smiled and replied, 'My friend, you are on the other side.'

You may feel that you have to change, when actually you just have to realise that perhaps you're fine just the way you are. You're running to achieve goals so that you can be peaceful and happy, but actually you're running away from the peace and happiness. Mindfulness is an invitation to stop running and rest. You're already on the other side.

Exploring the journey of a lifetime

After sailing for a long time, you finally see some land in the distance that's more beautiful than anything you've seen in your exploration. You decide to stop when you get there. The land looks so new and fresh, but at the same time, very familiar and cosy. As you draw closer, you discover that you're approaching your own house. Of all the places you've been and all the adventures you've had, you feel most at home here, where you left! However, the journey hasn't been fruitless. You've discovered much along the way, and had to travel that journey to discover what you most treasure.

Ultimately in meditation, you realise that you don't need to search for anything at all. Everything is okay just the way things are. You're already home. Each moment is magical, new and fresh. Each moment is a treasure never to be repeated again, ever. Your awareness is always shining, lighting up the world around you and inside you effortlessly. Awareness has no off or on switch – awareness is always effortlessly on. Although you experience ups and downs, pleasures and pain, you no longer hang on to things so much, and you therefore suffer less. This isn't so much a final goal as an ongoing journey of a lifetime. Life continues to unfold in its own way and you begin to grasp how to flow with life.

Buddha is quoted as saying:

> *The secret of health for both mind and body is not to mourn for the past, worry about the future, or anticipate troubles, but to live in the present moment wisely and earnestly.*

The journey of mindfulness is to discover how to live this way.

Chapter 2

Enjoying the Benefits of Mindfulness

*T*he enjoyment that comes from mindfulness is a bit like the enjoyment that comes from dancing. Do you dance because of the cardiovascular benefits, or for boosting your brain by following a tricky dance routine? When you dance with a goal or motive in mind, it kind of spoils it a bit, doesn't it? Dancing for the sake of dancing is far more fun. But of course, dancing for the sheer pleasure of it doesn't reduce the benefits of dancing on your mind and body – they're just the icing on the cake.

In the same way, be mindful for the sake of being mindful. Mindfulness is about connecting with your senses, being curious, exploring the inner working of the human mind. If you're too concerned about reaping the benefits of mindfulness meditation, you spoil the fun of it. The journey of meditation isn't to reach a certain destination – the journey *is* the destination. Keep this in mind as you read the various benefits of mindfulness described in this chapter and let the dance of mindfulness unfold within you. The benefits of mindfulness – relaxation, better mental and emotional health and an improved relationship with yourself and others – are just the added bonuses along the way. Read on to discover how mindfulness can help you.

Relaxing the Body

The body and mind are almost one entity. If your mind is tense with anxious thoughts, your body automatically tenses as well. They go together, hand in hand.

Why does your body become tense when you experience high levels of stress? The reason is mechanical and wired in the human body. When you experience stress, a chain reaction starts in your body, and your whole being prepares to fight or flee the situation. So a lot of energy surges through your body, which doesn't know what to do with this energy, so you tense up.

The aim of mindfulness isn't to make you more relaxed. *Trying* to relax just creates more tension. Mindfulness goes far deeper than that. Mindfulness, a mindful awareness, is about becoming aware and accepting of your moment-by-moment experience. So if you're tense, mindfulness means becoming aware of that tension. Which part of your body feels tense? What's its shape, colour, texture? What's your reaction to the tension, your thoughts? Mindfulness is about bringing curiosity to your experience. Then you can begin breathing into the tense part of your body, bringing kindness and acknowledging your experience – again, not trying to change or get rid of the tension. And that's it. Rest assured, doing this often leads to relaxation, but relaxation isn't the *aim*. See Chapter 12 for more on stress reduction.

Getting back in touch

As a baby, you were probably very much in touch with your body. You noticed subtle sensations, and may have enjoyed feeling different textures in the world around you. As you grew up, you learnt to use your head more and your body less. You probably aren't as in touch with your body as you were as a young child and don't notice those subtle messages that the body gives to you, through the mind. I'm sure that some people see the body as simply a vehicle for carrying the brain from one meeting to another!

In fact, the messages between your mind and body are a two-way process. Your mind gives signals to your body, and your body gives signals to your mind. You think, 'I fancy reading that *For Dummies* book' and your body picks it up. You feel hungry and your body signals to your mind that it's time to eat. What about the feeling of stress? If you notice the tension in your shoulders, the twitch in your eye or the rapid beating of your heart, again your body is sending signals to your mind.

But what if your mind is so busy with its own thoughts that it doesn't even notice the signals from your body? When this happens, you're no longer in touch with or looking after your body. Hunger and thirst, tiredness and stress – you're no longer hearing clearly your instinctual messages. This leads to a further disconnection between bodily signals and your mind, so things can get worse. Stress can spiral out of control.

Mindfulness emphasises awareness of your body. An important mindfulness meditation is the body scan (described in full in Chapter 6). In this meditation, you spend about 30 minutes or so simply being guided to pay attention to different parts of your body, from the tips of your toes to the top of your head. Some people's reaction is, 'Wow, I've never paid so much attention to my body, that was interesting!' or 'I now feel I'm moving back into my body'.

You may find the body scan a challenging experience if you're not used to being so in touch with your own body. Emotions you experienced in the past but weren't ready to feel, perhaps because you were too young, can be suppressed and trapped in the body. Sometimes, people suffer for years from a particular physical ailment but doctors are unable to explain the cause of it. Then, through counselling or meditation, the suppressed emotion arises into consciousness, which releases the emotion. The tightness in the body, or unexplained 'dis-ease', sometimes disappears with the release of the emotion. This is another example of how interconnected mind and body really are, and the benefits of getting back in touch with the body. Chapter 14 has more on healing the body through mindfulness.

The cracked pot

Once upon a time there was a water bearer who carried two pots of water to his teacher each day. Each day he would walk to the nearest stream, fill both pots with water, and walk back, one pot on each side of a pole he carried across his neck. One pot was cracked and so by the time the water bearer reached his teacher, it was only half full. This continued for two years, with the water bearer only bringing one and a half pots of water. The perfect pot was proud of its achievements. The cracked pot was sad that it could only do half the job it was supposed to do. One day, the cracked pot said to the water bearer, 'I feel so upset and ashamed. I'm imperfect and I can't hold a full pot of water. What use am I to anyone?' The water bearer told the cracked pot to look on the ground as he carried it. The cracked pot noticed the most beautiful wild flowers and plants on its side of the path. The water bearer explained, 'When I realised you were cracked, I decided to plant seeds on one side of the path, and every day, as you leak, you water that side of the path. If you weren't cracked, these gorgeous flowers wouldn't be here for all to enjoy.'

Sometimes you may think you're not perfect, or your mindfulness practice is not perfect, but how do you know? This story goes to show even a cracked pot can be seen as perfect, just as it is. In the same way, you're perfect just the way you are, with all your imperfections – that's what makes you unique.

Boosting your immune system

If something's wrong with your body, normally your immune system deals with it by fighting disease. Unfortunately, one aspect of the stress response is your immune system not working as hard. When threatened, your body puts all its resources into surviving that threat; energy required for digestion or immunity is turned off temporarily.

Stress isn't necessarily bad for you. If your stress levels are too low, you're unable to perform effectively and get bored easily. However, if you're stressed for sustained periods of time at high levels, your body's natural immune system is going to stop working properly.

Mindfulness enables you to notice subtle changes in your body. At the first sign of excessive stress, you can bring a mindful awareness to the situation and discover how to dissipate the stress rather than exacerbate it. In this way, mindfulness can really benefit your immune system.

Reducing pain

Amazingly, mindfulness has been proved to actually reduce the level of pain experienced in people practising it over a period of eight weeks. I've had clients who couldn't find anything to help them manage and cope with their pain until they began using mindfulness meditation.

When you experience pain, you quite naturally want to block that pain out. You tighten your muscles around the region and make an effort to distract yourself. Another approach is that you want the pain to stop, so you react towards the pain in an angry way. This creates greater tension, not only in the painful region, but in other areas of the body. Sometimes you may feel like fighting the pain. This creates a duality between you and your pain and you burn energy to battle with it. Or perhaps you react with resignation – the pain has got the better of you and you feel helpless.

Mindfulness takes a radically different approach. In mindfulness, you're encouraged to pay attention to the sensation of pain, as far as you can. So, if your knee is hurting, rather than distracting yourself or reacting in any other way, you actually focus on the area of physical pain with a mindful awareness. This means you bring attitudes like kindness, curiosity and acknowledgment towards the area of pain, as best you can. This isn't easy, but you can get better with practice. You can then consider the difference between the sensation of the physical pain itself, and all the other stuff you bring to the pain. You begin to understand the difference between *physical* pain and *psychological* pain. The physical pain is the actual raw sensation of pain in the body, whereas the psychological pain is the stress, anxiety and frustration generated. Through mindfulness, you begin to let go of psychological pain so that all that's left is the physical pain. When the psychological pain begins to dissolve, the muscle tension around the physical pain begins to loosen, further reducing the perception of pain. You begin to be able to accept the pain as it is in this present moment. Read Chapter 14 for more about mindfulness and physical healing.

Calming the Mind

Just as the aim of mindfulness isn't to relax the body, though this sometimes happens, so the aim of mindfulness isn't to calm the mind, though this sometimes happens too.

Your mind is like the ocean – occasionally wild, and at other times calm. Sometimes your mind goes from thought to thought without stopping to rest. At other times, your thoughts come slower and have more of a space between them. Mindfulness isn't so much about changing the rate of your thoughts, but about noticing the thoughts arising in the first place. By taking a step back from thoughts, you can hover above the waves. The waves are still there, but you have more possibility of watching the show rather than being controlled by the thoughts themselves.

Being too keen

A martial arts student went to his teacher and said earnestly, 'I'm devoted to studying your martial system. How long will it take me to master it?' The teacher's reply was casual, 'Ten years.' Impatiently, the student answered, 'But I want to master it faster than that. I'll work very hard. I'll practise every day, ten or more hours a day if I have to. How long will it take then?' The teacher thought for a moment and replied, 'Twenty years.'

What does this story mean to you? To me, it shows that hard work and attaining a goal don't necessarily go together. Sometimes, especially when practising something like mindfulness, you need simply to let things unfold in their own time. If you're anxious, you may just block your understanding.

Listening to your thoughts

Everything man-made around you was originally a thought in someone's head. Many people consider thought to be all-powerful. All your words, all your action and activities – everything is motivated by thought. So, being aware of the kind of thoughts going through your mind makes sense.

The brain easily gets into habitual patterns, as your thoughts travel their paths within the brain. *Neurons that fire together, wire together.* Each time you have a particular thought, or carry out a particular action, you slightly increase the chance of having the same thought again. Through repeated thinking or action, the connection between neurons strengthens. If you aren't mindful of these thoughts or actions, you may have all sorts of negative, untrue, unhelpful thoughts or behaviours that influence your life without you even being aware of them or questioning the truth or validity of them.

Mindfulness encourages you to watch your thoughts, emotions and actions; then you're better able to notice unhelpful thoughts and question their truth. Turn to Chapter 6 for a sitting meditation that includes mindfulness of thoughts.

Making better decisions

Every moment of every day you make decisions, whether you're aware of them or not. You made a decision to read this chapter. At some point, you'll decide to stop and do something else. More significant decisions you have to make have a bigger impact, and a 'good' decision is highly desirable. All that you do and have at the moment is partly due to the decisions you made in the past.

Awareness of your body can help you make better decisions – a gut feeling is a signal from your belly telling you what to do and has been found in some experiments to be faster and more accurate than logical thinking. Research shows a mass of nerves in the gut that's like a second brain. This intuition is routinely used by top CEOs of corporations to make critical decisions. For example, Michael Eisner, CEO of Walt Disney until 2005, says his body reacts when he hears a good idea. Sometimes he feels it in his stomach, sometimes his throat or his skin. Your unconscious mind has far more information than your conscious mind can handle. Making decisions just based on conscious logical thought misses out on the huge capacity of the subconscious brain. Mindfulness helps to deepen your level of awareness, and begin to tap into your intuitive, subconscious side.

Coming to your senses

One of the key ways of becoming more mindful and of calming the mind is to connect with your senses – sight, sound, touch, smell and taste. Consider the expressions, 'That was *sens*ible', 'I *sense* something's wrong', and 'She's come to her *senses*'. People's use of the word 'sense' shows we appreciate and value being in touch with our organs of perception. You know innately the value of connecting to your senses if you want to make a *sens*ible decision.

What is the benefit of purposefully connecting with your senses? Well, if you aren't paying attention to the stimulation coming through your five senses you're only paying attention to your thoughts and emotions. You're not aware of anything else. Your thoughts are mainly based on your experiences from the past, from memory. You may imagine something new, but on the whole, your mind reworks past experiences, or projects ideas into the future based on your past experiences. Emotions are also very much influenced by your thoughts. So, without paying attention to your senses, you're stuck with your own thoughts and emotions based on the past instead of the present.

By purposefully connecting with one of your senses, say, touch, you begin naturally to calm your mind a little. In mindfulness you can begin by focusing on your breathing. Focus on your belly stretching or your chest expanding or perhaps the movement of the air as it enters and leaves your body. By focusing on a particular sense, in this case the sense of touch, you're focusing your attention. Rather than your mind wandering wherever it pleases, you're gently training it to stay on one object, namely your breathing. And in the same way as you train a puppy to walk along a path and not keep running off, each time your attention strays, you bring it back, just as you would gently pull the puppy back to the path. You're discovering how to be gentle with yourself, as well as finding out to focus your attention. See Chapter 6 for a short mindful breathing meditation.

By coming to your senses mindfully you are:

- ✔ Training your attention to focus.
- ✔ Being kind to yourself when your mind wanders off.
- ✔ Realising that you've a certain amount of choice about what you pay attention to.
- ✔ Understanding that you can deliberately choose to shift attention away from thinking and into the senses.
- ✔ Calming your mind.

Creating an attentive mind

Attention is essential in achieving anything. If you can't pay attention, you can't get the job done, whatever the job is. Mindfulness trains your attention by sustaining your attention on one thing, or by switching the type of attention from time to time.

There are several types of attention, as shown in Figure 2-1:

✔ Narrow attention is focused and sharp, like the beam of a laser. You may use this type of attention when chopping vegetables or writing a letter.

✔ Wide attention is more open and spacious, like a floodlight. When you're driving, ideally your attention is open so you'd notice if a car moved closer to you from the side, or if children were playing up ahead.

✔ Outer attention is attention to the outer world through your senses.

✔ Inner attention is an awareness of your thoughts and feelings.

✔ Observer or witness awareness is your capacity to know what type of attention you're using. For example, if you're drawing a picture, you're aware that your attention is narrow. If you're walking through the countryside, you're aware that your attention is wide. For more on witness awareness, see the section 'Becoming Aware: Discovering Yourself' below.

All the different mindfulness meditations you read about in this book train your mind to be able to sustain attention in the various different ways mentioned in the preceding list.

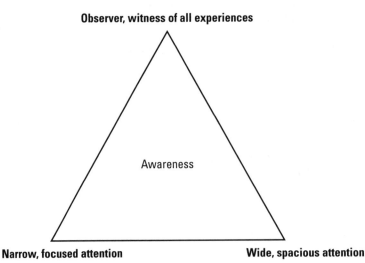

Observer, witness of all experiences

Awareness

Figure 2-1:
The different types of attention.

Narrow, focused attention   **Wide, spacious attention**

WISE WORDS

Empty your cup

A professor once went to visit a teacher of mindfulness. The professor was a world-famous scholar of mindfulness and had studied all the different ways, methods and techniques. He knew all the Eastern scriptures and Western science on the subject. He could answer any question on mindfulness with ease and a sense of pride. The teacher asked if he would like a cup of tea, and the professor said yes. The teacher began filling the cup until it was full and kept going. The tea was overflowing, and teacher continued to pour. 'What are you doing! The cup is already full!' exclaimed the professor, panicking. 'You are like this cup,' said the teacher calmly. 'How can I teach you anything of real value until you empty your cup?'

If you want to benefit from mindfulness, you need to put aside all your ideas about it, especially if you think you know what mindfulness is all about. Opinions, ideas and beliefs block the beauty and simplicity of mindfulness.

Soothing Your Emotions

Emotions are tremendously influential on your behaviour and thoughts. If you're feeling low, you're probably far more reluctant to go out with friends, or laugh at a joke, or work with zest. If you're feeling great, you're on top of things, everything feels easy and life flows easily.

How do you deal with emotions? Are you swept up by them, and just hope for the best? Mindfulness offers the opportunity to soothe and step back from emotional ups and downs.

Understanding your emotions

What is an emotion, a feeling or mood?

You experience emotion partly from a survival point of view. If you didn't feel scared when faced with a raging bull, you'd find yourself in lots of trouble. Other emotions, like happiness, help to create social ties with those around you, increasing your security. Even depression is thought to have evolved for your protection, reducing motivation and therefore the chance of experiencing harm or wasting energy through pursuing a goal.

Emotion comes from a Latin word meaning to 'move out'. If you observe emotions, you can discover certain important characteristics:

- ✔ Emotions are always changing. You aren't stuck with one emotion all your life, at the same intensity.

- ✔ Emotions are a very physical experience. If you're feeling anxious, you may feel a tingling in your stomach. If you're feeling angry, you may feel your breathing and heart rate go up.

- ✔ You can observe your own emotions. You can sense the difference between you and your emotions. You're not your emotions, you're the observer of your emotions.

- ✔ Emotions make a huge impact on your thoughts. When you're feeling down, you're likely to predict negative things about you or other people. When you're feeling happy, you're more likely to think positive thoughts, predict positive outcomes and look upon the past in a positive light too.

- ✔ Emotions tend to be pleasant, unpleasant or neutral.

Managing feelings differently

Take a few minutes to consider the following emotions, and how you deal with them:

- ✔ Anger
- ✔ Anxiety
- ✔ Fear
- ✔ Depression

Your approach may be to either avoid the emotion and pretend it isn't there, or to express your feelings to whoever is nearby. Mindfulness offers an alternative – a way of meeting emotions that enables you to see them in a different light. The idea is to acknowledge and give mindful attention to difficult feelings rather than avoid or react to them. Surprisingly, this tends to dissipate the strength and the pain of the emotion. See Chapters 6, 12 and 13 for ways of dealing with a variety of different emotions.

WISE WORDS

The guesthouse

This superb poem by Rumi (1207–1273) captures the attitude you're moving towards when dealing with emotions mindfully.

> This being human is a guesthouse.
>
> Every morning a new arrival.
>
> A joy, a depression, a meanness,
>
> some momentary awareness comes
>
> as an unexpected visitor.
>
> Welcome and entertain them all!
>
> Even if they're a crowd of sorrows
>
> who violently sweep your house
>
> empty of its furniture,
>
> still, treat each guest honourably.
>
> He may be clearing you out
>
> for some new delight.
>
> The dark thought, the shame, the malice,
>
> meet them at the door laughing,
>
> and invite them in.
>
> Be grateful for whoever comes,
>
> because each has been sent
>
> as a guide from beyond.

Becoming Aware: Discovering Yourself

Before examining my true nature, I used to believe that I was a tiny, completely independent and isolated human being living in the corner of a city on a planet called Earth. However, through mindfulness I began to discover a totally different and satisfying dimension of myself that I had overlooked. Understanding your true nature helps you to see things from a totally different perspective. Having a sense of this deeper dimension puts the waves of life's challenges into a much bigger context. If you're the ocean, what trouble do waves give you?

Inscribed above the ancient Greek temple of Apollo at Delphi is the phrase 'Know thyself', a vitally important concept for Greek philosophers like Socrates. But self-reflection isn't advocated so much in the twenty-first century!

Who are you? What is this incredible thing called life? What's going on? These are the questions that I've always grappled with.

Through practising mindfulness meditation and reflecting on the deeper questions of life, you may come to discover your own deep inner self. Through this process, you find deeper meaning in what you do in your work and leisure time, and how you relate to others.

The lion and the sheep

Mindfulness naturally leads to self-examination; examination of who is doing the mindfulness in the first place. The following story may help to illustrate the realisation that can take place.

A lion cub accidentally strayed away from its mother, and ended up with a flock of sheep. The lion cub grew up with the other sheep, ate what the other sheep ate and behaved like them too. As the lion grew up he continued to behave in the same way, frightened of the subtlest sounds. However, something just didn't feel right. One day, he looked into a still pool of water and saw a beautifully clear reflection of himself. He was a lion, not a sheep. Because he'd believed himself to be like the other sheep, he behaved and thought like one. Now he saw who he truly was, everything changed, and yet he was just the same as he always was. He returned to his pride and lived according to his true nature.

Mindfulness meditation helps you to see things in perspective. If you go from place to place, rushing to finish all that stuff on the to-do list, and when you're done, are so exhausted that you just collapse in front of the television, you may have a bit of a problem discovering who you truly are in the meantime. By taking some time to meditate, you're giving yourself the opportunity to stop and look at all these incessant thoughts and emotions that come and go, and discover who you really are.

This book describes one approach to discovering your true nature that I've found immensely liberating and fascinating. Self-discovery is a personal journey so you may have a totally different way of understanding your deep, inner being.

Read each of these paragraphs as slowly as you can. Notice your judgements and desire to agree or disagree with the statements. Try doing neither, and instead just read and reflect.

✔ **You are not your body.** Your body is made up of hundreds of millions of cells. Cells are dying and re-forming all the time. The cells are made up of atoms that are indistinguishable and are exchanging with all the atoms around you as you breathe, eat and excrete. Right now, you're digesting food, your nails and hair are growing, and your immune system is fighting any diseases within you. It's all just happening – you're not doing it. Even if your body became totally paralysed, the sense of you being there would still be present. The very fact that you say 'my body' suggests that the body is something you *have*, rather than your true inner self.

✔ **You are not your thoughts.** Thoughts keep coming, no matter how much you may meditate. You can be aware of your thoughts and, therefore, you are not your thoughts. If you were your thoughts, you wouldn't be able to notice them. The fact that you can observe your thoughts means they're separate and a space lies between you and what you think. In meditation, you can step back from your thoughts from time to time, but you can't control thoughts. Do you even know what you're going to think in the next few seconds? But you can be aware of your thoughts.

✔ **You are not your emotions.** Just as you can observe thoughts, you can also observe your emotions. Emotions arise, and eventually pass away. If you were your emotions, then your emotions would never pose any problem at all. You would be able to control emotions and wouldn't choose to have negative feelings.

So, what are you? What's left? What's your true identity? I call it the observer, or the witness. If you're the observer, you can't be that which you observe. You are awareness, presence, being and aliveness. Your essential nature is presence or awareness. Thoughts and ideas, emotions and images, desires, fears and actions arise *in you* but you're aware of the whole lot. You're aware of everything. Everything arises *in awareness*, in being. That is what you are. You aren't just the thought 'I am Shamash' or 'I am Jane'; you are that sense of presence that underlies all experience. Right now, you're digesting, your heart is beating and you're reading, all in awareness. You're just watching while the whole process is happening.

Here are some of the attributes of awareness:

✔ **You are always aware.** Sometimes that awareness is lost in thoughts and dreams, sometimes it's connected with the senses.

✔ **Awareness happens by itself.** Awareness is different to attention. Attention or *mindful* awareness is something to be cultivated and trained, which is what most of this book is about, but *pure* awareness is your inner self. To be aware takes no effort. You don't need to *do* awareness. Awareness is effortlessly operating right now as you read. You can't turn off or run away from awareness!

✔ **Awareness comes before thought.** As a baby, you had awareness without words and ideas. Thoughts and concepts come after awareness.

✔ **As awareness, you're both 'no-thing' and everything.** Without awareness, nothing would exist for you. With awareness, you're a part of everything.

Having read all these attributes of awareness, what's your reaction? Whether you believe these ideas or not isn't important – what *is* important is examining and exploring these ideas for yourself. As Socrates said, 'The unexamined life is not worth living'. I've personally found looking deeper into my identity to be completely transformative and liberating – mindful self-discovery is the ultimate therapy!

The story of the stonemason

Once upon a time a stonemason paused to rest from his hard work for a few minutes at the side of an enormous rock. He saw a lord and his servants pass underneath the shade of the trees nearby.

When the stonemason saw this rich lord with all his luxuries and comfort, his work suddenly felt much harder. 'Oh, if only I were a rich man,' he wondered, 'I would be so happy!' Suddenly a voice answered from the mountain: 'Your wish shall become reality; a rich man you shall be!'

When the stonemason returned home, he found a beautiful palace where his simple home had stood. The poor man was overflowing with joy, and before long his old life was completely forgotten. One day, when he was walking in the marketplace, he felt the sun burn on his face, and he wished he was as mighty as the sun itself. Immediately he became the sun.

As the sun, he felt all-powerful. His light shone around the entire world and his rays beamed on kings and cobblers alike. But before long, a cloud moved in front of him and obscured his light. 'What is this?' he wondered. 'A cloud is mightier than me! Oh, how I wish I were a cloud.'

And a cloud he became. He blocked the sun's beams, and for weeks he poured rain until the rivers overflowed their banks, and the crops of rice stood in water. Towns and villages were destroyed by the sheer power of the rain, but he noticed that only the great rock on the mountainside remained unmoved. 'What is this?' he cried. 'A rock is mightier than me! Oh how I wish I were a rock.'

And the rock he became, and he gloried in the power. Proudly he stood, and neither the heat of the sun nor the force of rain could move him. 'This is the best!' he said to himself. But soon he heard a strange noise at his feet, and when he looked down he saw a stonemason breaking him up, piece by piece. Then he cried in his anger: ' Oh, if only I were a stonemason!'

In that instant, he became the stonemason once again, and remained content as he was for the rest of his life.

Part II

Preparing the Ground for Mindful Living

The 5th Wave   By Rich Tennant

"Excuse me while I bring Roger into the here-and-now."

In this part . . .

You have the opportunity to create a solid foundation on which to build your practise mindfulness. Hone your motivation and commitment, and discover some powerful attitudes to supercharge your mindfulness. Learn how to shift modes of mind too, and how to simply go with the flow.

Chapter 3

Nurturing Your Motivation

. . . .

. . . .

*O*ne of the best ways of boosting your capacity to be mindful is to practise mindfulness meditation everyday. Establishing a daily habit of meditation isn't easy, but well worth the effort. With a clear and strong motivation to practise, you can develop the firm commitment necessary to engage in meditation regularly. Once the habit of daily meditation is created, the routine becomes as natural as having a shower – you now have a way of cleaning your mind everyday, not just your body.

This chapter explores what your deep intentions of mindfulness are, including a range of exercises and how you can you use them to motivate your daily meditative practice.

Exploring Your Intentions

The word 'intention' comes from the Latin *intendere,* meaning to direct attention. Intention is purpose – what you hope to achieve from a certain action. If you're driving to work, and your intention is to get there on time no matter what happens, you may drive recklessly and dangerously. If you're driving to work and your intention is to get there safely, you try to drive with a more focused attention, and at a safe and reasonable speed. Here's a more startling example. Imagine someone is cutting you with a knife, such as a surgeon who has to insert a blade and cut you open. As the intention of the surgeon is to help you to restore your health, most people are willing to undergo this seemingly horrendous procedure. However, a murderer may also use a blade, but with a far less positive intention, and you're unlikely to be so willing!

Intention shapes the nature of the whole action itself. Although the action may be the same (as with the example of cutting someone open), the intention itself strongly influences your moment-by-moment experience and state of mind. For these reasons, the right intention is vitally important in meditation. I'd go as far as to say that the nature of the intention itself strongly influences the quality of your meditative practice.

Clarifying intention in mindfulness

Dr Shauna Shapiro of Santa Clara University, together with several colleagues, came up with a helpful model to suggest how mindfulness works. They identify three key components: *intention, attention* and *attitude*. The components are required together and feed into each other when you engage in mindfulness. The components link in well with the often-used definition of mindfulness, which is: *paying attention in a particular way: on purpose, in the present moment and non-judgementally.* Breaking this down, you have:

- ✔ Paying attention – *attention*
- ✔ On purpose – *intention*
- ✔ In a particular way – *attitude*

These three components work together seamlessly to create the moment-to-moment experience that is mindfulness. Figure 3-1 shows the components of mindfulness working together.

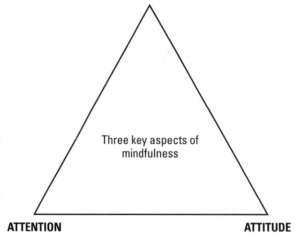

INTENTION

Three key aspects of mindfulness

Figure 3-1:
The three components of mindfulness.

ATTENTION   **ATTITUDE**

Intention is often a component that gets lost when people consider mindfulness, and yet it's vitally important. Intention sets the scene for what unfolds in the practice itself.

Intention evolves. One study has shown that people's intention in mindfulness is usually stress reduction and moves on to greater understanding of your thoughts and emotions, and finally towards greater compassion. For example, you may begin practising meditation to reduce your anxiety, and when that subsides, you practise to attain greater control over your emotions and eventually to be a more compassionate and kind person to your family and friends. What's *your* intention?

Mindfulness is being developed to relieve the suffering of a whole host of different conditions, from eating disorders to anxiety in pregnancy, from reducing students' stress to speeding up the healing process of psoriasis. These are all a wonderful flowering of applications of mindfulness, but keep in mind the original purpose and vision of mindfulness as a way of relieving *all* suffering, both yours and others, and developing a greater sense of compassion. Such a large and positive vision enlarges the practice of mindfulness for those who share those possibilities.

Finding what you're looking for

Meditative visualisation is a helpful exercise that may give you an insight into what your true and deep intentions in practising mindfulness are. When I first used this meditation, I was surprised and fascinated by the insights into my own deep motives.

You can read through these instructions and practise on your own or record them as an audio and listen to it as you practise. Alternatively, ask a friend to read out the meditation to you slowly.

Afterwards, do the writing exercise described in the next section.

Discovering your intention: Meditation

Find a comfortable position seated in a chair or sofa, or lying down. Choose a position in which you feel cosy and comfortable. Close your eyes.

> Imagine that you're sitting by the side of a beautiful expanse of water – a lake or lagoon, or perhaps a still, calm ocean. The place can be somewhere you've been before, seen before, or may be completely created in your imagination – it doesn't matter which. Find a place where you feel

calm and relaxed. The lake may have majestic trees around one side, and stunning mountains in the distance. The temperature is just about perfect for you, and a gentle breeze ensures that you feel refreshed. A flock of birds is flying across the horizon and you can sense a freshness in the air. Your body feels relaxed and at ease.

You look down and notice a pebble. You pick it up and look at it. It has a question engraved on it. The question is: 'Why do I want to practise mindfulness?' You look carefully at the question as you hold the pebble gently in your hand.

You throw the pebble out into the water. You watch the pebble as it soars through the air in an arc almost in slow motion and eventually makes contact with the surface of the water. You see the circular ripples radiate out. As the pebble contacts the water you continue to reflect on the question, 'Why do I want to practise mindfulness?'.

The pebble moves down into the water. You're able to see the pebble as it falls deeper and deeper into the water. As it continues to smoothly fall downwards in the deep water, you continue to watch it, and you continue to reflect on the question, 'Why do I want to practise mindfulness?'. You keep watching as the pebble falls, and you keep reflecting on the question.

Eventually, the pebble softly makes contact with the bottom and settles there. The question 'Why do I want to practise mindfulness?' is still visible. Reflect on that question for a few more moments.

Bring the visualisation meditation to a close, noticing the physical sensations of your body, taking a slightly deeper breath and, when you're ready, slowly opening your eyes. Record what you discovered in your journal, if you have one. This may help to reveal further insights as you write.

No right or wrong answers exist for this 'intention' meditation. Some people get clear answers about what they hope to get out of practising mindfulness, and others reflect on the question, yet no answers arise. Some people find that the answers they get at the surface of the lake are the more obvious ones but, as the pebble falls deeper, their reasons to practise clarify and deepen too. If the meditation was helpful, great; if not, don't be concerned – you have other exercises to do later in this chapter.

Discovering your intention: Sentence completion

Take a piece of paper, or your journal, and write as many answers as you can to the following questions in one minute, without thinking about it too much:

I want to practise mindfulness because . . .

I am hoping mindfulness will give me . . .

If I am more mindful I will . . .

The real reasons I want to practise mindfulness are to . . .

Ultimately mindfulness will give me . . .

Mindfulness is . . .

These sentence completion exercises may help to clarify your motivation and intentions of mindfulness.

Now read and reflect on your answers. Did any of your answers surprise you? Why did they? You may like to come back to these answers when you're struggling to motivate yourself to meditate – reading your answers can then be a way of empowering yourself to practise some meditation.

Developing a vision

A *vision* is a long-term aspiration: something you're willing to work towards. By having a clear vision, you have an idea of where you need to get to. Think of it in terms of any journey you make – you need to know two things: where you are now, and where you need to get to.

Mindfulness is about being in the present moment and letting go of goals. Why think about visions and intentions? Why not just be in the here and now and forget about aspirations? Well, the vision gives you the energy, the motivation and the strength to practise meditation, especially when you really don't feel like practising.

For example, your mind may be jam-packed with thoughts and ideas and opinions to such an extent that you can't easily calm down. Your vision may be to be a calm and collected person, someone who never really worries about things too much, and who others come to for advice. With this in mind, you know why you're practising meditation and *are committed* to sticking at it. This doesn't mean that the goal of each and every meditation is calmness, and that if you're not calm you've failed – a vision is bigger than that; a long-term objective rather than a short-term goal.

If you're not too sure of what your vision is, come back to this section after doing some mindfulness exercises or after dipping into other areas of this book, which may give you a clearer idea of a vision to work towards. The practice of meditation itself helps to develop an unambiguous vision as you begin to experience some benefits.

Try the following two exercises to help clarify your vision.

Write a letter to your future self

This is a wonderful way to develop a long-term vision of what you hope to achieve through mindfulness. Reflect on your future self in five or ten years. This is your chance to let go and dream. How would you feel? What sort of person do you hope to be? How do you cope with challenges in your life? Write a letter to yourself about it, or if you're a visual person, draw pictures. This vision gives your brain something to work towards, and the opportunity to begin discovering a path for you to tread to get there. Pin the letter up on the wall at home, or ask a good friend to post the letter back to you any time in the next year. Most people feel great receiving a letter from themselves dropping through the post, and the self-reflection always seems to arrive at the right time in your life.

Attend your own funeral

Try to overcome any reluctance about this exercise, because it's very moving and powerful. Imagine being at your own funeral service. You're aware of family and friends around you. Consider each person and imagine each of them saying what you'd *like* them to say about you. Really hear the positive things they're saying about you and your life. What do they value about you? What sort of aspects of your personality would you like them to talk about? What have they admired about you? After the exercise, think about it. How did you feel? What did people say about you?

The exercise helps to put things into context and clarifies your values; what's really important to you. How can you use what was said to create a vision of the kind of person that you want to become? How can that vision help motivate your meditation practice?

Ask yourself the following question every day for a couple of weeks: 'If today were the last day of my life, would I want to do what I'm about to do today?' Whenever the answer is 'No' for too many days in a row, you know that you need to change something. Even if you don't explicitly ask this question, you get a flavour of the value of considering death in order to help you wake up and focus on what's most important in life.

Preparing Yourself for Mindfulness

Letting go of a negative attitude towards meditation is helpful. If you go into meditation thinking that 'this probably isn't going to help me' as you practise and meet obstacles, you prove to yourself that it didn't work, you were right, and you instantly give up.

So when you cultivate a long-term vision for why you want to practise meditation, let it be just that – long-term. Let go in the here and now as you engage in the practice. Don't worry too much about whether or not you're moving towards your goal – trust that the process of meditation, practised by millions of people and supported scientifically by thousands of research papers, takes care of itself if you give it time, and stop questioning its value as far as you can.

In my experience of teaching mindfulness, a sceptical attitude towards mindfulness seems to 'work' best. People who say 'I'm not too sure if mindfulness will help me, but I'm going to give it a good go and see what happens' seem most likely to stick at it, and find it helps them.

Looking Beyond Problem-Solving

Mindfulness isn't a quick fix. You need to practise mindfulness on the good days and the bad ones – on days when you feel things are going okay, as well as when you feel anxious, stressed or depressed. Mindfulness is best cultivated slowly and steadily, day by day, so that when things become difficult or challenging for you, you can remember and use mindful awareness to bring your attention to your breathing, and soothe your mind.

Think of regular mindfulness meditation like putting on a safety belt in a car. You put the belt on every time you travel just in case you're in an accident. You don't put the belt on just before you crash – you'd be too late. The car journey is the same, whether you have a belt on or not, but the main difference is the preparation for what may happen. The safety belt of mindfulness helps to slow things down, so you can enjoy the view, and come to a safe stop when things become challenging.

Who knows? We shall see

One day, a student graduated with a first class honours degree from a top university. His friends and family celebrated and said how lucky he was. He was sure to land a great job. He replied, 'Who knows. We shall see.'

As soon as the party was over, the country slipped into a deep recession. People were getting laid off left, right and centre. No company was employing anyone. He applied for more than 50 jobs, to no avail. He didn't even get interviewed. His parents and partner felt sorry for him. He said, 'Who knows. We shall see'.

He decided to start up a business selling phones. At first, it didn't seem to work, but suddenly, as demand picked up, the business started to makes lots of money. He sealed a massive deal, and eventually become a millionaire. He bought a new house overlooking the sea. Others were amazed at his turn of fortune. He said, 'Who knows. We shall see.'

Unfortunately, all his savings were lost when a big bank failed. His house was repossessed and he had to move back with his parents. All those around him said how sorry they were about how things worked out. He smiled and said, 'Who knows. We shall see.'

He read in the paper that the couple who were now living in his old house were completely flooded. Due to rising sea levels, the foundations of the house became weak and had to be demolished. The insurance company didn't pay out and the couple lost everything. Everyone said how lucky the man was to leave when he did. He smiled and said, 'Who knows. We shall see.'

This story illustrates that you can judge problems in life as 'good' or 'bad', but you're not really seeing the big picture. No one knows what's going to happen next, and things may turn out to be okay. Try to keep an open mind in both your apparent fortune and misfortune.

Honing Your Commitment

Commitment is a pledge you make for a course of action. In this case your commitment is to mindfulness, developed through meditation and practised every day. Once you've decided to practise meditation, to commit is to follow through with your beliefs consistently. Commitment is also persistence with purpose. To achieve anything of significance, you need certain key commitments to stick to. Without commitment you can be easily swayed by passing feelings, and before long you forget the practices that you thought about doing or they become too far out of reach for you to resume in your life.

How do you make a commitment? The truth of the matter is that commitment is hard work. Just look at the number of people who struggle to stick to their New Year resolutions. However, the very fact that you make a commitment is the first step. Just because you failed to achieve your commitment, doesn't mean you should give up altogether. Say you want to stop eating chocolate. The first few days are fine, but then after a week, you see a delicious bar of your favourite chocolate lying on the kitchen table to tempt you, and without thinking, you begin devouring it. As you put the wrapper in the bin, you think that you've 'failed' and you may give up on the resolution altogether. Instead, realise that out of the last seven days of your resolution not to eat chocolate, you haven't eaten chocolate for six days. That's pretty good going – six out of seven! And try again tomorrow.

Commitment is most challenging when times are hard. When you've had a tough day, when everything seems to be going wrong, when the last thing you want to do is sit down and meditate, ironically that's when you need it most. Challenging days test your commitment to your original decision to practise every day. However, if you don't practise, even though you had every desire and squeezed every ounce of your commitment to practise but just didn't manage it, bring an attitude of curiosity and acceptance to the situation rather than beating yourself up about it. What's done is done. You wanted to practise but you didn't – the question is, what happened? What were the thoughts and feelings that led to your inaction? What's going through your mind right now as you ask yourself these questions?

Mastering self-discipline

The word *discipline* has negative connotations for some people, and can be a bit of a turn-off, which is a shame because self-discipline is important for a healthy lifestyle. Self-discipline is the ability to get yourself to do a certain action despite your emotional state at the time.

Imagine what you can achieve with perfect levels of self-discipline. No matter what you chose to do, you'd be able to do it. Say you wanted to become fitter. You'd just make that decision and you'd be guaranteed to follow through with the necessary regular exercise to ensure that it happened. This little example goes to show how amazingly powerful self-discipline can be, and why it's worth cultivating.

However, on its own, discipline can create a sense of cold, clinical action, almost too devoid of emotion. By combining this sense of discipline with your intentions and helpful attitudes (covered in Chapter 4), you can create a useful source of inspiration for your mindfulness practice.

Here are some tips for boosting your self-discipline for daily meditation:

- ✔ **Forgive yourself for the odd slip**. Remember, meditation is a long-term process. Don't just give up because of a lapse. If at first you don't succeed, find out why and try again!

- ✔ **Take things step by step.** Research has found that willpower is like a muscle. Willpower can become fatigued if you use it too much in a day, but can be strengthened over time. So don't try to transform your whole life in a day. You may want to start with a very short daily meditative practice.

- ✔ **Believe in yourself.** You can do it. Even if you suffer from attention disorders or you're ill, you can practise mindfulness, so believe that you're capable of making a commitment.

- ✔ **Ask for support.** Perhaps you can practise meditation with a partner or friend. Joining a meditation group can be a valuable support too.

- ✔ **Reward yourself.** You've probably given yourself a hard time on many an occasion for not doing something right, or well, or not being good enough, so why not reward yourself for doing something you're proud of? Creating a daily discipline of meditation is hard, so if you do manage for a week or even a few days, treat yourself to a little something!

Making a commitment that's right for you

One of the reasons people find it hard to stick to a commitment is because they're too ambitious. If you've never gone jogging before and you suddenly decide to run the marathon tomorrow, one of two things happen: you give up or you finish in a very injured and unhappy state. The knock-on effect is that you hate running or think that you were useless and can't run.

If you decide you're going to meditate for two hours a day for the rest of your life, no matter what happens, that may be tough. You need to take things easy and begin slowly. How do you decide what is the right commitment for you? Well, it depends what you want to get out of meditation. You can start with an eight-week commitment of practising meditation for 30 minutes per day and see how that goes. (See Chapter 9 for more about the eight-week routine).

Maybe two short meditations of ten minutes a day is more appropriate for your lifestyle, or even regular three-minute meditations throughout the day. Maybe you suffer from chronic pain or depression or want to develop yourself to a high level and wish to make a bigger commitment. That's fine of course, but start fairly modestly and build up your practising time. Meditation has no ideal minimum or maximum time in which to practise.

If you think that life is going well for you, and you just get slightly stressed from time to time, and want something to relax and focus you a bit more, then perhaps ten minutes of formal mindfulness meditation practice may be fine for you. If you suffer from medium to high levels of stress, anxiety, depression or ill health, turn to Chapters 12–14 for advice on the right commitment for you. Once the regular discipline of meditation becomes a habit, the effort of practice becomes easier. Cast your mind back to when you first learnt to brush your teeth. It was probably a real chore. Yes, it's good for your teeth, but you weren't interested – you wanted to play a game or watch

TV, not waste your time brushing your teeth. But now, if you don't brush your teeth for any reason, *it just doesn't feel right*. As you regularly practise meditation, you eventually find the same. You become nourished by the practice itself, and what may at times have felt difficult to do, now feels strange *not* to do. This is the sign that you've created a wonderful, positive way to uplift your health and wellbeing. Of course, at times you feel reluctant to practise, such as when you're reluctant to brush your teeth if you're really tired, but on the whole, you're now a keen meditator.

Your informal practice, which involves being mindfully aware of your day-to-day activities (see Chapter 8), will happen almost naturally if you regularly practise meditation for a set amount of time every day.

Inspiring you with extra motivation

Still struggling with the idea of self-discipline? Here are a final few thoughts to help you.

Think of your mind as being like a puppy. When you train a puppy, you need to be kind and gentle at first. If you put a leash on it and drag it hard from one place to another, the puppy won't learn. You'll probably upset it and will never train it well. However, if you let it do whatever it wants, you're also in trouble! The dog will be the master and rule the house. The young puppy learns that whatever it feels like doing at the time, it can do, making you feel very tired and frustrated with cleaning up and meeting its never-ending needs and desires. The puppy may end up eating too much and become sick. The middle way is best. You need to guide the puppy to do particular actions, and whenever it does them, you reward it. If the puppy does the wrong thing, you don't give it much attention and eventually it stops.

Nothing beats the real thing

I find that all the time I spend talking, writing or teaching mindfulness makes almost no difference to how mindful I am. The only thing that deepens my mindfulness is regular practice of mindfulness meditation itself. You may spend every waking hour reading, writing, studying and talking about meditation, but hardly ever practise it. And just as describing a mango isn't the same as tasting one, so talking or reading about meditation isn't the same as practising it. Reading about and discussing meditation may seem much more comfortable and easy than doing it, but unfortunately it makes no difference to your mind or body. So I recommend you aim at doing 'non-doing' everyday, for however long you decide.

Train your own mind in the same way. When your mind comes up with all sorts of ideas about what you could be doing instead of meditating, just kindly ignore it, without fighting or blocking the thoughts. Give your attention to the inner commitment to meditate, and reward that aspect of mind by meditating. Before long your puppy mind will be a well-trained and beautiful dog, behaving itself most of the time. You need lots of patience and progress may be slow, but the rewards make the puppy-training programme well worth it!

Each time you practise meditation, you're doing two things. First, you're becoming more mindful, which means more attentive, more compassionate and more positive emotionally. Secondly, you're increasing the chance of meditating again, on another day. This is because any new activity you take on, whether physical or mental, creates a new pathway in the brain. It's a bit like creating a new pathway through a forest. At first, walking through all the overgrowth is difficult. You need to push the overhanging branches out of way and step on the long grass under your feet. However, if you keep walking on that path, it becomes easier and easier. Soon enough, you don't need to battle anymore or think about which way to go next. The path is clear. It's the same with pathways in the brain. In fact, that's what commitment to an action creates in the brain – a pathway to greater mindfulness, awareness and 'aliveness'.

The donkey and the well

Once upon a time, a farmer's donkey fell into a well. The farmer tried all sorts of different ways to get the donkey out, to no avail. Eventually and regrettably, he gave up. The well needed filling up anyway, so he decided to bury the donkey. He convinced himself that the donkey wouldn't suffer any longer. He began shovelling soil into the well. At first the donkey was scared and brayed loudly but then calmed down and was silent. After shovelling for a while, the farmer decided to take a closer look inside, using a torch. The donkey was alive, and closer to the top of the well. Each time the farmer threw mud onto the donkey, he shook it off his back and stepped up onto the soil. Before long the donkey was able to step out of the well and into safety, as if nothing had happened.

The donkey was *motivated* to stay alive. If the donkey had thought, 'Oh no, I have no hope, I'm going to die,' then the donkey would have been buried. With the motivation and commitment to succeed in mindfulness you can come up with simple yet effective and creative solutions to challenges along the way.

Chapter 4

Growing Healthy Attitudes

· ·

· ·

> *The greatest discovery of our generation is that human beings can alter their lives by altering their attitudes of mind. As you think, so shall you be.*
>
> William James.

*T*he three important aspects to mindfulness are intention, attitude and attention (explained fully in Chapter 3). This chapter focuses on attitude.

When it comes to attitude, you have a choice. If you're aware of your outlook, you can begin to choose to change it for the better. Attitude isn't about what happens in your life, how successful you are, or even how you feel. You can be feeling the emotion of frustration, but think, 'Hey, at least I'm aware of it' or 'This is just a feeling' or 'This is a chance for me to understand the feeling of frustration'. Changing your attitude is difficult but *is* possible. By choosing mindful attitudes towards your moment-to-moment inner and outer experiences, you begin to release self-limiting beliefs, and live life with greater fluidity.

Think about singing. What's your attitude towards singing? Maybe you love it, and can't wait to jump up on the stage. If you don't care what other people think, or feel you're a great singer, then belting out your favourite song isn't a problem. However, if you think you must do it right, or worry about what others think, you may be more hesitant to sing and this affects your feelings, mood and how you actually sound.

Knowing How Attitude Affects Outcome

There once was a school that had six different ability groups for maths. Each year, the same maths teachers taught the same ability level in the subject. One year the head teacher decided to experiment. She picked a teacher at random, who turned out to be the teacher of the second from bottom set. The head told her how good she was and that she would give her the top set for maths next year. The teacher's attitude and expectations for the class totally changed when she received her new class. She knew that the top set should get the top grades as they always had. She taught them accordingly and sure enough, they achieved straight A grades. The amazing thing was that the class wasn't really the top set at all, but was the second from bottom set. Because the teacher had changed her attitude and expectations for the class, the students rose to the challenge and produced outstanding results. This experiment goes to show the power of attitude.

How does attitude affect the quality of mindfulness meditation? Well, if your attitude is 'Meditation is really hard', then you try very hard to get somewhere. If your attitude is 'Meditation is easy' and then struggle, you may begin to get frustrated. If your attitude is, 'I don't know how it'll go. I'm going to give it a good go and see what happens,' you're prepared for whatever arises.

Attitudes are the soil in which your mindfulness practices grow tall and strong. A rich, nutritious soil nourishes the seed of mindfulness and ensures that it grows well. Each time you practise mindfulness, you water the seed, giving it care and attention. However, if that soil deteriorates through unhelpful attitudes, then the young seedling will begin to wither. A plant needs regular watering to grow – a lack of care and attention results in it perishing.

Discovering Your Attitudes to Mindfulness

Attitudes can become habits; both good and bad habits. And attitudes, like habits, aren't easy to change. You need to work to improve your attitude. Begin by discovering what your current attitudes are towards meditation, stillness, silence and non-doing. Then, through understanding and effort, you can develop attitudes that are more conducive to a regular mindfulness practice.

Get pen and paper and answer the following ten questions to help you to find out your attitudes towards mindfulness meditation.

1. What do you hope to get out of practising mindfulness?

2. Why are you practising mindfulness?

3. What experiences do you expect to arrive at through practising mindfulness?

4. How long do you think it'll take before you notice the benefits of meditation?

5. What physical sensations do you expect during or after a meditation?

6. What are your past experiences of meditation? Do you continue to hold them or have you let them go?

7. How much effort are you willing to put into the practice? Will you meditate several times a day, or once a day, or once a week, or whenever you feel like it?

8. When you hear the word 'meditation' or 'mindfulness', what sort of thoughts and feelings arise?

9. How will you know that you're doing your meditation correctly?

10. What's the great thing about meditation?

Now, look at your answers. Do you notice any patterns? Are you very positive about the potential benefits of meditation? Are you negative about meditation? Or are you indifferent and do you just want to experiment, like being a scientist of your own mind?

Try to be non-judgemental towards your answers. See them as just the way things are. If you can't help being caught up in thinking, 'That's good' or 'Oh, that's a really bad attitude, what's wrong with me?', notice that too. Your mind is simply coming up with judgements.

Developing Helpful Attitudes

This section contains the key foundational attitudes that provide a base from which you can build a strong mindfulness practice. These attitudes help you to handle difficult sensations and emotions, overcome feelings of lethargy, and generate energy for taking action. Without these attitudes your practice may become stale and your intention may weaken, along with your power to pay attention in the present moment. Some helpful ways of approaching your practice are developed through experience; others are available right from the start.

Think of these key attitudes like strawberry seeds. If you're hoping to taste the delicious strawberries, you need to plant the seeds and water them regularly. In the same way, you need to water your attitudes regularly, by giving them your mindful attention. Then you can enjoy the fruit of your efforts in the form of a sweet, delicious strawberry. I'm a sucker for strawberries.

Although the attitudes identified in this section seem separate, they feed into and support each other. Any one of these, pursued and encouraged to grow, inadvertently supports the others.

Understanding acceptance

Acceptance turns out to be one of the most helpful attitudes to bring to mindfulness. Acceptance means perceiving your experience and simply acknowledging it rather than judging it as good or bad. For some people, the word 'acceptance' is off-putting – replace it with the word 'acknowledgement', if you prefer.

By acceptance, I don't mean resignation. I don't mean, 'If you think you can't do something, accept it' – that would be giving up rather than accepting. I'm talking about your experience from moment to moment.

For example, when you feel pain, whether it's physical, such as a painful shoulder, or mental, such as depression or anxiety, the natural reaction is to try to avoid feeling the pain. This seems very sensible because the sensation of physical or mental pain is unpleasant. You ignore it, distract yourself, or perhaps even go so far as turning to recreational drugs or alcohol to numb the discomfort. This avoidance may work in the immediate short term, but before long, avoidance fails in the mental and emotional realm. By fighting the pain, you still feel the pain, but on top of that, you feel the emotional hurt and struggle with the pain itself. Buddha called this the 'second arrow'. If a warrior is injured by an arrow and unleashes a series of thoughts like 'why did this happen to me' or 'what if I can never walk again', that's a 'second arrow'. You may inflict this on yourself each time you feel some form of pain or even just a bit of discomfort, rather than accepting what has happened and taking the next step. Avoidance – running away – is an aspect of the 'second arrow' and compounds the suffering. Acceptance means stopping fighting with your moment-to-moment experience. Acceptance removes that second arrow of blame, criticism or denial.

Perhaps you sit down to meditate and feel bombarded by thoughts dragging you away again and again. If you don't accept the fact that your mind likes thinking, you become more and more frustrated, upset and annoyed with yourself. You want to focus on the meditation but just can't.

In the above example:

- ✔ First arrow – lots of thoughts entering your mind during meditation.

- ✔ Second arrow – not accepting that thoughts are bound to come up in meditation. Criticising yourself for having too many thoughts.

- ✔ Solution – to acknowledge and accept that thoughts are part and parcel of meditation. You can do this by gently saying to yourself 'thinking is happening' or 'it's natural to think' or simply labelling it as 'thinking . . . thinking'.

By *acknowledging* the feeling, thought or sensation and going into it, the experience changes. Even with physical pain, try experimenting by actually feeling it. Research has found that the pain reduces. But remember, you're not acknowledging it to get rid of the feeling. That's not acceptance. You need to try to acknowledge the sensation, feeling or thought *without trying to change it* at all. Pure acceptance of it, just as it is. Maybe even relaxing into the discomfort. One way to relax into the discomfort is by courageously turning to the sensation of discomfort, and simultaneously feeling the sensation of your own breath. With each out-breath, allow yourself to move closer and soften the tension around the discomfort.

If all this acceptance or acknowledgement of your pain seems impossible, just try getting a sense of it and make the tiniest step towards it. The smallest step towards acceptance can set up a chain of events ultimately leading towards transformation. Any tiny amount of acceptance is better than none at all.

Another aspect of acceptance is to come to terms with your current situation. If you're lost, even if you have a map of where you want to get to, you have no hope of getting there, *if you don't know where you are to start with*. You need to know and accept where you are before you can begin working out how to get to where you want to be. Paradoxically, acceptance is the first step for any radical change. If you don't acknowledge where you are and what's currently happening, you can't move on appropriately from that point.

Here are some ways you can try to cultivate acceptance:

- ✔ Gently state the label of the experience you aren't accepting. For example, if you're not accepting that you're angry, state in your mind, to yourself, 'I'm feeling angry at the moment... I'm feeling angry'. In this way, you begin to acknowledge your feeling.

- ✔ Notice which part of your body feels tense and imagine your breath going into and out of the area of tightness. As you breathe in and out, say to yourself, 'It's okay. It's already here... It's already here'.

✔ Consider how much you accept or acknowledge your current thoughts/ feelings/sensation on a scale of 1 to 10. Ask yourself what you need to do to increase your acceptance by 1, and then do it as best you can.

✔ Become really curious about your experience. Consider: 'Where did this feeling come from? Where do I feel it? What's interesting about it?'. In this way, the curiosity leads you to a little more acceptance.

In the realm of emotions, the quickest way to get from A to B isn't to try and force yourself to get to B, but to accept A. Wholehearted acceptance leads to change automatically.

Discovering patience

Helen Keller, the American deaf blind political activist is quoted as saying, 'We could never learn to be brave and patient, if there were only joy in the world.' The quote makes a valid point. If every time you meditated, you were filled with joy and peace, you wouldn't need that wonderful attitude of patience. The reality is that challenging thoughts and emotions sometimes arise in meditation, like in any activity. The important thing is how you meet and welcome those feelings.

Although you can experience the benefits of meditation after a short period of time, research shows that the more time you dedicate to cultivating mind-fulness, the more effective the result. Meditation is a training of the mind and training takes time.

If you're a naturally rather impatient person, meditation is the perfect training for you. Patience, like all the attitudes I talk about in this section, is a state you can develop through regular effort. Attitudes are muscles you can train in the gym of the mind.

Here are some ways you can develop your patience:

✔ Whenever you're in any situation and begin to experience impatience, see this as an opportunity to practise mindfulness of thoughts. This means becoming fascinated by the kind of thoughts that are popping into your head. Are they all true? What effect are the thoughts having on your emotional state? What are the thoughts all about?

✔ The next time you're driving and see a yellow light, safely stop if you can rather than speeding through. See how that makes you feel. Repeat several times and notice if it becomes easier or more difficult to be patient.

✔ Rather than frantically choosing the shortest queue at the supermarket checkout, just choose the nearest one. Connect with any feelings of impatience that arise and bring a sense of curiosity to your experience, rather than immediately reacting to your impatience.

✔ When having a conversation with someone, spend more time listening rather than speaking. Let go of your initial urges to speak, and listen more. Listening can take tremendous effort, and is excellent patience training. Each time you practise, you train your brain to become slightly more patient.

Seeing afresh

Seeing afresh is normally referred to as the *beginner's mind* and was first used by the Zen master Suzuki Roshi. He once said: 'In the beginner's mind there are many possibilities, but in the expert's there are few.' What does that mean?

Consider a young child. Children, if they're fortunate enough to be brought up lovingly, are the greatest mindfulness teachers in the world! They're amazed by the simplest thing. Give them a set of keys and they stare at it, notice the wide range of colours reflected in them, shake them and listen to the sound – and probably giggle too. Then, of course, they taste the keys! Children epitomise the beginner's mind. They see things as if for the first time because they're not filled with ideas, concepts, beliefs, names or thoughts about what's the right or wrong thing to do. Babies don't intellectualise. They connect with the raw sensory data entering their mind, and love it. Young children, if lovingly brought up, are naturally mindful, and that mindfulness is a true joy for them.

You can see life in a similar way. You can cultivate this attitude of the beginner's mind, of seeing things afresh – you just need to make a little effort. Try this exercise:

1. Sit or lie down in a relaxed and comfortable posture and close your eyes.

2. Now imagine you've been blind from birth. You've never experienced colour before. You've heard people talking about it, but you can't even imagine colour. Spend at least five minutes doing this. When you find your mind wandering off into thoughts, gently guide it back to this exercise.

3. When you're ready, gently open your eyes, as if you're seeing for the first time. See with the beginner's mind. Enjoy the range of colours and forms in front of you. Notice how your mind automatically names

different objects. Bring the attention back to the awareness of the variety of colours, shadows, reflections. You may even begin to notice things you've never noticed before – that's a sign that you're engaging with the beginner's mind and seeing afresh.

4. Continue with this beginner's mind attitude as you go about your activities today, and be with each experience as if for the first time.

When you experience the state of the beginner's mind, you live in a world of fascination, curiosity, creativity, attention and fun. You're continuously discovering and looking out with the eyes of a child. You're in 'don't know' mind. When you think, 'I know what's going to happen' or 'I know what the breath feels like', you stop looking. You don't know what's going to happen, you just think you do. Each moment is fresh. Each moment is different and unique. Each moment is the only moment you have.

If you're a beginner to meditation, you're in an enviable position. You really are in the beginner's mind! However, by the time you practise your second meditation, you may begin comparing it to your first one – 'It was better last time', or 'Why can't I concentrate now?' or 'This is it. I've got it!'. You start to compare, conceptualise or condemn. When this happens, try to let it go – as much as you can – and bring your attention back to the here and now, the present moment, as if you're engaging in this for the very first time. I'm not saying that the beginner's mind is an easy attitude, but it's fundamental to sustaining a long-term meditative discipline.

Finding trust

Without a certain degree of trust, mindfulness meditation is challenging. This is because trust helps you to continue believing in the process of meditation when you feel that nothing's happening, or something 'wrong' is happening. For example, if you're meditating and you suddenly feel bored, you need to trust that this is just another feeling, and that by continuing to practise meditation, that feeling may go away or may not. Or, you may find that by the end of a meditation, you feel a bit worse than when you started. Without trust you won't be able to see that this is just a temporary experience which, like all experiences, won't last forever.

Trust takes time to develop in relationships. You can't expect to meet people and immediately trust them. You need to see how they behave, what they say, and how they treat you and others. With time, with patience, trust grows. And with that growing trust, the relationships deepen, mature and become more meaningful. A relationship that lacks in trust has little beauty. With trust comes warmth, friendship and a feeling of connection – you feel at ease and comfortable in a trusting relationship. Your relationship with meditation is similar. You may not trust in the process to begin with, but with patience and dedicated, regular practice, you may begin to trust it. The more you trust in its power to heal and restore you, the more you relax into it, and allow meditation to happen to you, in a sense, rather than trying to *do* meditation. Meditation is an act of non-doing, or being, which arises out of the security of trust.

Here are some ways of building your trust:

✔ Decide how long you're going to try meditation for, and stick to it. So, if you want to try meditation for four weeks, for 20 minutes a day, just do it. Be prepared to find some days harder to practise than others, and begin to trust in the process.

✔ If you're scientifically minded, look up all the research on mindfulness and meditation, in this book or elsewhere. This may help to convince you to stick to the discipline.

✔ If you know someone else who regularly practises meditation, ask her about her relationship with it. Consider meditating with her to help you.

✔ Give meditation time. Be patient with it as far as you can, and your trust will naturally grow with time.

✔ Try trusting your own experience, in the here and now. What is your intuition trying to tell you?

Practising curiosity

Einstein was a master of curiosity. He thought curiosity is an essential part of a fulfilling life. Einstein is quoted as saying: 'The important thing is not to stop questioning. Curiosity has its own reason for existing. One cannot help but be in awe when he contemplates the mysteries of eternity, of life, of the marvellous structure of reality. It is enough if one tries merely to compre-hend a little of this mystery every day. Never lose a holy curiosity.'

Curiosity is the basis of all true learning. If you're curious, you want to find out something new – you want to gain some new knowledge. A curious person is fully connected with her senses. If you're curious, you look around intently and earnestly, to see something you haven't seen before. You ask lots and lots of questions, both of yourself and others. These can be ques-tions like, 'Why is the sky blue?' or, 'Why is that shadow over there faint, whereas this one is much darker?' Or it may be questions about yourself, like, 'I wonder why I feel tired after eating X' or, 'Where do thoughts come from?' or, 'What happens to the feeling of frustration if I try to feel it in the body and breathe into it?'

Bringing curiosity to your mindfulness practice is especially helpful. In fact, with curiosity, mindfulness automatically arises – you naturally begin to pay attention, and with a sense of wonder, to notice what's happening. Take the example of thought – if you're really curious about the types of thought that you have over a period of ten minutes, you pay attention and watch thoughts in your mind as best you can. If your curiosity is genuine, you'll probably keep watching those thoughts until that curiosity is satisfied.

How can you develop curiosity in meditation? I'd say, by asking questions. Here are some questions you can ask yourself before a meditation to get you started. Then, try to come up with some of your own – your own curiosity is more powerful than anything I give to you.

- ✔ What happens if I meditate every day for 20 minutes for four weeks, whether I feel like it or not?

- ✔ What effect occurs if I put more effort into my meditation? What if I put in less effort?

- ✔ What if I sit or lie down really still, even if I have the urge to move – what happens then?

- ✔ Where in the body do I feel positive emotions? Where do I feel negative ones? What shape and colour do the emotions have, if any?

- ✔ What effect does having a gentle smile whilst meditating have on my practice?

I could go on and on with thousands of questions to ask. Ask yourself a question and investigate. Feed your curiosity and see what you discover. Allow your curiosity to spread from your meditation practice to your day-to-day living. Become curious about your thoughts, emotions and physical sensations rather than just ignoring them, or trying to instantly change them.

Meditation is like a laboratory, where you come up with ideas, observe, watch, see what happens and perhaps draw conclusions. Keep asking yourself questions, and keep going in that way. Meditation gives the opportunity to find out about yourself and the workings of your own mind and heart, and when you understand that, you understand not only yourself, but everyone else, because everyone has essentially the same processes going on. Humans are far more similar than you may think.

Letting go

Imagine I told you to hold a glass of water absolutely still. In fact, imagine I said that I'd give you whatever you wanted if you held the glass of water perfectly still. You'd probably try very hard and the glass might look quite still, but if you, or anyone else, looked really carefully at the water you'd notice that it was still moving. I suspect that the harder you tried to hold the glass still, the more you'd shake it, as you felt more worried or nervous about being 100 per cent still. The best way for the glass of water to be still would be for you to *let it go* and put it down on a solid surface. Then, the water would stop moving.

Nature has many beautiful examples of letting go. Apple trees need to let go of their fruit so that the seeds inside can germinate. Animals need to let go of their young so they can find out how to fend for themselves. Young birds need to let go of any fear they feel when they first jump off a branch to begin to fly. You're always letting go of each breath of air to make room for the next one. This last example shows that you naturally know how to let go all the time, in one sense. Remember this the next time you're struggling to let go.

Letting go is the essence of meditation. Thoughts, emotions, ideas, opinions, beliefs, emotions, sensations are all to be observed, explored and then let go.

People often think they've 'got it'. They know how to 'do meditation'. This is a mistake. As soon as you think you've got 'it', whatever you think 'it' is, you're probably mistaken. You have an *idea* of what meditation is about, but ideas are just that: ideas. Ideas are not facts. Reality is in a state of flux and change from moment to moment. You'd be better off thinking you have an idea of how to meditate, and the idea may turn out to be right or wrong – you're going to find out and see what happens. This links up with the beginner's mind that I discuss earlier.

How do you let go? Imagine you're holding a tennis ball in your hands, and you're asking me how to let go. Letting go isn't something you do. Letting go is about stopping the doing. To let go of something, you stop holding on to it. The first step is to realise you're holding on to the object in the first place. If you're walking around holding a tennis ball, you can't let go if you don't know that the ball is in your hands. Once you know that the ball is there, and feel the tension in your hands, you automatically let go.

Here is a short meditation based on the practice of letting go. Have a go and see what arises for you.

1. Find a comfortable posture. You don't even need to close your eyes if you don't want to for this exercise.

2. Notice, right now, the position of your body. Can you feel any physical tension in the body? Which parts feel warm, and which ones cold? Does the tension have a shape, a colour, a texture? Be aware of what they are. What happens to the tension and tightness as you become aware of them? Do they release or stay there?

3. Become aware of any emotions that are touching you at the moment. What happens when you observe them? Get a sense of how strong the emotion is. Don't *try* to let go. Putting effort into letting go just creates more tension – instead, become aware of it and allow the emotion to take its own course. Let the emotion let go of itself if it wants to. If the feeling lingers on, can you be okay with that, and accept it as it is?

4. At the end of this short meditation, see if you're willing to let go of anything that you found out – anything that you're now holding on to, trusting that you have within you all that needs to be known.

Developing kindness

Kindness is my religion.

Dalai Lama.

This is one of the most important of all attitudes you can bring to your mindfulness practice. Your awareness of the breath, or body or sounds, or whatever you're paying attention to, can have a quality to it. The quality can be cold, harsh and incisive, or it can be warm, kind, friendly, forgiving, caring, gentle – in other words, loving. By bringing a sense of friendliness to your experience, the experience, whether it's pleasant, unpleasant or neutral, transforms.

Because kindness is such an important attitude, I go into this in more detail in the next section.

Figure 4-1 is the tree of mindfulness. The growth and development of the tree of mindfulness represents your own inner capacity to be mindful. Watering the roots represents the effort you make to cultivate the mindful attitudes and practise mindfulness. The fruit represents the benefits you naturally gain from the effort you put into being mindful. 'As you sow, so shall you reap' is the essence of mindfulness – this is why the fruit from your own tree of mindfulness is the same as the roots.

Over time, as you continue to look after the tree of mindfulness within you, the tree strengthens and matures. Your roots grow deep into the earth and your tree stands firmly earthed to the ground, offering shade to those around quite naturally. Meditation is firmly established within your being.

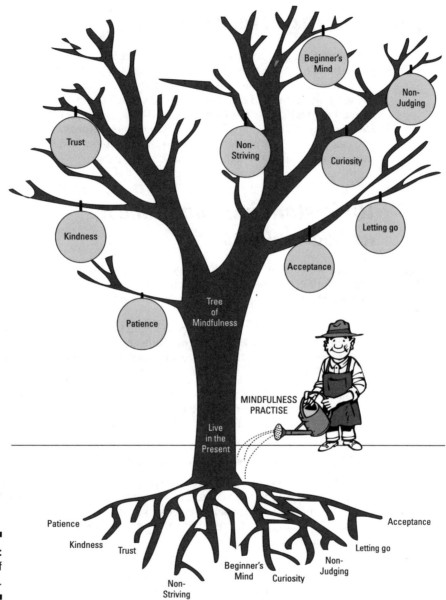

Figure 4-1:
The tree of
mindfulness.

Appreciating 'Heartfulness'

With attentiveness, a marksman can shoot an innocent person; a thief can plot a bank robbery; a drug baron can count his money. But this isn't true mindfulness – mindfulness is not pure attention alone. In Eastern language, the word for mind and heart is often the same word, which is *heartfulness*. Instead of *Mindfulness For Dummies,* this book could just as easily be called *Heartfulness For Dummies.* Heartfulness is giving attention to anything that you can perceive with a sense of warmth, kindliness and friendliness, and thereby avoid self-criticism and blame.

Understanding mindfulness as heartfulness

Here are some ways of specifically generating warmth and friendliness, along with attention. You need to give each of these exercises at least five minutes for best effect. Try to generate an intention rather than a feeling.

- ✔ Look at something in front of you in the same way as you may look into the eyes of a beautiful child, or a flower. Bring a sense of affection to your visual perception, whatever that may be, for a few minutes. Note what happens.

- ✔ Listen to your favourite piece of relaxing music. This may be a piece of classical music, New Age music, or perhaps it's the sounds of nature, such as birds singing or the wind rustling the trees.

- ✔ Smell the aroma in the room around you or of the food on your plate, in the same way that you smell the most beautiful scent of a perfume.

- ✔ When you next eat, take a few moments to feel your breath. You may find this difficult as the habit is to dive in and munch, but hold back if you can. Now remember how lucky you are to have some food to eat at all. Chew each morsel fully before you tuck into your next helping. Savour the taste.

- ✔ Notice the sense of touch as you walk from one place to another. Slow down as much as you can, and feel the sensations in the feet. Imagine your feet are kissing the earth with each step you take. Visualise yourself walking on precious ground, and allow yourself to be fully immersed in the sense of contact.

- ✔ Listen to any negative thoughts or emotions in yourself. Perhaps you're habitually critical of yourself for having these feelings. Try a radically different approach – befriend them. Bring a sense of warmth and kindness to your anger, jealousy or frustration. Listen to yourself compassionately as you would to a good friend – with care and understanding. What happens?

Developing an Attitude of Gratitude

Gratitude is considered by some as the greatest of all emotions that can be cultivated. Recent studies are beginning to show that gratitude has a unique relationship with wellbeing, and can explain aspects of wellbeing that other personality traits cannot. An attitude of gratitude goes hand in hand with mindfulness.

You're grateful when you're aware of what you do have rather than what you don't. The effect of this is an opening of the heart. When you're aware with an open heart, you're in a deeper mindful mode.

Gratitude is a skill that you can develop. If you're bad at tennis or the piano, with practice you get better. The same is true of gratitude. Through repeated effort you can develop, strengthen and intensify gratitude. Flex your gratitude muscle by trying this exercise, which is almost guaranteed to make you more grateful!

1. Think of something you're ungrateful for. Perhaps you're ungrateful in your job, a relationship, or your place of residence.

2. Now think of all the things that are good about it. Give yourself two minutes and challenge yourself to come up with as many good things as possible. For example, if you're not happy with your job: Does it pay you money? Do you get time off? Is there a pension or medical plan that goes with it? Are there any colleagues you like? Do you get breaks? Does it make being at home more pleasurable? Think of as many positive aspects for which you're grateful. To supercharge this exercise rather than just thinking about it, write it down. Be aware that you may have to overcome some resistance to doing this, especially if you really are very ungrateful about the situation.

3. Try this exercise again for other areas of your life. See what effect that has on them. Again, remember that the exercise takes some effort, but the rewards make it worthwhile.

4. Commit to doing this regularly for a week or month on a daily basis and you may find yourself being naturally more grateful for all sorts of other things too, including meditation.

Letting go through forgiveness

When someone has hurt you, or you've done something wrong, you have a conflict in your mind. You probably feel annoyed or even angry at others or yourself. This harmful state of mind requires forgiveness for you to enable greater wellbeing and less ill will for yourself. Being annoyed with someone else hurts you rather than anyone else. You may enjoy hearing about others forgiving in situations of hatred, but when you're called upon to do so yourself, you're stuck. You may find yourself in anger, depression or hatred. Many studies now show that releasing and letting go of past hurts through forgiveness leads to a longer and happier life.

Try this approach to begin allowing in forgiveness:

- ✔ Understand that hating someone else doesn't actually hurt that person at all.

- ✔ List all the beneficial things that have emerged from a situation. Try to see the situation from a totally different perspective. Ask a trusted friend to help you if you want.

- ✔ Be compassionate with yourself. If you've been ruminating over a problem for some time, perhaps now's the time to let it go. You don't deserve all this hurt you're carrying around with you.

- ✔ Understand that the story you're telling yourself is just that: a story. This pain and hurt may be repeating itself in your mind through a story. Try letting go of the story, or seeing the story from another person's perspective. Something may shift to help you to forgive.

- ✔ Wish the person well. If someone has hurt you, counteract that with some loving-kindness meditation. Wish the person well just as you may wish yourself or a friend well. Use the loving-kindness meditations in this book to help you.

An alternative practice would be to do a forgiveness meditation. You may choose to record and play this back whenever you feel it appropriate.

1. Sit in a comfortable and relaxed position. Let your eyes close if that's okay with you, and allow your breath to find a natural rhythm.

2. Imagine or feel the breath going into your heart. Become aware of and feel the obstructions you've created in your heart due to a lack of forgiveness, whether for yourself or others. Become mindful of the heartache from a lack of forgiveness in your core.

3. Now you can *ask forgiveness of others*. Say to yourself, 'Let me become aware of the many ways that knowingly or unknowingly I've caused

others pain and suffering though my own fear, pain or anger. Visualise each person who comes to mind – feel the sorrow and pain they feel due to your words and actions. Now, finally, release this sadness, sorrow and heartache by asking for forgiveness. As you imagine or feel each person's presence, say to them: 'I ask for your forgiveness. Forgive me.' Repeat this slowly as many times as you feel appropriate, speaking from the heart.

4. Now you can move on to *forgiving yourself*. You've hurt yourself in many ways through thoughts, words or actions. You may have done this consciously or unconsciously, without even knowing it. Allow yourself to become mindful of any unkindness you've directed towards yourself. Feel the suffering you've caused yourself and begin to release this by saying: 'For all the ways I have been causing suffering to myself through thoughts, words or actions, consciously or unconsciously, I forgive myself. I forgive myself as far as I can.'

5. Now you can move on to *forgive other people* who have hurt you. You've been hurt by many people through their words or actions, knowingly or unknowingly. They've caused you suffering in your being to different degrees. Imagine the ways they've done this. Become aware and feel the pain others have caused you and allow yourself to let go of this sadness from your heart with the words: 'I have been hurt by others many times, in many ways, due to the pain, sorrow, anger or misunderstanding of others. I've carried this suffering in my being for longer than enough. As far as I'm ready to, I offer my forgiveness. To those I've hurt, I forgive you.' Repeat these phrases if you want.

With time and practice, you may feel a shift in your heart and be able to forgive. If the shift doesn't happen, notice how you feel and be soft and kind with yourself. Let the forgiveness be genuine. Forgiveness takes time, so be patient and practise the meditation regularly. With regular commitment, you're able to release yourself from the sorrow you're carrying through gentle forgiveness.

Tackling Unhelpful Attitudes

Just as you have helpful attitudes to cultivate in your mindfulness practice, you also have unhelpful attitudes that you'd be better off staying away from. For example, if you're a bit of a perfectionist and are worried you're going to fall asleep in your meditation, you don't need to start panicking, or worrying when you start struggling to stay awake. You just need to become aware of the perfectionist mindset and, as best you can, let the unhelpful approach go.

The most unhelpful thing you can do with mindfulness is not to practise. Once you begin practising regularly, in no matter how small a way, you may begin to discover which attitudes to nurture in your meditation and which are unhelpful.

Avoiding 'quick-fix' solutions

If you want a quick fix for all your problems, you've come to the wrong place. *Mindfulness is simple but not easy*. Mindfulness is a powerful process that takes time, and a certain type of effort, energy and discipline. You find quick fixes in the domain of TV advertising, billboards, and the Internet. Unfortunately, in my limited experience of instant happiness, it's just that – instantly present and instantly gone. I know that temptations are great, and marketing companies spend billions to work out how to convince you to part with your hard-earned cash.

However, you can integrate meditation practices into your life in short bursts. You don't have to sit for hours and hours in the lotus posture. One minute of fully focused attention on your breath on a daily basis can begin to shift something within you. The more you put in, the more you get out. Five minutes is better than one minute. Thirty minutes is better than five. You need to decide what's right for you – trust in yourself to make a decision and stick to that choice for a period of time.

Overcoming perfectionism

'I'll meditate as soon as I've sorted my life out', 'I'll do the course when things are totally settled', 'I'll practise mindfulness when I have no more problems in my life'. These excuses are common, and on the whole, unconstructive. Sometimes you do need to allow major events in your life to settle before you work on a new skill like mindfulness. However, you can't wait for life to become perfect. You don't have time to waste. If you've found a way to systematically and thoroughly create a meaningful way of producing further health and wellbeing in your life, why not take the first step? Yes, you may get it wrong, and make mistakes, but imperfection, mistakes and stumbles are an integrated part of the process of finding out about anything. No child ever began to walk without falling. No driver ever learns to drive without stalling. Take the first step today.

Finding out from failure

Failures are finger posts on the road to achievement.

CS Lewis.

There's no such thing as a bad meditation. There's no failure in meditation. I list here some experiences that people *think* made them fail at meditation, and reasons why they aren't 'failures':

- 'I couldn't concentrate. My mind was all over the place.' You can't concentrate continuously. Sooner or later your mind goes into thoughts, dreams, ideas or problems. The nature of the mind is to wander off. Lack of concentration is an integral part of meditation.

- 'I couldn't sit still.' Your body is designed to move. However, through training, slowly but surely, you're able to sit still for longer. If sitting really isn't for you, remember you can do mindfulness while you move. Try walking meditation (Chapter 6), exercises that integrate awareness, like yoga or tai chi, or any other action you choose in a mindful and therefore meditative way.

- 'I felt bored/tired/frustrated/angry/annoyed/jealous/excited/empty.' You're going to feel a variety of emotions in your meditation, just as you do in your everyday life. The difference is, instead of reacting to them automatically, you've got the valuable opportunity to watch them rise and fall. In the long run, these emotions will probably calm down a bit, but in the meantime you need simply to be aware of them – if you can, enjoy the show!

- 'I had the experience of X (replace X with *any* negative experience), which I didn't like.' People have both pleasant and unpleasant experiences in meditation. The experience may be anything from deep sadness to feeling you're disappearing, or your arms may feel as if they're floating up. Your mind is releasing knots within your psyche out into your conscious mind, and freeing you from your own conditioning. This is part and parcel of the process – let the process unfold by itself if you feel you can.

If you find yourself becoming very concerned or frightened in your meditation, and if the feelings are ongoing, you may need professional support for what's coming up for you. Get in touch with your doctor or suitable therapist.

Love is a powerful attitude

Once there was a little girl who was ill. She needed a blood transfusion but had a rare blood type. The doctors searched for a blood match but to no avail. They then thought of testing her younger, six-year-old brother, and fortunately he was a match. The doctors and his mother explained to the boy that they needed his blood so that they could give it to his sister to help her get better. The boy looked concerned and said that he needed to think about it, which surprised them. After some time, he returned and agreed. The doctors laid the brother down on a bed next to his sister, and began transferring some blood. Before long his sister began to get better. Then, suddenly, the boy called the doctor over and whispered in his ear, 'How long do I have left to live?'. The boy thought that by giving blood, he'd die, which of course he wouldn't. That was why he took some time to decide before saying yes to giving his blood to his sister.

Chapter 5

Humans Being Versus Humans Doing

*A*s human beings, people love doing stuff. You go to work, have hobbies, socialise and become adept multi-taskers trying to fit everything into the day. But what about the *being* in human being?

Every day, in everything you do, your mind switches between *doing* mode and *being* mode. This doesn't mean that you switch between, say, typing an email and staring into space. Instead, it means *being* in the moment as you're *doing* a task. One mode of mind isn't better than the other. They're both helpful in different ways. However, using the wrong mode of mind for a particular situation can cause difficulties.

In this chapter, I explain how spending some of your time just *being* has huge and far-reaching advantages. I also tell you how to 'just be it'.

Delving into the Doing Mode of Mind

You know the feeling. You've got to get the kids ready, drop them off at school, pay the gas bill, pop that letter in the post, renew the car insurance and make sure that you call your sister to see if she's feeling better. You're exhausted just thinking about everything! But you know you have to do it all. Your mind is in *doing* mode.

Doing mode is a highly developed quality in humans. You can think and conceptualise how you want things to be, and then work methodically in order to achieve them. That's part of the reason why people have been able to design computers and land on the moon – the products of doing mode.

Doing mode is certainly not a bad thing. If you want to get the shopping done, you need some doing mode! However, sometimes doing mode goes too far, and you start doing more and more without taking a break. That can certainly be draining.

The hallmarks of the doing mode of mind are:

- ✔ **You're aware of how things *are*, and how they *should* be.** For example, if you need to renew your home insurance, you're aware that you currently haven't renewed the insurance, and that you need to at some point soon.

- ✔ **You set a goal to fix things.** If you're in doing mode, you're setting goals as to the way things should be. This problem-solving happens all the time without you being conscious of it. In the home insurance example, your goal may be to call several insurance companies or visit several websites to find the right deal for you.

- ✔ **You try harder and harder to achieve your goal.** In doing mode, you feel driven. You know what you want and you try hard to get it. Doing mode is all about getting to the destination rather than considering anything else. So, if an insurance company puts you on hold for too long you begin to feel tense and frustrated. In this driven state of mind, you don't come up with creative solutions such as calling a different company or just trying at a quieter time.

- ✔ **Most of your actions happen automatically.** You're not really aware when you're in doing mode. You're completing tasks on automatic pilot. Thoughts pop into your head, emotions emerge and you act on them largely unconsciously. If the person you're speaking to on the telephone is rude, you may automatically react, making you both feel bad, rather than considering that the phone operator may have had a really long and bad day too.

- ✔ **You're not in the present moment.** When engaged in doing mode, you're not connected with your senses, in the now. You're thinking about how things should be in the future, or replaying events from the past. You're lost in your head rather than focused in the moment. Whilst you're placed on hold on the telephone, your mind may wander into anxious thoughts about tomorrow's meeting rather than just taking the chance to have a break and look at the sky, or gaze at the beautiful tree through the window.

Doing mode isn't just the mode you're in when you're doing stuff. Even when you're sitting on the sofa, your mind can be spinning. You're in doing mode. Trying to run away from negative emotions or towards pleasant ones is also part of doing mode's speciality.

Doing mode is most unhelpful when applied to emotional difficulties. Trying to get rid of or suppress emotions may seem to work in the very short term, but before long the emotions rise up again. Being mode is a more helpful state of mind for understanding and finding out about emotions, particularly negative ones. See the later section 'Dealing with emotions using being mode'.

Cruising on auto-pilot

Aeroplanes have a button called automatic pilot. When pilots push that button, they don't have to consciously control the aircraft – the plane flies by itself. People can also run on auto-pilot when they're in doing mode, although I haven't found the button for it yet! You may have had the experience when going to fetch something from another room. You walk down the stairs and into the room and . . . your mind's gone blank! You wandered off somewhere internally and forgot what you wanted. Or you're driving somewhere different and end up unconsciously driving to work. Oops! That's human auto-pilot in action.

Auto-pilot has some advantages, which is why it has evolved in humans. Once something has become automatic, you don't need to consciously think about it again, and can give your attention to something else. Auto-pilot also saves some energy. Imagine if you had to think about every movement of your body when you were driving or walking – activities that involve hundreds of muscles; thinking in this way would be very tiring. In fact, you say someone has learnt something properly if he can do it automatically without thinking about it.

The problems of automatic pilot are that:

✔ **You can get trapped in auto-pilot.** You can spend your whole life in doing mode. With everything happening automatically, you have a lack of connection with the beauty of life. The blue sky, the green trees, the flight of a bird, the eyes of a child become just ordinary or you don't even notice them. This kind of living leads to a sense of dissatisfaction.

✔ **You don't have a choice.** Auto-pilot is particularly dangerous in the field of thoughts and emotions. You may be thinking 'I'm useless', 'I'm unlovable' or 'I can't do that' automatically without even noticing it. Thoughts have a huge effect on emotions, especially if you believe the thoughts to be true. Automatic negative thoughts lead to unhelpful and difficult emotions. All you notice is that you're suddenly really low, or angry, or tired. However, if you're conscious of these negative thoughts, you have a choice as to whether you believe them or not.

Embracing the Being Mode of Mind

Society values people achieving goals. You see people in the papers who have record amounts of money, or who've climbed the highest mountain. How many times has someone made the headlines for living in the moment?!

People are very familiar and almost comforted by the doing mode of mind. To stop doing so much, whether physically or mentally, isn't easy. Doing feels attractive and exciting. However, people are beginning to realise that too much doing is a problem. In fact a whole philosophy has arisen and lots of books have been written all about how you can slow down.

On the surface, the realm of *being* appears lifeless and boring. In actual fact, this couldn't be further from the truth. Being mode is a nourishing and uplifting state of mind that's always available to you, in the midst of busy activity. You can be trading in the stock market and conscious of your physical, emotional and psychological state of mind – you're in being mode. Being mode isn't easy to cultivate, yet the rewards of accessing this inner resource far outweigh any difficulties in reaching it.

The hungry tigers

The classic story of the hungry tigers points towards a different way of living.

One day a man was walking through a forest when a tiger spotted him and chased after him. The man ran out of the forest as fast as he could to escape the hungry beast. Eventually he stumbled and fell off the edge of a cliff. As he fell he managed to catch a vine, but continued to dangle precariously over the high drop. The tiger continued to watch him from above. Another pack of hungry tigers paced below the man. Then a mouse popped out of a crevice in the cliff. The mouse started gnawing the vine the man was clinging to. Suddenly, the man saw a beautiful plump strawberry glistening in the light. He plucked it and popped it into his mouth. How wonderful it tasted!

You can interpret this story in many ways. I like to think of the tiger above as worries about the past and the high drop to the tigers below as concerns about the future. The suggestion is to come to your senses – enjoy the strawberry of the present moment, and engage in being mode! The story also offers hope: no matter how bad your past or future appears to be, you may be able to take some pleasure through connecting with senses in the here and now.

Here are some of the qualities of the being mode of mind:

- **You connect with the present moment.** When you're in being mode, you're mindful of sight, sound, smell, taste and touch. You're not thinking about the past or future.

- **You acknowledge and allow things to be as they are.** You're less goal-oriented. You have less of a burning desire for situations to change. You accept how things are before moving to change anything. Being mode doesn't mean resignation, it means active acceptance of the way things are at the moment. If you're lost but you have a map, the only way of getting anywhere is to know where you are to start with. Being mode is about acknowledging where you are.

- **You're open to pleasant, unpleasant and neutral emotions.** You're willing to open up to painful and unpleasant sensations or emotions without trying to run away from them. You understand that avoiding an emotion just locks you into it more tightly.

The being mode of mind is what mindfulness endeavours to cultivate. Being mode is about allowing things to be as they are already. When you stop trying to change things, paradoxically they change by themselves. As Carl Jung said: 'We cannot change anything until we accept it.'

Accepting a situation or emotion just to make it go away doesn't really work, and misses an important point. For example, say you're feeling a bit sad. If you acknowledge it with a secret desire that it will go away, you haven't fully accepted it yet. Instead, accept an emotion wholeheartedly if you can – emotions are here to teach us something. Listen to your emotions and see what they have to say.

Combining Being and Doing

Think of your mind as like the ocean. The waves rise and fall but the still, deep waters are always there underneath.

You're tossed and turned in the waves when you're on the surface in doing mode. The waves aren't bad – they're just part of the ocean. Going further down, the waves of doing rest on the still waters of being, as shown in Figure 5-1. Being is your sense of who you are. Being is characterised as a state of acceptance, a willingness to be with whatever is. Being is tranquil, still and grounding.

Doing
More likely to be restless, dissatisfied, conceptual, focused on outer world, avoiding negative experiences and goal orientated.

Figure 5-1:
The ocean of doing and being.

Being
Your inner sense of awareness, allowing, acceptance, peace, stillness and silence which is ever present, underneath the doing.

Experience itself is neither doing nor being mode. You determine the mode by how you react or respond to the experience. Doing is getting actively involved in the experience in order to change it in some way. Being is simply seeing it as it is. That lack of fixing can result in a sense of calmness even when things are tricky.

Switching from doing to being doesn't require years of mindfulness training. It can happen in a moment. Imagine walking to work and worrying about all the things that you need to get done, and planning how you'll tackle the next project with the manager away on holiday. Suddenly you notice the fiery red leaves on a tree. You're amazed at the beauty of it. That simple connection with the sense of sight is an example of being mode. The mode of mind changes by shifting the focus of attention to the present moment. You're no longer on automatic pilot with all its planning, judging, criticising and praising. You're in the present moment. Even something as seemingly mundane as feeling your feet in contact with the ground as you walk is a move towards being mode too. Changing modes may not seem easy at first, especially when you're preoccupied by thoughts, but it gets easier through practice.

The key to a mindful way of living is to integrate both doing and being modes of mind into your life. Become aware of which mode you're operating in and make an appropriate choice about which is most helpful for the situation. You need to know where you are on the map before you can move on. Doing mode is important. You need to plan what you're going to do today, what food to buy, how to give feedback to a colleague and how best to respond when your children start arguing. These activities make you human. However, as a human *being*, you need to integrate a being mode of mind into your doing in order to be fully awake to your life.

Overcoming Obsessive Doing: Distinguishing Wants from Needs

One of the most common addictions people have is work. What started as a 9 a.m. to 5 p.m. job can easily become a 5 a.m. to 9 p.m. job. Naturally, you need to work and earn enough cash to pay the bills. However, before you know it, you're trying to earn a bit more than you actually need. And then your neighbour gets that new car, and you're tempted to do the same. So you do, but it's a touch out of your budget. You go for that promotion, but you need to put in lots more hours – it's a slippery slope to more and more doing. If working long hours is what you want, you're fine but if it's too much for you, or the long hours are having a negative impact on your relationships, consider looking into a different way of living.

You're excessively doing when your balance is tipped towards your *wants* rather than your *needs*. You need to keep a balance between what you want out of life and what you actually need. I define wants as desires that aren't really essential to your life, but that you seem to chase after, like an even bigger house or wanting absolutely everyone to like you. Needs are your basic necessities such as food, shelter, clothing and a sense of security. Here are some suggestions for reducing your wants and so helping you to make doing mode easier:

- Make a list of all the things you need to do today. Then prioritise. Ensure that you put mindfulness on the list too. That goes at the top!

- Put some things on your to-do list that aren't urgent but fun, like reading you favourite novel or taking the kids to the cinema. Non-urgent activities give you a chance to have a breather from energy-draining doing mode.

- Think about people you know who rarely rush from place to place. Ask them how they get everything done, or just spend more time with them.

- Simplify your life. Remember who and what's most important in your life and let go of the rest. As American writer and naturalist Henry David Thoreau said: 'Life is frittered away by detail. Simplify, simplify.'

- Switch television channels when adverts come on. Adverts are designed to ignite dissatisfaction in you, making you want more, more, more.

- Invoke the being mode of mind whenever you're doing things. Connecting with your breath or the senses is a helpful way of accomplishing this.

Being in the Zone: The Psychology of Flow

Have you ever noticed that when you're eating your favourite food, you forget all your worries and problems? The experience is so lovely that the sense of who you are, what you do, where you come from, and whatever the plan is for tomorrow all vanish for a moment. In fact, most pleasures that you engage in result in you letting go of the sense of 'you' with all your problems and issues.

Imagine skiing downhill at high speed. You sense the wind whooshing past you, feel the cool mountain breeze, and enjoy the deep blue colour of the sky. You're *in the zone*; in the moment, at one with all around you. When you're in the zone, you let go of doing mode and come into being mode – the present moment.

This 'in the zone' state of mind is called 'flow' by psychologist Mikhail Csíkszentmihályi . But what's flow got to do with the being mode of mind? Surely being in the zone is always about doing? Not quite. Practising mindfulness helps to generate flow experiences directly. Everything you do, you can do in the moment, giving you a deeper sense of aliveness.

Here's what you experience when you're in a state of flow:

- ✔ You feel at one with the world.
- ✔ You let go of your sense of an individual and any worries and problems.
- ✔ You're completely focused.
- ✔ You feel very satisfied with what you're doing.
- ✔ You're happy, although you don't really notice it at the time because you're so engrossed in whatever you're doing.

Understanding the factors of flow

Csíkszentmihályi found some key factors that accompany an experience of flow. I've adapted them here so you can generate a flow experience in anything. As long as you do a task mindfully, it's potentially going to be a flow experience.

Here are some of key factors of flow and how you can generate them using mindfulness:

✔ **Attention.** Flow experiences need attention. Mindfulness is all about attention, and mindfulness increases your level of attention with practice. Through regular mindfulness practice, your brain becomes better at paying attention to whatever you choose to focus on, making a flow experience far more likely. When driving, you simply pay attention to your surroundings rather than letting your mind wander off.

✔ **Direct and immediate feedback.** Flow needs direct feedback as to how you're doing. When you're practising mindfulness, you're getting immediate feedback because you know at any time if you're paying attention or if your mind has wandered off for the last few minutes. So, if driving, you notice when your mind has drifted into dreaming about what's for dinner tonight, and you bring your attention gently back to the here and now.

✔ **Sufficiently challenging task.** Mindfulness is an active process of repeatedly rebalancing to come back to the present moment while the mind – doing what minds do – wants to pull you away into other thoughts. To drive in a mindful way from work to home would be a suitable challenge for anyone, potentially creating a flow experience.

✔ **Sense of personal control.** When you're mindful of your thoughts and feelings that are arising, you've created a choice. You don't have to react to them or do what they tell you to do. This generates a sense of control, as you become aware of the choices you have. If whilst driving, someone cuts in front of you, you've got the choice to either react and feel annoyed, or practise letting it go. Even if you do react, you can notice how you react and what effect the reaction has on your thoughts and feelings.

✔ **Intrinsically rewarding.** As you carry out a task you're doing it for the sake of itself. If you're driving your car to get home as fast as possible to have your cup of tea, you're not going to be in a flow experience. If you drive to simply enjoy each moment of the journey, that's different. You can feel the warmth of the sunshine on your arm, appreciate the colour of the sky whilst sitting in traffic and marvel at the miracle of the human body's ability to do such a complex task effortlessly. You're in a flow experience.

Normally, mindfulness would make you a safer driver rather than a more dangerous one. However, begin by being mindful of safer tasks like washing dishes or going for a walk before you attempt mindfulness of driving, just so you get used to being mindful. Don't use mindfulness of driving if you find the experience distracting.

Discovering your flow experiences

Everyone's had flow experiences. By knowing when you've been in flow, you can encourage more opportunities to experience it in the future. The following are some typical activities that people often find themselves flowing in. You may even find something here to try yourself:

- **Reading or writing.** When you're fully engaged in a good book full of fascinating insights or a challenging storyline, you're in flow. You forget about everything else and time flies by. When writing in flow, words simply pop into your head and onto your page with effortless ease. You stop criticising what you're creating, and enjoy seeing the report or book pouring out of you. I've discovered how to do this myself by writing whatever words arise into my awareness first, and avoiding all self-judgement. Then I go back and edit the writing later on. In this way, the writing seems to flow naturally. This is an example of mindful writing.

- **Art or hobbies (such as drawing, painting, dancing, singing or playing music).** Most artistic endeavours involve flow. You're directly connected with your senses and people often describe themselves as being 'at one with the music'. If you're doing a particular hobby because you're forced to, it may or may not be a flow experience as the intrinsic motivation isn't there.

- **Exercise (walking, running, cycling, swimming and so on).** Some people love exercise so much that they get addicted to it. The rush of adrenaline, the full focus in the present moment, and the feeling of exhilaration makes for a flow experience.

- **Work.** Perhaps surprisingly, you can be in flow at work. Research has found that people are happier at work than they are in their leisure time. Work encourages you to do something with a focused attention, and often involves interaction with others. You need to give something of yourself. This can set the stage for flow. In contrast, watching TV at home can drain your energy, especially if you're watching unchallenging programmes.

- **Anything done mindfully.** Remember, anything that you do with a mindful awareness is going to generate a flow state of mind, from making love to making a cup of tea.

Encouraging a Being Mode of Mind

Generally speaking, most people spend too much time in doing mode and not enough in being mode. Doing mode results in chasing after goals that may not be what you're really interested in. Being mode offers a rest – a chance to let go of the usual, habitual patterns of the mind and drop into the awareness that's always there.

You can be in being mode even though you're doing something. Being mode doesn't necessarily mean that you're doing nothing. You can be busy working hard in the garden, and yet if your attention is right in the moment, and you're connecting directly with the senses, you can be in being mode.

Here are ten ways of switching from doing mode to being mode:

✔ When walking from place to place, take the opportunity to feel your feet on the floor, see the range of different colours in front of you, and listen to the variety of different sounds.

✔ When moving from one activity to another, take a moment to rest. Feel three complete in-breaths and out-breaths or more if you have time.

✔ Establish a regular meditation routine using formal mindfulness meditation practices (for more on this, head to Chapter 6).

✔ Use the three-minute mini-meditation several times a day (see Chapter 7).Whenever you catch yourself becoming excessively tense or emotional, use the mini-meditation to begin moving towards being mode and opening up to the challenging experience, rather than reacting to try to avoid or get rid of the experience.

✔ Avoid multitasking whenever you can. Doing one thing at a time with your full and undivided attention can engage being mode. Doing too many things at the same time encourages your mind to spin.

✔ Find time to do a hobby or sport. These activities tend to involve connecting with the senses, which immediately brings you into being mode. Painting, listening to music or playing an instrument, dancing, singing, walking in the park, and many more activities all offer a chance to be with the senses.

✔ When taking a bath or shower, use the time to feel the warmth of the water and the contact of the water with your skin. Allow all your senses to be involved in the experience; enjoy the sound of the water and breathe in the scent of your favourite soap or body wash.

✔ When you're eating, pause before your meal to take a few conscious breaths. Then eat the meal with your full attention.

✔ Treat yourself to a day of mindfulness once in a while. Wake up slowly, feel your breath frequently, and connect with your senses and with other significant people around you as much as you can.

Dealing with emotions using being mode

Using doing mode in the area of thoughts and emotions is like using the wrong remote control to change the channel on your television. No matter how hard you push the buttons, the channel isn't going to change – and pushing the buttons harder just makes you more tired and breaks the remote control. You're using the wrong tool for the job.

Say you're feeling sad today. Doing mode may feel the emotion and use the problem-solving, goal-oriented mind to try to fight it, asking, 'Why am I sad? How can I escape from it? What shall I do now? Why does this always happen to me?' Doing mode sets thoughts spinning in your head, which just makes you feel worse.

Next time you have an uncomfortable feeling like sadness, anger, frustration or jealousy, try this exercise to get into being mode:

1. **Set your intention.** Let your intention be to feel the emotion and its effects as best you can with a gentle curiosity. You're not doing so as a clever way to get rid of it. You're just giving yourself space to learn from the emotion rather than running away.

   All emotions, no matter how strong, have a beginning and an end.

2. **Feel the emotion.** Feel the emotion with care, kindness and acceptance, as best you can. Open up to it. Notice where the emotion manifests itself in your body. Breathe into that part of your body and stay with it. Allow the emotion to be as it is. You don't need to fight or run away. Be with the experience.

3. **De-centre from the emotion.** Notice that you can be aware of the emotion, without being the emotion itself – create a space between you and the feeling. This is an important aspect of mindfulness. As you observe the feeling, you're separate from it in the sense that you're free from it. You're watching it. It's like sitting on a riverbank as the water rushes by rather than being in the river itself. As you watch the water (emotion) pass by, you're not in the river itself. Every now and then, you may feel like you've been sucked into the river and washed downstream. As soon as you feel this, simply step back out of the river again. Figure 5-2 illustrates this idea.

4. **Breathe.** Now simply feel your breath. Be with each in-breath and each out-breath. Notice how each breath is unique, different and vital for your health and wellbeing. Then continue with whatever you need to do in a mindful way.

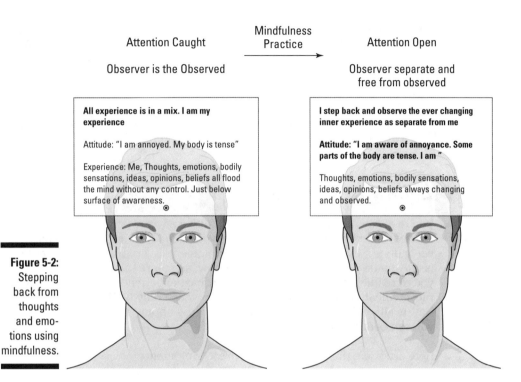

Attention Caught

Observer is the Observed

Mindfulness Practice →

Attention Open

Observer separate and free from observed

All experience is in a mix. I am my experience

Attitude: "I am annoyed. My body is tense"

Experience: Me, Thoughts, emotions, bodily sensations, ideas, opinions, beliefs all flood the mind without any control. Just below surface of awareness.

I step back and observe the ever changing inner experience as separate from me

Attitude: "I am aware of annoyance. Some parts of the body are tense. I am "

Thoughts, emotions, bodily sensations, ideas, opinions, beliefs always changing and observed.

Figure 5-2: Stepping back from thoughts and emotions using mindfulness.

Finding time to just be

Are you a busy bee? Do you have too much to do to have time to be? One of the attractive things about mindfulness is that you don't have a fixed amount of time that you're 'supposed' to practise for. Your daily practice can be meditating for one minute or one hour – it's up to you. The other great thing about mindfulness is that you can simply be mindful of your normal everyday routine and in that way build up your awareness and *being* mode. That takes no time at all; in fact, it can save time because you're more focused on your activities.

These mindful practices require almost no time at all:

✔ When waiting in a queue, rather than 'killing' the time, engage your awareness. Notice the colours and sounds around you. Or challenge yourself to see if you can maintain the awareness of your feet on the floor for ten full breaths.

✔ When you're stopped at a red traffic light you have a choice. You can get yourself frustrated and impatient, or you can do traffic light meditation! Close your eyes and nourish yourself with three mindful breaths – very refreshing!

✔ The next time the phone rings, let it ring three times. Use that time to breathe and smile. Telesales companies know that you can 'hear the smile' on the phone and ask employees to smile when they're on a call. You're in a more patient and happy state of mind when you speak.

✔ Change your routine. If you normally drive to work, try walking or cycling for part of it. Speak to different friends or colleagues. Take up a new hobby. When you change your habit, you're engaging different pathways in the brain. You instinctively wake up to the moment and just be.

Living in the moment

You're always in the present moment. You've never been in any other moment. Don't believe me? Every time your mind worries about the past, when does it do it? Only in the present moment. Every plan you've ever made is only made in the present too. Right now, as you're thinking about what you're reading, and comparing it to your past experience, you're doing so in this moment, now. Your plans for tomorrow can only be thought about now. Now is all you're ever in. So what's all the fuss about? The question is how you can connect with the here and now.

Here are some tips for living in the present moment:

✔ **Focus on whatever you're doing.** When you type, feel the contact between your fingers and the keyboard. When you drive, try giving it your full attention rather than allowing your mind to wander. When drinking tea, do some mindful drinking. Feel the sensations as the cup comes towards your mouth, and enjoy the refreshing taste of tea. Living in the present is trickier than it sounds but each time you try, you get a little bit better. Slowly but surely, you start really living in the moment.

✔ **Reduce activities that draw you out of the moment.** I found that watching too much television sent my mind spinning, so I got rid of it. For you, you may need to reduce the time you spend surfing the Internet or chatting for hours online. Or it may be as simple as stopping lying in bed in the morning for too long, allowing you time to worry unnecessarily about the day. Nothing's wrong with any of these activities, but they don't encourage moment-by-moment living. They capture your attention and lead to a passive state of mind. Switching from channel to channel while slumped on the sofa drains your energy much faster than an activity done with a gentle awareness.

✔ **Establish a daily mindfulness practice.** Doing so strengthens your ability to stay in the present rather than being drawn into the past or pulled into the future. The strength of your daily habit extends into your everyday life, without you even trying. You hear the sound of that bird in the tree, or find yourself listening intently to your colleague in an effortless way. Now mindfulness becomes fun.

✔ **Look deeply.** Consider and reflect on all the people and things that came together in each moment. For example, you're reading this book. The book's paper came from trees which needed sunshine and rain, soil and nutrients. The book was edited, marketed, printed, transported and distributed and sold by people. It also required the invention of the printing press, language and more. You were taught English by someone to enable you to understand the words. This awareness of all that's come together and been provided for you to enjoy naturally creates gratitude and present moment awareness. This is called *looking deeply*. You're connecting in the moment, and also seeing the bigger picture of how things have come together in an interconnected way. Looking deeply isn't thinking about your experience, but seeing your experience in a different way. You can try it in any situation – it transforms your perspective, and perspective transforms experience.

Part III
Practising Mindfulness

The 5th Wave   By Rich Tennant

"Helen, you're drifting."

In this part . . .

You get down to some proper mindfulness practice here. Discover the delights of practising mindfulness not only when you set time aside for it, but in your normal everyday living. Find out how to design a mindfulness routine that's right for you by doing an eight week mindfulness course, and know how to avoid the common pitfalls in the mindfulness game.

Chapter 6

Getting Into Formal Mindfulness Meditation Practice

. . . .

In This Chapter

▶ Trying eating, walking and body scan mindfulness meditation practices

▶ Breathing and walking in a mindful way

▶ Understanding and overcoming pitfalls

. . . .

*M*editation is like diving to the bottom of the ocean, where the water is still. The waves (thoughts) are at the surface, but you're watching them from a deeper, more restful depth. To submerge to that peaceful depth takes time. Extended meditations in these formal practices offer the diving equipment for you to safely reach those tranquil places.

Formal practice is mindfulness meditation you specifically make time for in your day – it doesn't mean you need to put on a suit or a posh dress though! You decide when and how long you're going to meditate, and you do it. A formal mindfulness routine lies at the heart of a mindful way of living. Without such a routine, you may struggle to be mindful in your daily life. This chapter explores some formal meditation practices, from sitting to walking.

Preparing Your Body and Mind for Mindfulness Meditation

Here are some useful pointers on preparing yourself to practise meditation:

✔ You can practise the meditation any time and anywhere that suits you. For more help on deciding times and places to practise, see Chapter 9.

> ✔ Avoid meditating immediately after a big meal, or when you're feeling very hungry; your stomach may then become the object of your attention rather than anything else.
>
> ✔ You can sit on a chair or the floor to meditate. For more on sitting postures, see further on in this chapter.

Savouring Eating Meditation

Try this eating meditation the first time you practise mindfulness. Starting with eating meditation demonstrates the simplicity of meditation. Mindfulness meditation isn't about sitting cross-legged for hours on end, it's about the awareness you bring to each present moment. Meditation is about living with an open and curious awareness. Anything done with mindful awareness is meditation, including eating, driving, walking, talking and much more.

Try the following exercise:

1. **Place a raisin in your hand.** Imagine you dropped in from outer space and have never seen or tasted a raisin before. Spend a few minutes looking at the colour and texture of the raisin. Explore the creases and folds of its skin, how it catches the light as you rotate it and how much varying detail it contains. Observe the skill in your fingers to be able to delicately hold and rotate the raisin precisely and at will.

2. **Bring the raisin towards your nose.** Feel the sensations in your arm as you bring the raisin towards your nose. As you breathe, notice if the raisin has a scent, and the quality of it. Notice how you feel if the raisin doesn't have a scent. Spend a few minutes doing this.

3. **Hold the raisin to your ear.** Rotate it gently between your thumb and finger and listen to the sound it produces, if any. Perhaps it makes a quiet crackling sound or no noise at all. When you've done this, bring your arm back down.

4. **Rotate the raisin between your fingers and thumb.** Notice the texture of the raisin. Close your eyes to tune into the sense of touch more deeply. Feel the shape of the object and its weight. Gently squeeze the raisin and observe if you can get a sense of its inner contents.

5. **Bring the raisin towards your mouth.** Are you salivating? If so, your body has already begun the first stage of digestion. Touch the raisin gently onto your upper and lower lips to see what sensations you can detect. Place the raisin on your tongue. Do you have a sense of relief

now, or frustration? Feel the weight of the raisin on your tongue. Move the raisin around your mouth, noticing how skilled your tongue is at doing this. Place the raisin between two teeth and slowly bring your teeth together. Observe the phenomenon of tasting and eating. Spot the range of experiences unfolding, including a change in taste, and the fluxing consistency of the raisin as it slowly breaks up and dissolves. Be aware of yourself chewing and how you automatically start to swallow. Stay with the experience until you've finished eating the raisin.

6. **Notice the aftertaste in your mouth having finished eating the raisin.**

Now, reflect on these questions:

✔ How do you feel having done that exercise?

✔ What effect will this process have on your experience of eating raisins?

✔ What did you notice and find out?

There's no correct experience in this eating meditation. Different people have different experiences. You probably found it wasn't your normal experience of eating. The first thing to discover about all meditation is that *Whatever your experience is, is your experience and is correct and valid.*

By connecting with the senses, you move from automatic pilot mode to a mindful mode (refer to Chapter 5 for more about mental modes). In other words, rather than eating the raisin while doing something else and not even noticing the taste of the raisin, you deliberately turn your attention to the whole process of eating.

You may have found the taste of the raisin to be more vivid and colourful than usual. Perhaps you noticed things about raisins that you hadn't noticed before. Mindfulness reveals things you didn't notice, and transforms the experience itself, making for a deeper experience. If this is true of eating something ordinary like a raisin, consider what effect mindfulness could have on the rest of your experiences!

You may have noticed that you were thinking during the exercise, and perhaps you felt you couldn't do the mindful eating properly because of thinking. Don't worry – you're *always* thinking, and it's not going to stop any time soon. What you can do is begin to become aware that it's happening and see what effect that has.

Relaxing with Mindful Breathing Meditation

If you're keen to try a short ten-minute sitting mindfulness meditation, this one's for you. This meditation focuses your attention on the breath and enables you to guide your way back to your breathing when your attention wanders away.

Here's how to practise ten minutes of mindful breathing:

1. Find a comfortable posture. You can be sitting up in a chair, cross-legged on the floor, or even lying down (see the later section 'Finding a posture that's right for you'). Keep your spine straight if you can (if you can't, choose whatever posture suits you). Close your eyes if you want to.

This is an opportunity to be with whatever your experience is from moment to moment. This is a time for you. You don't need to achieve anything. You don't need to try too hard. You simply need to be with things as they are, as best you can, from moment to moment. Relax any obvious physical tensions if you can.

2. Become aware of the sensations of breathing. Feel your breath going in and out of your nostrils, or passing through the back of your throat, or feel your chest or belly rising and falling. As soon as you've found a place where you can feel your breath comfortably, endeavour to keep your attention there.

Before long, your mind may take you away into thoughts, ideas, dreams, fantasies and plans. That's perfectly normal and absolutely fine. Just as soon as you notice that it's happened, gently guide your attention back to your breath. Try not to criticise yourself each time your mind wanders away. Understand that it's all part of the meditation process. If you find yourself criticising or getting frustrated, try gently smiling when you see that your mind has wandered away. Then guide your attention back to your breath.

3. Continue to stay with the meditation, without trying to change the depth or speed of your breathing.

4. After ten minutes, gently open your eyes.

All the timings suggested in this book are for guidance only. You can be flexible and reduce or increase the time you meditate depending on your circumstances. I would suggest you decide how long you're going to practise meditating before each sitting, and then stick to your decision. You can use an alarm with a gentle ring, or perhaps a countdown timer on your phone to indicate when you've finished. This avoids having to keep opening your eyes to check that you need to bring the meditation to a close.

A cure for breathing boredom

A meditation student went up to her teacher and said that she was bored of feeling the breath. Could a different technique make breathing more interesting? The teacher replied, 'Yes. Close your mouth and breathe with your nose. Then take your left arm and with the thumb block your left nostril. With your index finger block the other nostril. You can no longer breathe. In less than a minute, you'll be more interested in breathing than anything else in the whole world. Try it for just 30 seconds and you'll find it hard to think about anything else but breathing.'

Remember how important your breathing is, and try not to take it for granted. Breathing is special.

If that was one of the first times you've practised meditation, you're starting a journey. The meditation may have felt fine or awful. That doesn't matter too much. What matters is your willingness to accept whatever arises, and keep practising. Starting meditation is a bit like going to the gym for the first time in months – the experience can be unpleasant to begin with! Keep practising and try not to judge it as a good or bad meditation – there's no such thing. And remember, there's nothing to be frightened about in meditation either – if you feel too uncomfortable, you can simply open your eyes and stop the meditation.

Engaging in Mindful Movement

Moving and stretching in a slow and mindful way is a wonderful preparation for more extended meditation exercises. Movement can also be a deep formal meditation in itself, if you approach it with full awareness.

When practising mindful movement, tune into the sensations of your breath as you move and hold different postures. Become aware of thoughts and emotions that arise, notice them, and shift your awareness back to the body. Be mindful of where a stretch is slightly out of your comfort zone and begins to feel uncomfortable. Explore what being at this *edge* of your comfort zone feels like. Notice if you habitually drive yourself through the pain, or if you always avoid the discomfort. Be curious about your relationship with movement and stretching and bring a playful attitude to your experience.

Practising mindful movement has many benefits. You can:

> ✔ **Explore limits and discomfort**. When you stretch, you eventually reach a limit, beyond which the discomfort becomes too intense (the edge). Mindfulness offers the opportunity to explore your mind's reactions as you approach your edge. Do you try to push beyond it, often causing injury, or do you stay too far away, avoiding the slightest discomfort? By

approaching the edge with a mindful awareness, you open up to uncomfortable physical sensations rather than avoiding them.

You can transfer this skill of mindful awareness to your experience of difficult thoughts and emotions, encouraging you to stay with them and acknowledge them, and see what effect mindfulness has on them.

✓ **Tune into the sensations in your body and out of the usual wandering mind**. By focusing in on the range of feelings and sensations in your body, you bring yourself into the present moment. Mindful movement shows you a way of coming into the here and now. Most of the other formal meditation practices involve being still, and you may find movement an easier door into mindful practice.

✓ **Discover how to be mindful while your body is in motion**. You can transfer this discovery into your daily life and become more mindful of all the movement you do, such as walking, cooking, cleaning and getting dressed. You're training your mind to be mindful in your day-to-day activities.

✓ **Gain an understanding about life through movement practice**. When trying to balance in a yoga posture, notice how your body isn't stiff or still, but continuously moving and correcting to maintain your balance. Sometimes you lose your balance and have to start again. In the same way, living a life of balance requires continuous correction, and sometimes you get it wrong. You just need to start again.

Consider other lessons about life you can take from doing a sequence of mindful yoga, or any other mindful movement. Think about how you cope with the more challenging poses, or how you may compare yourself to others, or compete with yourself.

Breathing into different parts of your body

In mindfulness practice, I often mention 'breathing into' your toes or fingers or your discomfort. What does that mean? Your lungs don't extend into your toes! Here's how you breathe into a particular part of the body:

1. Feel the sensations in the particular part of the body you're working on.

2. As you breathe in, imagine your breath going from your nose up or down into that part of your body or experience.

3. When you breathe out, sense your breath going out of that part of the body and back out of your nose. Allow the sensations in that part of the body to gently soften as you do this.

If this technique doesn't really work for you, try feeling the part of the body you're working on at the same time as feeling your breathing. Over time, this idea of breathing into your experience may naturally begin to make some sense. If it doesn't, don't worry.

Trying Out the Body Scan Meditation

The body scan is a wonderful meditation to start your journey into contemplative practices. You normally do the body scan lying down, so you get a sense of letting go straight away.

Practising the body scan

Set aside at least half an hour for the body scan. Find a time and a place where you won't be disturbed, and where you feel comfortable and secure. Turn off any phones you have.

This is a time totally set aside for yourself, and to be with yourself. A time for renewal, rest and healing. A time to nourish your health and wellbeing. Remember that mindfulness is about being with things as they are, moment to moment, as they unfold in the present. So, let go of ideas about self-improvement and personal development. Let go of your tendency for wanting things to be different from how they are, and allow them to be exactly as they are. Give yourself the space to be as you are. You don't even need to try to relax. Relaxation may happen or it may not. Relaxation isn't the aim of the body scan. If anything, the aim is to be aware of your experience, whatever it may be. Do whatever feels right for you.

The body scan practice is very safe. However, if the body scan brings up feelings that you can't cope with, stop and get advice from a mindfulness teacher or professional therapist. However, if you can, open up to the feelings and sensations and move in close – by giving these feelings the chance to speak to you, you may find that they dissipate in their own time.

1. Loosen any tight clothing, especially around your waist or neck. You may like to remove your shoes.

2. Lie down on your bed or a mat with your arms by your sides, palms facing up, and legs gently apart. If you feel uncomfortable, place a pillow under your knees, or just raise your knees. Experiment with your position – you may even prefer to sit up. You can place a blanket over yourself, as your body temperature can drop when still for an extended time.

3. Begin by feeling the weight of your body on the mat, bed or chair. Notice the points of contact between that and your body. Each time you breathe out, allow yourself to sink a little deeper into the mat, bed or chair.

4. Become aware of the sensations of your breath. You may feel the breath going in and out of your nostrils, or passing through the back of your

throat, or feel the chest or belly rising and falling. Be aware of your breath wherever it feels most predominant and comfortable for you. Continue for a few minutes.

5. When you're ready, move your awareness down the left leg, past the knee and ankle and right down into the big toe of your left foot. Notice the sensations in your big toe with a sense of curiosity. Is it warm or cold? Can you feel the contact of your socks, or the movement of air? Now expand your awareness to your little toe, and then all the toes in-between. What do they feel like? If you can't feel any sensation, that's okay. Just be aware of lack of sensation.

6. As you breathe, imagine the breath going down your body and into your toes. As you breathe out, imagine the breath going back up your body and out of your nose. Use this strategy of breathing into and out of each part to which you're paying attention (see the nearby sidebar 'Breathing into different parts of your body').

7. Expand your awareness to the sole of your foot. Focus on the ball and heel of the foot. The weight of the heel. The sides and upper part of the foot. The ankle. Breathe into the whole of the left foot. Then, when you're ready, let go of the left foot.

8. Repeat this process of gentle, kind, curious accepting awareness with the lower part of the left leg, the knee and the upper part of the left leg.

9. Notice how your left leg may now feel different to your right leg.

10. Gently shift your awareness around and down the right leg, to the toes in your right foot. Move your awareness up the right leg in the same way as before. Then let it go.

11. Become aware of your pelvis, hips, buttocks and all the delicate organs around here. Breathe into them and imagine you're filling them with nourishing oxygen.

12. Move up to the lower torso, the lower abdomen and lower back. Notice the movement of the lower abdomen as you breathe in and out. Notice any emotions you feel here. See if you can explore and accept your feelings as they are.

13. Bring your attention to your chest and upper back. Feel your rib cage rising and falling as you breathe in and out. Be mindful of your heart beating if you can. Be grateful that all these vital organs are currently functioning to keep you alive and conscious. Be mindful of any emotions arising from your heart area. Allow space for your emotions to express themselves.

14. Go to both arms together, beginning with the fingertips and moving up to the shoulders. Breathe into and out of each body part before you move to the next one, if that feels helpful.

15. Focus on your neck. Then move your mindful attention to your jaw, noticing if it's clenched. Feel your lips, inside your mouth, your cheeks, your nose, your eyelids and eyes, your temples, your forehead and

checking if it's frowning, your eyes, the back of your head, and finally the top of your head. Take your time to be with each part of your head in a mindful way, feeling and opening up to the physical sensations with curiosity and warmth.

16. Imagine a space in the top of your head and soles of your feet. Imagine your breath sweeping up and down your body as you breathe in and out. Feel the breath sweeping up and down your body, and get a sense of each cell in your body being nourished with energy and oxygen. Continue this for a few minutes.

17. Now let go of all effort to practise mindfulness. Get a sense of your whole body. Feel yourself as complete, just as you are. At peace, just as you are. Remember this sense of being is always available to you when you need it. Rest in this stillness.

18. Acknowledge the time you've taken to nourish your body and mind. Come out of this meditation gently, being aware of the transition into whatever you need to do next. Endeavour to bring this mindful awareness to whatever activity you engage in next.

Appreciating the benefits of the body scan meditation

The body scan meditation has many benefits:

✔ **Getting in touch with your body.** You spend most of your time in your head, constantly thinking, thinking, thinking. By practising the body scan, you're connecting with your own body, and disconnecting from your mind with all its ideas, opinions, beliefs, judgements, dreams and desires. Thinking is a wonderful and precious aspect of being human but by connecting with the sensations in the body, you tune into the intelligence and wisdom of the body. Hearing what the body has to say is fascinating if you listen carefully and give it the space to express itself. The body scan helps you acknowledge that understanding and insight comes not only from the thinking brain but from the whole body, a supremely intelligent system from which you can discover so much.

✔ **Letting go of doing mode and coming into being mode.** As you lie down to do the body scan you can completely let go physically. Your mind can follow on from this and also begin to let go of thinking on automatic pilot. Through the body scan you begin to move from the autopilot doing mode of mind into the being mode of mind, which is about allowing things to be just as they are (see Chapter 5 for more).

✔ **Training your attention.** The body scan alternates between a wide and a narrow focus of attention; from focusing on your little toe all the way through to the entire body. The body scan trains your mind to be able to move from detailed attention to a wider and more spacious awareness from one moment to the next. In other words, you're more able to zoom in and out of an experience – a skill you can use outside of meditation.

✔ **Releasing emotions stored in the body.** Stressful events experienced from childhood, such as divorce or extreme discipline, cause great fear and can get locked and stored in the body as physical tension, an absence of sensation, or as a dysfunctional part of the body, such as problems with digestion. The body scan helps to release that stored-up emotion and tension. Some clients have had years of physical ailments relieved through the regular practice of the body scan meditation.

✔ **Using the body as an emotional gauge.** Practising the body scan and becoming increasingly aware of your body enables you to become more sensitive to how your body reacts in different situations throughout the day. If you become stressed or nervous about something, you may be able to notice this earlier through the body, and so be able to make an informed choice as to what to do next. Without that awareness, you don't have a choice and face the possibility of unnecessarily spiralling down into unhelpful emotions and a tense body. For example, if you notice your forehead tightening up or your shoulders tensing in a meeting, you can do something about it, rather than letting it unconsciously build and build.

Diaphragmatic breathing

Diaphragmatic or *belly breathing*, rather than just chest breathing, is the type of breathing that takes place when you're relaxed and calm. You can see it in babies and young children when they breathe. Their bellies come out as they breathe in, and go back in when they breathe out. This belly breathing is caused by a deep, relaxed breath in which the diaphragm goes up and down, pushing the stomach in and out. When you practise diaphragmatic breathing, you nourish your body with greater levels of oxygen, and the breathing is easier for the body. Many people find it therapeutic, and it is emphasised in yoga too. Try taking a few belly breaths before you start your meditation to help lead you into a more focused state of mind.

Here's how to do diaphragmatic breathing (see Figure 6-1):

1. Loosen any tight clothing, especially around your waist.

2. Get into a comfortable position, sitting or lying down.

3. Place one hand on your chest and the other on your belly.

4. As you breathe in and out, allow the hand on your belly to gently rise up and down while keeping the hand on the chest relatively still. Diaphragmatic breathing may take some practice at first, but in time it becomes easy and natural. Practise as often as you want, and it soon becomes a healthy habit.

Figure 6-1:
An example
of how to
encourage
diaphrag-
matic
breathing.

Overcoming body scan obstacles

The body scan seems easy on the surface. All you need to do is lie down, pop on the CD, and guide your awareness through your body. In reality you're doing a lot more than that. If you've spent your life ignoring your body, trying a different approach takes both courage and determination. Problems may arise. Perhaps:

- You felt more pain in your body than you normally do.
- You wanted to stop the body scan.
- You couldn't concentrate.
- You fell asleep.
- You became more anxious, depressed or frustrated than when you started.
- You couldn't do the body scan.
- You didn't like the body scan.
- You couldn't stop crying.
- You couldn't see the point of the body scan.

All these are common experiences. Of course, experiences of pleasure and peace occur too! Remember the following sentence when you begin to struggle with the body scan, and other long meditations:

You may not always like it – you just need to keep at it.

Enjoying Sitting Meditation

Sitting meditation is simply being mindful in a sitting position. In this section I share some common sitting postures and guide you through seated practice. Once you establish yourself in the practice, you can adapt it in any way that suits you.

Try sitting meditation after a couple of weeks' practising the body scan every day (explained in the previous section). The body scan helps you to begin getting accustomed to paying attention to your breath and your body in an accepting and kindly way. You also begin to understand how easily the mind wanders off, and how to tenderly bring the attention back. The sitting meditation continues to develop your attention, bringing a wider range of present moment experiences to be mindful of. Although your mind still strays into thoughts, you begin to shift your *relationship* to thoughts, which is a small but fundamental shift.

Finding a posture that's right for you

When sitting for meditation, imagine yourself as a mountain: stable, grounded, balanced, dignified and beautiful. Your outer posture is more likely to be translated in your inner world, bringing clarity and wakefulness.

Sit on a chair or on the floor, in any posture, as long as you can sit with your back as straight as you can manage.

Ensure that your hips are several inches above your knees by sitting on a cushion or pillow. This helps to straighten your back, which keeps you more aware, awake and mindful.

Sitting on a chair

In a quest for comfort, you may have become accustomed to slouching on chairs. Over time, slouching causes damage to your back. You may habitually lean against the chair with an arched back and crooked neck, which isn't conducive to sitting meditation. When you sit away from the back of the chair and support your own weight, you're making a statement to yourself: 'I'm making an effort to meditate. I'm supporting myself.' Making this statement tends to have a positive effect on the meditation itself.

Here's how to sit on a chair for meditation (see Figure 6-2):

1. Try putting a couple of magazines, wooden blocks or perhaps even telephone directories underneath the back two legs of the chair. By giving your chair a slight tilt forwards you help to make your back straight naturally, without much effort.

2. Place your feet flat on the floor, or on a cushion on the floor if the chair is too high. Your knees need to be at more than about ninety degrees so that your hips are above your knees.

3. Position your hands on your knees face down, face up or place your hands in each other. If your hands are facing up, you may find it comfortable to allow your thumbs to gently touch each other. Some people also like to allow the hands to rest on a small cushion on their legs to prevent the shoulders dragging downwards.

4. Imagine that your head is a helium-filled balloon. Allow your head to lift naturally and gently and straighten your spine without straining. You want to achieve an upright back without tension. Picture the vertebrae as stacked coins. Tuck in your chin slightly.

5. Lean forwards and backwards a few times until you find the middle balance point – at this position your head neither falls back nor forward but is naturally balanced on the neck and shoulders. Then lean to the left and right to find the point of balance again. Now relax any extra tension in the body. You're ready to meditate!

Sitting on the floor

You can also do seated meditation sitting in the more traditional posture on the floor. Some people find sitting on the floor more grounding and stable. However, sitting in the most comfortable posture for you is more important than anything else.

On the floor, you can do the *kneeling posture,* shown in Figure 6-3, in which you support your buttocks using a meditation stool or a cushion. If you use a meditation stool, ensure that you have a cushion for it too, or you may find it uncomfortable.

It's important to find a stool or cushion at the right height for you. Too high and your back will feel strained and uncomfortable. Too low and you're more likely to slump and feel sleepy.

Figure 6-2:
Sitting on
a chair for
meditation.

Here are the instructions for the kneeling posture:

1. Begin by shaking your legs, and rotating your ankles to prepare yourself for the posture.

2. Kneel on a carpet or mat on the floor.

3. Raise your buttocks up and place the kneeling stool between your lower legs and your buttocks.

4. Gently sit back down on the kneeling stool. Place a cushion on top of the kneeling stool if you haven't already done so, to make the posture more comfortable for yourself.

5. Shift your body around slightly to ensure you're in a posture that feels balanced and stable for you. You don't need to be overly rigid in your posture.

The other position is the *Burmese posture*. This simply involves sitting on a cushion, and placing both lower legs on the floor, one folded in front of the other (shown in Figure 6-4).

Here are the Burmese posture instructions:

1. Shake your legs, rotate your ankles and have a stretch, however feels right for you. This helps to prepare your body to sit.

2. Place a mat or soft blanket on the ground. On top of that, place a firm cushion, or several soft cushions on top of each other.

3. Sit down by placing your buttocks on the cushion. Allow your knees to touch the ground. If your knees don't touch the ground, either use more cushions or try one of the other postures suggested in this section.

4. Allow the heel of your left foot to be close to or to gently touch the inside thigh of your right leg. Allow the right leg to be in front of the left leg, with the heel pointing towards your lower left leg. If your legs aren't that supple, adjust as necessary, always ensuring you're comfortable.

5. Invite your back to be quite straight but relaxed too. Gently rock back and forth to find the point where your head is balanced on your neck and shoulders. Tuck your chin in slightly, so the back of your neck isn't straining.

6. Place your hand on your knees facing down, or up with thumb and first finger gently touching. Alternatively, place a small cushion in your lap, and place your hands on the cushion in any way that feels right for you. I find the cushion helps to prevent my shoulders being dragged forward and down.

7. Meditate to your heart's content.

You'll find it more comfortable to sit on a firm meditation cushion, often called a *zafu*. Ordinary cushions on their own are too soft. The zafu helps to raise your hips above your knees, making the sitting position more stable. Alternatively, use lots of small cushions or fold a large cushion to give you better support. Find a position you're happy with.

Figure 6-3:
Kneeling
position
with a medi-
tation stool.

Figure 6-4:
The
Burmese
position.

Practising sitting meditation

The mindful sitting practice I describe here comprises several stages. To begin with, I recommend that you just do the first stage – mindfulness of breath – daily. Then, after about a week, you can expand the meditation to include mindfulness of breath and body, and so on.

Practising mindfulness of breath

1. Find a comfortable upright sitting posture on the floor or in a chair. Ensure that your spine is straight if you can.

2. The intention of this practice to be aware of whatever you're focusing on, in a non-judgemental, kind, accepting and curious way. Remember that this is a time set aside entirely for you, a time to be aware and awake to your experience as best you can, from moment to moment, non-judgementally.

3. Become aware of the feeling of your breath. Allow your attention to rest wherever the sensations of your breath are most predominant. This may be in or around the nostrils, as the cool air enters in and the warmer air leaves the nose. Or perhaps you notice it most in your chest as the rib cage rises and falls. Or maybe you feel it most easily and comfortably in the area of your belly, the lower abdomen. You may feel your belly move gently outwards as you breathe in, and back in as you let go and breathe out. As soon as you've found a place where you can feel the breath, simply rest your attention there for each in-breath and each out-breath. You don't need to change the pace or depth of your breathing, and you don't even need to think about it – you simply need to feel each breath.

4. As you rest your attention on the breath, before long your mind will wander off. That's absolutely natural and nothing to worry about. As soon as you notice it's gone off, realise that you're already back! The fact that you've become aware that your mind has been wandering is a moment of wakefulness. Now, simply label your thought quietly in your own mind. You can label it 'thinking, thinking' or if you want to be more specific: 'worrying, worrying' or 'planning, planning'. This helps to frame the thought. Then gently, kindly, without criticism or judgement, guide your attention back to wherever you were feeling the breath. Your mind may wander off a thousand times, or for long periods of time. Each time, softly, lightly and smoothly direct the attention back to the breath, if you can.

5. Continue this for about ten minutes, or longer if you want to.

At this point you can stop or carry on to the next stage which is mindfulness of both breath and body.

6. Expand your awareness from a focused attention on the breath, to a more wide and spacious awareness of the body as a whole. Become aware of the whole body sitting in a stable, balanced and grounded presence, like a mountain. The feeling of breathing is part of the body, so get a sense of the whole body breathing.

7. When the mind wanders off into thoughts, ideas, dreams or worries, gently label it and then guide the attention back to a sense of the body as a whole, breathing as in Step 4.

8. Remember that the whole body breathes all the time, through the skin. Get a sense of this whole body breathing.

9. Continue this open, wide, curious, kind and accepting awareness for about ten minutes or longer if you feel like it. If certain parts of your body become uncomfortable, choose to breathe into that discomfort and note the effect of that, or slowly and mindfully shift your bodily position to relieve the discomfort. Whatever you choose, doing it mindfully is the important bit.

At this point you can stop or carry on to mindfulness of sounds.

10. Let go of mindfulness of breath and body and become aware of sounds. Begin by noticing the sounds of your body, the sounds in the room you're in, the sounds in the building and finally the furthest sounds outside. Let the sounds permeate into you rather than straining to grasp them. Listen without effort – let it happen by itself. Listen without labelling the sound, as best you can. For example, if you hear the sound of a plane passing or a door closing or a bird singing, listen to the actual sound itself – its tone, pitch and volume – rather than thinking 'oh, that's a plane'.

11. As soon as you notice your thoughts taking over, label the thought and tenderly escort the attention back to listening.

12. Continue listening for ten minutes or so.

At this point you can stop or carry on to mindfulness of thoughts and feelings.

13. When you're ready, turn your attention from the external experience of sound to your inner thoughts. Thoughts can be in the form of sounds you can hear or in the form of images you can see. Watch or listen to thoughts in the same way you were mindful of sounds – without judgement or criticism, and with acceptance and openness.

14. Watch thoughts arise and pass away like clouds in the sky. Neither force thoughts to arise nor push them away. As best you can, create a distance, a space, between you and your thoughts. Notice what effect this

has, if any. If the thoughts suddenly disappear, see if you can be okay with that too.

15. Another way of watching thoughts is to imagine that you're sitting on the bank of a river. As you sit there, leaves float on the surface and continuously drift by. Place each thought that you have onto each leaf that passes you. Continue to sit and observe them passing by.

16. Every so often your attention may get stuck in a train of thought. Your mind just works that way. As soon as you notice this, calmly take a step back from your thoughts and watch them once again from a distance, as best you can. If you criticise yourself for your mind wandering, observe that as just a thought too.

17. Now try turning towards emotions. Notice whatever emotions arise and whether they're positive or negative. As far as you can, open up to the emotion and feel it. Notice where that emotion manifests itself in your body. Is it new or familiar? Is there just one emotion there or several layers? Do you feel like running away from the emotion, or staying with it? Breathe into the feeling as you continue to watch it. Observe your emotion in a curious, friendly way, like a young child looking at a new toy.

18. Continue to practise for ten minutes or so. These subtle activities take time to develop. Just do your best and accept however you feel they've gone, whether successful at focusing or not.

At this point you can stop or carry on to choiceless awareness.

19. *Choiceless awareness* is simply an open awareness of whatever arises in your consciousness. It may be sounds, thoughts, the sensations in your body, feelings, or the breath. Just be aware of it in an expansive, receptive and welcoming way. Put the welcome mat out for your experience. Notice whatever predominates most in your awareness and let it go again.

20. If you find your mind wandering (and it's particularly easy to get swept up and away into thoughts when practising this), come back to mindfulness of breath to ground yourself before trying again. Become curious about what's happening for you, rather than trying to change anything.

21. Practise for about ten minutes, then begin to bring the sitting meditation to a close. Gently congratulate yourself for having taken the time to nourish your health and wellbeing in this practice, for having taken time out of doing mode to explore the inner landscape of being mode, and allow this sense of awareness to permeate whatever activities you engage in today.

Overcoming sitting meditation obstacles

One of the most common problems with sitting meditation is posture. After sitting for some time, the back or knees or other parts of the body start to ache. When this happens, you have two choices.

- ✔ **Observe both the discomfort as well as your mind's reaction to it, while remaining sitting still.** I recommend this if the discomfort doesn't hurt too much. Mindfulness is about welcoming experiences, even if they feel unpleasant at first. What does the discomfort feel like exactly? What's its precise location? What do you think about it? As all experience is in a state of flux and change, you may find that even your feeling of physical discomfort changes.

- ✔ By discovering how to stay with these sensations your meditation skills flow into your everyday life. You can manage other difficult emotions and challenging problems in the same welcoming, curious and accepting way, rather than fighting them. Your body and mind are one, so by sitting still, your mind has a chance to stabilise and focus too.

- ✔ **Mindfully move the position of your body.** If your bodily discomfort is overwhelming, you can, of course, move your body. You may be sitting in an unsuitable posture. However, if possible, try not to react quickly to the discomfort. Instead, shift your position slowly and mindfully. In this way, you enfold your shift of position into the practice. You're responding instead of reacting, which is what mindfulness is about. Responding involves a deliberate choice by you – you feel the sensation and make a conscious decision as to what to do next. Reacting is automatic, lacks control and bypasses an intentional decision by you. By becoming more skilful in responding to your own experience in meditation, your ability spills out into everyday life – when someone frustrates you, you can respond to them whilst in control of yourself rather than reacting in an out of control way.

Besides posture, frustration can arise from the practice itself. You're so used to judging all your experiences, that you judge your meditation too. But mindfulness means non-judgemental awareness. *Bad meditation doesn't exist – there's no such thing.* Sometimes you can concentrate and focus your mind, and other times it's totally wild. Meditation is like that. Trust in the process, even if it feels as if you're not improving. Mindfulness works at a level both above and below the conscious mind, so on the surface of things it may seem as though you're not getting anywhere. Don't worry – each meditation is a step forwards because you've actually practised.

Stepping Out with Walking Meditations

Walking meditation is meditation in which the process of walking is used as a focus. The ability to walk is a privilege and a miraculous process that you can feel grateful for.

Imagine being able to walk to work in a meditative, calm and relaxed way, arriving at your destination refreshed and energised. You can walk in a stress-free way with walking meditation. My students often say walking meditation is one of their favourite practices. The walking gives them time out from an over-occupied mind. Meditative walking is also a good way of preparing for the other, more physically static meditations.

Examining your walking habits

You probably rarely just walk. You may walk and talk, walk and think, walk and plan, or walk and worry. Walking is so easy that you do other things at the same time. You probably walk on automatic pilot most the time. However, you can get into negative habit patterns and end up spending all your time planning when you walk and rarely just enjoying the walking itself.

When you walk, you're normally trying to get somewhere. That makes sense, I know. In walking meditation, you're not trying to get anywhere. You can let go of the destination and enjoy the journey, which is what all meditations are about.

Practising formal walking meditation

In this section I describe a formal walking meditation, which means you make special time and space to practise the exercise. You can equally introduce an awareness of your walking in an informal way, when going about your daily activities. You don't have to slow down the pace at which you walk for that.

To practise formal walking meditation, sometimes called mindful walking, try the following steps:

1. Decide how long you're going to practise. I suggest ten minutes the first time, but whatever you feel comfortable with. Also choose where to practise. The first time you try it, practise walking *very* slowly, so a quiet room at home may be best.

2. Stand upright with stability. Gently lean to the left and right, forwards and backwards, to find a central, balanced standing posture. Let your knees unlock slightly, and soften any unnecessary tension in your face. Allow your arms to hang naturally by your sides. Ensure that your body

is grounded, like a tree, firmly rooted to the ground with dignity and poise.

3. Become aware of your breath. Come into contact with the flow of each inhalation and exhalation. Enjoy breathing.

4. Now slowly lean onto your left foot and notice how your sensations change. Then slowly shift your weight onto your right foot. Again perceive how the sensations fluctuate from moment to moment.

5. When you're ready, gradually shift most of your weight onto your left foot, so almost no weight is on the right foot. Slowly take your right heel off the ground. Pause for a moment here. Notice the sense of anticipation about something as basic as taking a step. Now lift your right foot off the ground and place it heel first in front of you. Become aware of the weight of your body shifting from the left to the right foot. Continue gradually to place the rest of the right foot flat and firmly on the ground. Notice the weight continue to shift from left to right.

6. Continue to walk in this very slow, mindful way for as long as you want. When you finish, take some time to reflect on your experience.

Trying alternative walking meditations

Here are a couple of other ways of practising walking meditation which you can use whilst moving at your own pace:

Walking body scan

In this walking meditation you gradually move your awareness up your body as you walk, from your feet all the way to the top of your head.

1. Begin by walking as you normally would.

2. Now focus on the sensations in your feet. Notice how the weight shifts from one foot to the other.

3. Continue to move your mindful attention up your body. Feel your lower legs as you walk, then your upper legs, noticing their movement.

4. Now observe the movement and sensations in the area of the hips and pelvis.

5. Continue to scan your awareness to the lower, and then upper torso, then your arms, as they naturally swing to help you keep balance.

6. Observe the sensation in your shoulders, your neck, your face, and then the whole of your head.

7. Now get a sense of the body as a whole as you continue to stroll, together with the physical sensation of the breath. Continue this for as long as you wish.

Walking and smiling

This is a practice recommended by world-famous mindfulness teacher Thich Nhat Hanh. This mindfulness exercise is about generating positive feelings as you walk. Try the following as an experiment. Have fun with it:

1. Find a place to walk, by yourself, or with a friend. Try to find a beautiful place to walk if possible.

2. Remember that the purpose of walking meditation is to be in the present moment, letting go of your anxieties and worries. Just enjoy the present moment.

3. Walk as if you're the happiest person on earth. Smile – you're alive! Acknowledge that you're very fortunate if you're able to walk.

4. As you walk in this way, imagine you are printing peace and joy with every step you take. Walk as if you're kissing the earth with each step you take. Know that you're taking care of the earth by walking in this way.

5. Notice how many steps you take when you breathe in, and how many you take when you breathe out. If you take three steps with each in-breath, in your mind say 'in – in – in' as you breathe in. And if you take four steps as you breathe out, say 'out – out – out – out'. Doing so helps you to become aware of your breathing. You don't need to control your breathing or walking; let it be slow and natural.

6. Every now and then, when you see a beautiful tree, flower, lake, children playing, or anything else you like, stop and look at it. Continue to follow your breathing as you do this.

7. Imagine a flower blooming under each step you take. Allow each step to refresh your body and mind. Realise that life can only be lived in the present moment. Enjoy your walking.

Overcoming walking meditation obstacles

Walking meditation doesn't create as many issues as the other meditations. However, here are a couple that often crop up, with ideas to solve them:

- ✔ **You can't balance when walking very slowly.** Walking straight at a very slow pace is surprisingly tricky. If you think that you may fall over, use a wall to support yourself. Additionally, gaze at a spot in front of you and keep your eyes fixed there as you walk forwards. As you practise, your balance improves.

- ✔ **Your mind keeps wandering off.** Walking meditation is like all other mindfulness practices. The mind becomes distracted. Gently guide your attention back to the feeling of the feet on the floor, or the breath. No self-criticism or blaming is required.

Generating Compassion: Metta Meditations

Metta is a Buddhist term meaning loving-kindness or friendliness. Metta meditation is designed to generate a sense of compassion both to yourself and to others. All mindfulness meditations make use of an affectionate awareness, but metta meditations are specifically designed to deepen this skill and direct it in specific ways.

Many religious traditions and ancient cultures emphasise the need to love and care for yourself and those around you. When you're feeling particularly harsh and self-critical, metta meditation can act as an antidote and generate feelings of friendliness and affection. The reason metta meditation works is due to an important aspect of human beings: you can't feel both hatred and friendliness at the same time – by nourishing one, you displace the other. Metta meditation is a gentle way of healing your inner mind and heart from all its pain and suffering.

 If you're new to meditation, try some of the other meditations in this book first. When you've had some experience of those meditations, you're ready to try the metta meditation. Take your time with it – work through the practice slowly and regularly and you're sure to reap the benefits.

Meeting the Olympic meditators

Metta meditation is a skill you can develop in the same way as you can become skilful at tennis or driving – brain scans of experienced meditators have proven it. Renowned brain scientist Professor Richard Davidson and his team of neuroscientists at the University of Wisconsin – Madison in the United States have shown that short-term meditators can become more compassionate through metta-type meditations. Long-term, so-called 'Olympic meditators', who've spent over 10,000 hours meditating (not all at the same time!), have amongst the highest levels of wellbeing and compassion ever recorded in brain scans! In brain scan experiments, these expert meditators stepped out of uncomfortable and noisy scientific experiments after hours of testing with a smile on their faces – a reaction not seen before by scientists. The scientists proved that a sense of compassion is the most positive of positive emotions and is extremely powerful and healing for both body and mind.

Practising loving-kindness meditation

Here's a guided metta meditation. Work through it slowly, taking it step by step. If you don't have the time or the patience to do all the stages, do as many as you feel comfortable with. Be gentle with yourself, right from the beginning.

1. You can practise loving-kindness in a seated or lying down position. You can even practise it while walking. What's most important isn't the position you adopt, but the intention of kindness and friendliness you bring to the process. Make yourself warm and at ease. Gently close your eyes, or keep them half open, looking comfortably downwards.

2. Begin by feeling your breath. Notice the breath sensation wherever it feels most predominant for you. This awareness helps create a connection between your body and mind. Continue to feel your breath for a few minutes.

3. When you're ready, see if certain phrases arise from your heart for what you most deeply desire for yourself, in a long-lasting way and which you can ultimately wish for all beings. Phrases like:

   May I be well. May I be happy. May I be healthy. May I be free from suffering.

4. Softly repeat the phrases again and again. Allow them to sink into your heart. Allow the words to generate a feeling of kindness towards yourself. If that doesn't happen, don't worry about it – your intention is more important than the feeling. Just continue to repeat the phrases lightly. Let the phrases resonate.

5. Now bring to mind someone you care about; a good friend or person who inspires you. Picture the person in your mind's eye and inwardly say the same phrases to him or her. Don't worry if you can't create the image clearly. The intention works by itself. Use phrases like:

   May you be well. May you be happy. May you be healthy. May you be free from suffering.

   Send loving-kindness to the person using these words.

6. When you're ready, choose a neutral person; someone you see daily but don't have any particular positive or negative feelings towards. Perhaps someone you walk past every morning or buy coffee from. Again send a sense of loving-kindness using your phrases:

   May you be well. May you be happy. May you be healthy. May you be free from suffering.

7. Now choose a person you don't get on with too well. Perhaps someone you've been having difficulties with recently. Say the same phrases again, from the mind and heart. This may be more challenging.

8. Now bring all four people to mind: yourself, your friend, your neutral person and your difficult person. Visualise them or feel their presence. Try to send an equal amount of loving-kindness to them all by saying:

   May we be well. May we be happy. May we be healthy. May we be free from suffering.

9. Finally, expand your sense of loving-kindness outwards, towards all living beings. Plants, animals of the land, air and sea. The whole universe. Send this sense of friendliness, care, loving kindness and compassion in all directions from your heart.

   May all be well. May all be happy. May all be healthy. May all be free from suffering.

If the metta phrases I've suggested don't work for you, then here are other suggestions. Choose two or three and use them as your metta phrases. Or you can be creative and come up with your own too:

- ✔ May I be at peace with myself and all other beings.

- ✔ May I accept myself just as I am.

- ✔ May I find forgiveness for the inevitable hurt we bring to one another.

- ✔ May I live in peace and harmony with all beings.

- ✔ May I love myself completely just as I am now no matter what happens.

- ✔ May I be free from the suffering of fear and anger.

- ✔ May I love myself unconditionally.

Metta meditation can be a profoundly healing practice. Be patient with yourself and practise it slowly and lovingly. Let the phrases come from your heart and see what happens.

Once you become experienced at this meditation, you can even practise it whilst walking. However, remember to keep your eyes open or you may mindfully bump into something!

Overcoming metta meditation obstacles

You may experience a few specific problems with metta meditation. Some common issues with suggestions for overcoming them include:

✔ **You can't think of a specific person.** If you can't think of a suitable friend, or neutral person, or someone you're having difficulties with, don't worry. You can miss that step for now, or just choose anyone. The intention of loving kindness is more important than the specific person you choose.

✔ **You say the phrases but don't feel anything.** This is perfectly normal, especially when you start. Imagine the phrases coming out of your chest or heart, rather than your head, if you can. Again, the feeling isn't as important as your attitude of friendliness in the practice. The feelings may come in the future, or may not – you don't need to worry about that.

✔ **Your mind keeps wandering off.** This is simply the nature of mind, and happens in all meditations. As always, as soon as you notice, kindly and gently bring your attention back to the practice. Each time you bring it back, you're strengthening your mind to pay attention.

✔ **You feel very emotional.** Feeling emotional is a very common reaction. You may not be used to generating feelings in this way, and it can unlock deep-seated emotions. If you can, try to continue with the practice. If your emotions become overwhelming, try just the first phase, sending metta towards yourself, for the whole meditation. Doing just one phase for a whole meditation is perfectly fine. Alternatively, stop the practice and come back to it later on, when it feels more appropriate.

Chapter 7

Using Mindfulness for Yourself and Others

*Y*ou require a lot of looking after. If you malnourish your body and mind, things begin to go wrong. You need to eat a balanced diet and exercise regularly to maintain optimum health and wellbeing. You need to have the right amount of work and rest in your life. And you need to challenge yourself intellectually, to keep your mind healthy. You need to socialise and also save some time just for you. Achieving all this perfectly is impossible, but how can you strive to take care of yourself without becoming overly uptight and stressed?

Mindfulness can help you look after both yourself and others. Being aware of your thoughts, emotions and body, as well as the things and people around you, is essential. This awareness enables you to become sensitive to your own needs and those of others around you, therefore encouraging you to meet everyone's needs as far as possible.

A caring, accepting awareness is the key to healthy living. Mindfulness is the best way to develop awareness. This chapter details suggestions for looking after yourself and others through mindfulness.

Using a Mini Meditation

You don't need to practise meditation for hours and hours to reap its benefits. Short and frequent meditations are an effective way of developing mindfulness in your everyday life.

Introducing the breathing space

When you've had a busy day, you probably enjoy stopping for a nice hot cup of tea or coffee, or other favourite beverage. The drink offers more than just liquid for the body. The break gives you a chance to relax and unwind a bit. The three-minute mini meditation, called the *breathing space* (illustrated in Figure 7-1 and 7-2), is a bit like a tea break, but as well as relaxation, the breathing space enables you to check what's going on in your body, mind and heart – not getting rid of feelings or thoughts, but looking at them again from a clearer perspective.

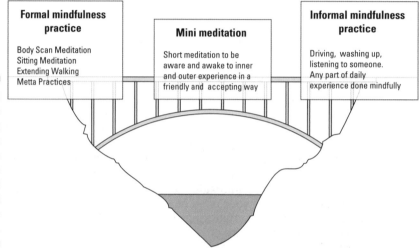

Figure 7-1: How the breathing space acts as a bridge between formal and informal mindfulness practice.

Formal mindfulness practice

Body Scan Meditation
Sitting Meditation
Extending Walking
Metta Practices

Mini meditation

Short meditation to be aware and awake to inner and outer experience in a friendly and accepting way

Informal mindfulness practice

Driving, washing up, listening to someone. Any part of daily experience done mindfully

TRY THIS

Tree, rope or wall? Describing an elephant

Six blind people were asked to determine what an elephant looks like. Each of them was guided to the elephant and felt a different part. One felt a leg and said that the elephant was like a pillar. One felt the trunk and said that the elephant was like the branches of a tree. One felt the tail and said that the elephant was like a rope. Another felt the ear and said that the elephant felt like a fan. The one who felt the belly thought the elephant felt like a wall. And the one who felt the tusk said that the elephant was like a solid pipe. Then they all started arguing, insisting that they were right about the nature of the elephant. A wise person happened to be passing (they always do in these stories) and said that they were all right to a certain extent. If they felt other parts of the elephant they would get a different perspective.

The moral of the story? Meditation enables you to see both your outer and inner experience fully, shifting your perspective and helping you to resolve inner and outer conflicts. You begin to understand how other people can be restricted by their views because that is all they know – they're just feeling one part of the elephant. This insight can result in greater compassion and understanding.

Practising the breathing space

You can practise the breathing space almost any time and anywhere. The meditation is made up of three distinct stages, which I call A, B and C to help you to remember what to practise at each stage. The exercise doesn't have to last exactly three minutes – you can make it longer or shorter depending on where you are and how much time you have. If you only have time to feel three breaths that's okay; doing so can still have a profound effect. Follow these steps:

1. Sit upright with a sense of dignity, but don't strain your back and neck. If you can't sit upright, try standing upright; lying down on your back or even curling up is acceptable. Sitting up straight is helpful because it sends a positive message to the brain – you're doing something different.

2. Practise the A step for about a minute or so, then move on to B for a minute, ending with C also for a minute – or however long you can manage.

   ✔ **Step A: Awareness.** Reflect on the following questions, pausing for a few seconds between each one:

   • *What bodily sensations am I aware of at the moment?* Feel your posture, become aware of any aches or pains, or any pleasant sensations. Just accept them as they are, as far as you can.

   • *What emotions am I aware of at the moment?* Notice the feelings in your heart or belly area or wherever you can feel emotion.

   • *What thoughts am I aware of, passing through my mind at the moment?* Become aware of your thoughts, and the space between you and your thoughts. If you can, simply observe your thoughts rather than becoming caught up in them.

   ✔ **Step B: Breathing.** Focus your attention in your belly area, the lower abdomen. As best you can, feel the whole of your in-breath and the whole of each out-breath. You don't need to change the rate of your breathing – just become mindful of it in a warm, curious and friendly way. Notice how each breath is slightly different. If your mind wanders away, gently and kindly guide your attention back to your breath. Appreciate how precious each breath is.

   ✔ **Step C: Consciously expanding.** Consciously expand your awareness from your belly to your whole body. Get a sense of your entire body breathing (which it is, through the skin). As the energy settles in your body, notice its effect. Accept yourself as perfect and complete just as you are, just in this moment, as much as you can.

Imagine the breathing space as an hourglass. The attention is wide and open to start with and then narrows and focuses on the breath in the second stage, before expanding again with more awareness and spaciousness.

The breathing space meditation encapsulates the core of mindfulness in a succinct and portable way. The full effects of the breathing space are:

- **You move into a restful 'being' mode of mind.** Your mind can be in one of two very different states of mind: *doing* mode or *being* mode. Doing mode is energetic and all about carrying out actions and changing things. Being mode is a soothing state of mind where you acknowledge things as they are (for lots more on being and doing mode, refer to Chapter 5).

- **Your self-awareness increases.** You become more aware of how your body feels, the thoughts going through your mind and the emotion or need of the moment. You may notice that your shoulders are hunched, or your jaw is clenched. You may have thoughts whizzing through your head that you hadn't even realised were there. Or perhaps you're feeling sad, or are thirsty or tired. If you listen to these messages, you can take appropriate action. Without self-awareness, you can't tackle them.

- **You create more opportunities to make choices.** You make choices all the time. At the moment, you've chosen to read this book and this page. Later on you may choose to go for a walk, call a friend or cook dinner. If your partner snaps at you, your reaction is a choice to a certain extent too. By practising the breathing space, you stand back from your experiences and see the bigger picture of the situation you're in. When a difficulty arises, you can make a decision from your whole wealth of knowledge and experience, rather than just a fleeting reaction. The breathing space can help you make wiser decisions.

- **You switch off automatic pilot.** Have you ever eaten a whole meal and realised that you didn't actually taste it? You were most likely on automatic pilot. You're so used to eating, you can do it while thinking about other things. The breathing space helps to connect you with your senses so that you're alive to the moment.

  Try this thought experiment. Without looking, remember if your wrist watch has roman numerals or normal numbers on it. If you're not sure, or got it wrong, it's a small indication of how you're operating on automatic pilot. You've looked at your watch hundreds of times, but not really looked carefully (I explain more about automatic pilot in Chapter 5).

- **You become an observer of your experience rather than feeling trapped by it.** In your normal everyday experience, no distance exists between you and your thoughts or emotions. They just arise and you act on them almost without noticing. One of the key outcomes of the breathing space is the creation of a space between you and your inner world. Your thoughts and emotions can be in complete turmoil, but you simply observe and are free from them, like watching a film at the cinema. This seemingly small shift in viewpoint has huge implications, which I explore in Chapter 5.

✔ **You see things from a different perspective.** Have you ever taken a comment too personally? I certainly have. Someone is critical about a piece of work I've done, and I immediately react, or at least feel a surge of emotion in the pit of my stomach. But you have other ways of reacting. Was the other person stressed out? Are you making a big deal about nothing? The pause offered by the breathing space can help you see things in another way.

✔ **You walk the bridge between formal and informal practice.** Formal practice is where you carve out a chunk of time in the day to practise meditation. Informal practice is being mindful of your normal everyday activities. The breathing space is a very useful way of bridging the gap between these two important aspects of mindfulness. The breathing space is both a formal practice because you're making some time to carry it out, and informal because you integrate it into your day-to-day activities.

✔ **You create a space for new ideas to arise.** By stopping your normal, everyday activities to practise the breathing space, you create room in your mind for other things to pop in. If your mind is cluttered, you can't think clearly. The breathing space may be just what the doctor ordered to allow an intelligent insight or creative idea to pop into your mind.

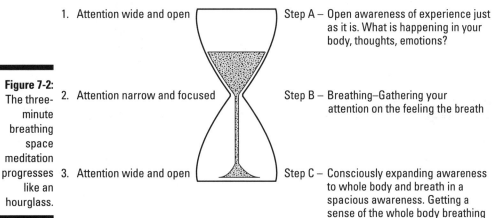

1. Attention wide and open — Step A – Open awareness of experience just as it is. What is happening in your body, thoughts, emotions?

2. Attention narrow and focused — Step B – Breathing–Gathering your attention on the feeling the breath

3. Attention wide and open — Step C – Consciously expanding awareness to whole body and breath in a spacious awareness. Getting a sense of the whole body breathing

Figure 7-2: The three-minute breathing space meditation progresses like an hourglass.

Using the breathing space between activities

Aim to practise the breathing space three times a day. Here are some suggested times for practising the breathing space:

✔ **Before or after meal times.** Some people pray with their family before eating a meal to be together with gratitude and give thanks for the food. Doing a breathing space before or after a meal gives you a set time to practise and reminds you to appreciate your meal too. If you can't manage three minutes, just feel three breaths before diving in.

✔ **Between activities.** Resting between your daily activities, even for just a few moments, is very nourishing. Feeling your breath and renewing yourself is very pleasant. Research has found that just three mindful breaths can change your body's physiology, lowering blood pressure and reducing muscle tension.

✔ **On waking up or before going to bed.** A short meditation before you jump out of bed can be a wholesome experience. You can stay lying in bed and enjoy your breathing. Or you can sit up and do the breathing space. Meditating in this way helps to put you in a good frame of mind and sets you up for meeting life afresh. Practising the breathing space before going to bed can calm your mind and encourage a deeper and more restful sleep.

✔ **When a difficult thought or emotion arises.** The breathing space meditation is particularly helpful when you're experiencing challenging thoughts or emotions. By becoming aware of the nature of your thoughts, and listening to them with a sense of kindness and curiosity, you change your relationship to them. A mindful relationship to thoughts and emotions results in a totally different experience.

Using Mindfulness to Look After Yourself

Have you ever heard the safety announcements on a plane? In the event of an emergency, cabin crew advise you to put your own oxygen mask on first, before you help put one on anyone else, even your own child. The reason is obvious. If you can't breathe yourself, how can you possibly help anyone else? Looking after yourself isn't just necessary in emergencies. In normal, everyday life, you need to look after your own needs. If you don't, not only do you suffer, but so do all the people who interact or depend on you. Taking care of yourself isn't selfish – it's the best way to be of optimal service to others. Eating, sleeping, exercising and meditating regularly are all ways of looking after yourself and hence others.

Exercising mindfully

You can practise mindfulness and do physical exercise at the same time. In fact, Jon Kabat-Zinn, one of the key founders of mindfulness in the West, trained the USA Mens Olympic Rowing Team in 1984. A couple of the men won gold – not bad for a bunch of meditators!

Regular exercise is beneficial for both body and mind, as confirmed by thousands of research studies. If you already exercise on a regular basis, you know the advantages. If not, and your doctor is happy with you exercising, you can begin by simply walking. Walking is an aerobic exercise and a great way to practise mindfulness (see Chapter 6 for a walking meditation). Then you can build up to whatever type of more strenuous exercise you fancy. Approach each new exercise with a mindful attitude – be curious of what will happen, stay with uncomfortable sensations for a while, explore the edge between comfort and discomfort and look around you.

To start you off, here are a few typical physical exercises, and ideas about how to suffuse them with mindfulness:

Mindful running

Leave the portable music player and headphones at home. Try running outside rather than at the gym – your senses have more to connect with outside. Begin by taking ten mindful breaths as you walk along. Become aware of your body as a whole. Build up from normal walking to walking fast to running. Notice how quickly your breathing rate changes, and focus on your breathing whenever your mind wanders away from the present moment. Feel your heart beating and the rhythm of your feet bouncing on the ground. Notice if you're tensing up any parts of your body unnecessarily. Enjoy the wind against your face and the warmth of your body. Observe what sort of thoughts pop up when you're running, without being judgemental of them. If running begins to be painful, explore whether you need to keep going or slow down. If you're a regular runner, you may want to stay on the edge a little bit longer; if you're new to it, slow down and build up more gradually. At the end of your run, notice how you feel. Try doing a mini meditation (described in the first section) and notice its effect. Keep observing the effects of your run over the next few hours.

Mindful swimming

Begin with some mindful breathing as you approach the pool. Notice the effect of the water on your body as you enter. What sort of thoughts arise? As you begin to swim, feel the contact between your arms and legs and the water. What does the water feel like? Be grateful that you can swim and have access to the water. Allow yourself to get into the rhythm of swimming. Become aware of your heartbeat, breath rate and the muscles in your body. When you've finished, observe how your body and mind feel.

Mindful cycling

Begin with some mindful breathing as you sit on your bike. Feel the weight of your body, the contact between your hands and the handlebars, and your foot on the pedal. As you begin cycling, listen to the sound of the wind. Notice how your leg muscles work together rapidly as you move. Switch between focusing on a specific part of your body like the hands or face, to a wide and spacious awareness of your body as a whole. Let go of wherever you're headed and come back to the here and now. As you get off your bike, perceive the sensations in your body. Scan through your body and detect how you feel after that exercise.

Preparing for sleep with mindfulness

Sleep, essential to your wellbeing, is one of the first things to improve when people do a course in mindfulness. People sleep better, and their sleep is deeper. Studies found similar results from people who suffered from insomnia who did an eight-week course in MBSR (mindfulness-based stress reduction).

Sleep is about completely letting go of the world. Falling asleep isn't something you *do* – it's about *non-doing*. In that sense sleep is similar to mindfulness. If you're *trying* to sleep, you're putting in a certain effort, which is the opposite of letting go.

Here are some tips for preparing to sleep using mindfulness:

✔ Stick to a regular time to go to bed and to wake up. Waking up very early one day and very late the next confuses your body clock and may cause difficulties in sleeping.

✔ Avoid over-stimulating yourself by watching television or being on the computer before bed.

✔ Try doing some formal mindfulness practice like a sitting meditation or the body scan (refer to Chapter 6) before going to bed.

✔ Try doing some yoga or gentle stretching before going to bed. I've noticed cats naturally stretch before curling up on the sofa for a snooze. This may help you to relax and your muscles unwind.

✔ Do some mindful walking indoors before bed. Take five or ten minutes to walk a few steps and feel all the sensations in your body as you do so.

✔ When you lie in bed, feel the in-breath and the out-breath. Rather than trying to sleep, just be with the breathing. Count your out-breaths from one to ten. Each time you breathe out, say the number to yourself. Every time your mind wanders off, begin again at one.

✔ If you're lying in bed worrying, perhaps even about getting to sleep, accept your worries. Challenging or fighting thoughts just makes them more powerful. Note them, and gently come back to the feeling of the breath.

If you seem to be sleeping less than usual, try not to worry about it too much. In fact, worrying about how little sleep you're getting becomes a vicious circle. Many people sleep far less than eight hours a day and most people have bad nights once in a while. Not being able to sleep doesn't mean something is wrong with you and lack of sleep is not the worst thing for your health.

Looking at a mindful work-life balance

Work-life balance means balancing work and career ambitions on the one side, and home, family, leisure and spiritual pursuits on the other. Working too much can have a negative impact on other important areas.

Try this little meditation to help reflect on and improve your work-life balance:

1. Sit in a comfortable upright posture, with a sense of dignity and stability.

2. Become aware of your body as a whole, with all its various changing sensations.

3. Guide your attention to the ebb and flow of your breath. Allow your mind to settle on the feeling of the breath.

4. Observe the balance of the breath. Notice how your in-breath naturally stops when it needs to, as does the out-breath. You don't need to do anything – it just happens. Enjoy the flow of the breath.

5. When you're ready, reflect on this question for a few minutes:

   What can I do to find a wiser and healthier balance in my life?

6. Go back to the sensations of the breathing. See what ideas arise.

7. Bring the meditation to a close and jot down any ideas that may have arisen.

Refer to *Work-Life Balance For Dummies* by Jeni Mumford for more on this topic.

Using Mindfulness in Relationships

Humans are social animals. People's brains are wired that way. Operating outside of relationships, alone, is very difficult. Research into positive psychology, the new science of wellbeing, shows that healthy relationships impact happiness more than anything else. Psychologists have found that wellbeing isn't so much about the quantity of relationships but the quality. You can develop the quality of your relationships through mindfulness.

Starting with your relationship with yourself

Trees need to withstand powerful storms, and the only way they can do that is by having deep roots for stability. With shallow roots, the tree can't really stand upright. The deeper and stronger the roots, the bigger and more plentiful are the branches that the tree can produce. In the same way, you need to nourish your relationship with yourself to effectively branch out to relate to others in a meaningful and fulfilling way.

Here are some tips to help you begin building a better relationship with yourself by using a mindful attitude:

- **Set the intention.** Begin with a clear intention to begin to love and care for yourself. You're not being selfish by looking after yourself; you're watering your own roots, so you can help others when the time is right. You're opening the door to a brighter future that you truly deserve as a human being.

- **Understand that no one's perfect.** You may have high expectations of yourself. Try to let them go, just a tiny bit. Try to accept at least an aspect of yourself you don't like, if you can. The smallest of steps makes a huge difference. Just as a snowball starts small and gradually grows as you roll it through the snow, so a little bit of kindness and acceptance of the way things are can start off a positive chain reaction to improve things for you.

- **Step back from self-criticism.** As you practise mindfulness, you become more aware of your thoughts. You may be surprised to hear a harsh, self-critical inner voice berating you. Take a step back from that voice if you can, and know that *you are not your thoughts*. When you begin to see this, the thoughts lose their sting and power. (The sitting meditation in Chapter 6 explores this.)

- **Be kind to yourself.** Take note of your positive qualities, no matter how small and insignificant they seem, and acknowledge them. Maybe you're polite, or a particular part of your body is attractive. Or perhaps you're generous or a good listener. Whatever your positive qualities are, notice them rather than looking for the negative aspects of yourself or what you can't do. Being kind to yourself isn't easy, but through mindfulness and by taking a step-by-step approach, it's definitely possible.

✔ **Forgive yourself.** Remember that you're not perfect. You make mistakes, and so do I. Making mistakes makes us human. By understanding that you can't be perfect in what you do, and can't get everything right, you're more able to forgive yourself and move on. Ultimately, you can only learn through making mistakes – if you did everything correctly, you'd have little to discover about yourself. Give yourself permission to forgive yourself.

✔ **Be grateful.** Develop an attitude of gratitude. Try being grateful for all that you do have, and all that you can do. Can you see, hear, smell taste and touch? Can you think, feel, walk and run? Do you have access to food, shelter and clothing? Use mindfulness to become more aware of what you have. Every evening before going to bed, write down three things that you're grateful for, even if they're really small and insignificant. Writing gratitude statements each evening has been proven to be beneficial for many people. Try this for a month and continue if you find the exercise helps you in any way.

✔ **Practise metta/loving kindness meditation.** This is probably the most effective and powerful way of developing a deeper, kinder and more fulfilling relationship with yourself. Refer to Chapter 6 for the stages of the metta practice.

Mindfulness and me

Before I discovered the art of mindfulness and meditation, I was a bit of a perfectionist. I worked very hard to get the top marks at school and when I went to university I continued the habit. I was being too hard on myself. I searched for ways of reducing the stress and eventually found meditation. I was very reluctant and sceptical at first – I spent a year deciding whether or not to learn it though a course. Meditation and mindfulness seemed too mystical and spiritual for my scientific mind. In the end I gave it a go and haven't looked back since! As I practise, it changes my relationship to myself. I don't feel the driving need to be absolutely brilliant in the work I do, which for some may sound like a bad thing. For me, that means I have more time for myself. I'm a bit kinder to myself. I'm on a journey and certainly haven't 'got there' (I don't think that I or anyone can be perfect in that sense). More recently, I've discovered not to take mindfulness too seriously. Mindfulness is not a religion or philosophy, but a creative way of living that each person uses in his own way. By having a light-hearted approach, I am more relaxed about my own thoughts, words and actions and I allow life to unfold in a more natural way. If I remember to be mindful, that's great, but if I forget or have a lapse, that's human and not a problem at all.

Engaging in deep listening

Deep or mindful listening occurs when you listen with more than your ears. Deep listening involves listening with your mind and heart – your whole being. You're giving completely when you engage in deep listening. You let go of all your thoughts, ideas, opinions and beliefs and just listen.

Deep listening is healing. By healing I mean that the person being listened to can feel a great sense of release and let go of frustrations, anxieties or sadness. Through deep listening, true communication occurs – people want to be listened to more than anything else.

Deep listening comes from an inner calm. If your mind is wild, it's very difficult to listen properly. If your mind is in turmoil, go away to listen to your breathing or even to your own thoughts. By doing so you give your thoughts space to arise out of the unconscious, and you thereby release them.

Here's how to listen to someone deeply and mindfully:

- Stop doing anything else. Set your intention to listen deeply.
- Look the person in the eye when he speaks.
- Put aside all your own concerns and worries.
- Listen to what the person is saying and how he's saying it.
- Listen with your whole being, your mind and heart, not just your head.
- Observe posture and tone of voice as part of the listening process.
- Notice the automatic thoughts popping into your head as you listen. Do your best to let them go and come back to listening.
- Ask questions if necessary, but keep them genuine and open rather than trying to change the subject. Let your questions gently deepen the conversation.
- Let go of judgement as far as you can. Judging is thinking rather than deep listening.
- Let go of trying to solve the problem or giving the person the answer.

When you give the other person the space and time to speak without judging, he begins to listen to himself. What he's saying becomes very clear to him. Then, quite often, the solution arises naturally. He knows himself far better than you do. By jumping straight into solutions, you only reduce the opportunity that person has to communicate with you. So, when listening, simply listen.

Arguing with monks

Researchers wanted to see the effect of an argument and confrontation on an experienced meditator. They chose a monk who had extensive meditative practice behind him. The researchers found the most confrontational university professor to argue with the monk. They measured the men's blood pressure and heart rates during the conversation. The professor's heart beat started off very high, but the monk's stayed calm. As the conversation went on, the professor became calmer and calmer (but still didn't want to stop talking!). In this way, if you remain peaceful and calm, having established a mindfulness routine, you can spread a sense of wellbeing quite naturally as you talk to others. Your relationships flourish in this way.

Being aware of expectations

Think about the last time you were annoyed by someone. What were your expectations of that person? What did you want him to say or do? If you have excessively high expectations in your relationships, you're going to find yourself frustrated.

Expectations are ideals created in your mind. The expectations are like rules. I expect you to behave, or to be quiet, or to make dinner every evening, or to be funny, not angry or assertive. The list is endless.

The more expectations you have of others, the more difficult your relationships become – both for you and other people. If a person doesn't meet your expectations, you may react with anger, sadness, frustration or jealousy. These emotions are natural to a certain extent, but if you experience them too frequently or too intensely, too much negative emotion harms your health and wellbeing. And just because you have high expectations or react emotionally when your expectations aren't met, doesn't mean the other person is going to change, especially if you treat that person with emotional outbursts.

The next time you're about to feel annoyed, angry or sad about an expectation of yours not being met, try the following mindfulness exercise. The practice helps you to move from an emotional or verbal reaction, to a mindful and balanced response.

1. **Don't speak yet.** A negative reaction just fuels the fire.

2. **Become aware of your breathing without changing it.** Is it deep or shallow? Is it slow or rapid? If you can't feel it, just count the out-breaths from one to ten.

3. **Notice the sensations in your body.** Do you feel the pain of the unful-filled expectation in your stomach, shoulders or somewhere else? Does it have a shape or colour?

4. **Imagine or feel the breath going into that part of the body.** Feel it with a sense of kindness and curiosity. Breathe into it and see what happens.

5. **Take a step back.** Become aware of the space between you, the observer, and the thoughts and feelings, which are the observed. See how you're separate and therefore free of them. You're going into observer mode, taking a step back, having a bird's-eye view of the whole situation from a bigger perspective. This is much easier to say than do but, bit by bit, through practice, you can do it.

6. **If necessary, go back to that person and speak from this wiser and more composed state of mind.** Don't speak unless you're settled and calm. Most of the time, speaking in anger may get what you want in the short term, but in the long term, you leave people feeling upset. Play this by ear.

Looking into the mirror of relationships

Relationship is a mirror in which you can see yourself.

J. Krishnamurti

All relationships are a mirror, whether with a partner or work colleague, that help you to see your own desires, judgements, expectations and attach-ments. Relationships give an insight into your own inner world. What a great learning opportunity! You can think of relationships as an extension of your mindfulness practice. You can observe what's happening, both in yourself and the other person, with a sense of friendly openness, with kindness and curiosity. Try to let go of what you want out of the relationship, just as you do in meditation. Let the relationship simply be as it is, and allow it to unfold moment by moment.

Here are some questions to ask yourself as you observe the mirror of relationships:

- ✔ **Behaviour.** How do you behave in different relationships? What sort of language do you use? What's your tone of voice like? Do you always use the same words or sentences? What happens if you speak less, or more? Notice your body language.

- ✔ **Emotions.** How do you feel in different relationships? Do certain people or topics create fear or anger or sadness? Get in touch with your emo-tions when you're with other people, and see what the effect is. Try not to judge the emotions as good or bad, right or wrong – just see what they do.

✔ **Thoughts.** What sort of thoughts arise in different relationships? What happens if you observe the thoughts as just thoughts, and not facts? How are your thoughts affected by how you feel? How do your thoughts affect the relationship?

Being mindful in a relationship is more difficult than it sounds. You can easily find yourself caught up in the moment and your attention is trapped. Through regular mindfulness practice, your awareness gradually increases and becomes easier. Although mindfulness in relationships is challenging, it's very rewarding too.

Taking responsibility for your emotions

'You make me angry.' 'You're annoying me.' 'You're stressing me out.'

If you find yourself thinking or saying sentences like these, you're not really taking responsibility for your own emotions. You're blaming someone else for the way you feel. This may seem perfectly natural. However, in truth, no one can affect the way you feel. *The way you feel is determined by what you think about the situation.* For example, say I accidentally spill a cup of tea on your work. If you think that I did it on purpose, you may think 'you damaged my paperwork deliberately, you idiot' and then feel angry and upset. You blame me for your anger. If you see it as an accident and think that I may be tired you think, 'It was just an accident – I hope he's okay', and react with sympathy. The emotion is caused by your thought, not by the person or the situation itself.

Rather than blame the other person for your anger, actually feel the emotion. Notice when it manifests in your body if you can. Observe the effect of breathing into it. Watch it with a sense of care. This transforms your relationship to the anger from hate to curiosity, and thereby transforms the anger from a problem to a learning opportunity.

Meeting difficult people anew

Relationships are built on the history between you and the other person, whoever that may be. Whenever you meet another human being, your brain automatically pulls out the memory file on the person, and you relate to him with your previous knowledge of him. This is all very well when you're meeting an old and dearly loved friend for example, but what about when you need to deal with someone you've had 'difficulties with in the past? Perhaps you may have had an argument or just don't seem to connect?

When dealing with difficult people it's worth remembering you have two ways of meeting another human being. The first way is to see your ideas, memories, thoughts, opinions and beliefs about that person. The other way is to actually see that person as he is, without the judgements and ideas and stories. This is meeting anew, meeting afresh, as if for the first time. Mindfulness is about meeting *all* experience afresh. When you connect with your senses, you're no longer in the realm or ideas, opinions and beliefs. You're in the field of the present moment. Meeting another human being in that way, you can't help but feel a warmth towards him as well as a sense of wonder.

Here are some ways of dealing with difficult relationships:

✔ Take five mindful breaths or carry out a mini meditation (check out Chapter 8) before meeting the other person. This may help prevent the feeling of anger or frustration becoming overpowering.

✔ Observe the difference between your own negative image about the person, and the person himself. As best you can, let go of the image and meet the person as he is by connecting with your senses when you meet him.

✔ Buddha is quoted as saying, 'Remembering a wrong is like carrying a burden on the mind.' Understanding this, try to forgive whatever has happened in your relationship and see if that helps.

✔ See the relationship as a game. Mindfulness is not to be taken too seriously, and nor are relationships. Often relationships become stagnant because you're both taking things too seriously – allow yourself to lighten up.

✔ Consider: what's the worst that may happen? That question usually helps to put things back in perspective. You may be overestimating how bad the other person is, or the worst that he can realistically do to you.

✔ Become curious about the kind of thoughts that arise in your head when you meet the difficult person. Are the thoughts part of a familiar pattern? Can you see them as merely thoughts rather than facts? Where did you get these ideas from? This is an example of mindfulness of thoughts – becoming curious about your thinking patterns and noticing what's happening. You're not trying to fix or change – that happens by itself if you observe the current thought patterns clearly.

Relationships are difficult. Don't be too hard on yourself if things don't work out. You have your own character and sometimes you just don't connect with another. Let go of the negatives from the past, as best you can, and follow your instincts. Allow things to unfold in their own, natural way as best you can.

Lake meditation: Discovering acceptance

This meditation is normally done lying down, but you can do it in any posture that's comfortable for you. Close your eyes softly. Feel your breathing for a few minutes. Now, when you're ready, imagine a beautiful lake. The lake is perfectly still and calm. The surface of the lake is so still, it looks like a polished mirror. Majestic mountains are in the background, and the sky is predominantly blue, with a few small, white, fluffy clouds. The sky and mountains are reflected in the lake. Around the sides of this wonderful lake are old, mighty trees, with branches leaning out over the lake. A few birds fly across the lake in the distance. When the wind blows, small ripples and larger waves whip up on the surface, reflecting a dance of glints across the water. You're aware that as the seasons change, the lake embraces the rain and fallen leaves, and in the winter may freeze on the surface. Deep under the surface, little changes or moves, and the water continues to teem with life. The lake openly accepts whatever is offered to it.

Now, when you're ready, allow yourself to merge and become one with the lake. As you lie or sit, you allow yourself to be the lake itself, if that makes sense to you. You're both the deep, still lake underneath, and the ripples on the surface. Just allow yourself to absorb the slightest sense of what this may mean for you. In your compassion, kindness and gentleness, you're supporting this body of water. As the weather changes, the water becomes muddied and gathers twigs and leaves. Can you softly allow all this to happen and continue to just be the lake? Appreciate how the changing conditions of the lake give it character, charm and richness. Allow yourself to feel your own tranquillity and serenity underneath the turbulent surface. Is that possible to some extent? Are you able to allow the continual change that persistently unfolds around and in the lake to be part of the natural process of nature, and even embrace the beauty of it in yourself?

If you find it helpful, use this image of the lake to enrich your meditation practice from time to time. Even bringing it to mind as you go about your daily activities helps you to perceive life from a place of acceptance and peacefulness. Evoke the memory of how the lake can be both still, deep and unmoving underneath and disturbed at the surface. Recognise the continually fluxing thoughts and feelings of the mind and heart, and identify with the awareness that's both always there and just behind them. See your story, your world, your ideas, thoughts, dreams, opinions and beliefs as part of that vast awareness but not all of it. Enjoy the vision of the lake as it effortlessly reflects the sun and sky, birds and bees, plants and animals during the day, and the exquisite pale moon and twinkling stars at night, in the dark, cool sky – ever present, always changing, and yet always the same.

Chapter 8

Using Mindfulness in Your Daily Life

*M*indfulness is portable – you can be mindful anywhere and every-where, not only on the meditation cushion or yoga mat. You can engage in a mindful state of mind while giving a presentation, feeding the cat, or hugging a friend. By cultivating a mindful awareness, you deepen your day-to-day experiences and break free from habitual mental and emotional patterns. You notice that beautiful flower on the side of the road, you become aware and release your tense shoulders when thinking about work, and you give space for your creative solutions to life's challenges. All the small changes you make add up. Your stress levels go down, your depression becomes a bit more manageable and you begin to be more focused. You need to put in some effort to achieve this, but a totally different effort to the kind you're probably used to – you're then bound to change in a positive way. This chapter offers some of the infinite ways of engaging this ancient art of mindfulness in your daily life.

Using Mindfulness at Work

Work. A four-letter word with lots of negative connotations. Many people dislike work because of the high levels of stress they need to tolerate. A high level of stress isn't a pleasant or healthy experience, so welcome any way of managing that stress with open arms.

In many countries, managing the level of stress that employees face, and taking active steps to reduce stress, is a legal obligation. If you think that you're suffering from work-related stress, you need to consider talking to your manager or other appropriate person about the situation. Poor management standards are linked to unacceptably high levels of stress, and changes need to be made to ensure that stress is kept at reasonable levels according to the Health and Safety Executive in the UK.

So how can mindfulness help with work?

- ✔ Mindfulness is proven to lower levels of stress, anxiety and depression.
- ✔ Mindfulness leads to a greater ability to focus, even when under pressure, which then results in higher and more creative productivity and efficiency.
- ✔ Mindfulness improves the quality of relationships, including those at work.

Mindfulness isn't simply a tool or technique to lower stress levels. Mindfulness is a way of being. Stress reduction is the tip of the iceberg. One business organisation I trained aptly said: 'Mindfulness goes to the heart of what good business is about – deepening relationships, communicating responsibly, and making mindful decisions based on the present facts, not the limits of the past.' When employees understand that giving mindful attention to their work actually improves the power of their brain to focus, their work becomes more meaningful and inspiring.

Beginning the day mindfully

Watching the 100-metres race in the Olympics, you see the athletes jump up and down for a few minutes before the start, but when they prepare themselves in the blocks, they become totally still. They focus their whole beings completely, listening for the gunfire to signify the start. They begin in stillness. Be inspired by the athletes – begin your day with an inner stillness, so you can perform at your very best.

Start the day with some mindfulness meditation. You can do a full formal meditation such as a body scan or a sitting meditation (both these meditations are in Chapter 6), or perhaps some yoga or stretching in a slow and mindful way. Alternatively simply sit up and feel the gentle ebb and flow of your own breath, or listen to the sounds of the birds as they wake up and chirp in the morning. Other alternatives include waking up early and eating your breakfast really slowly and mindfully (see the raisin exercise in Chapter 6), or perhaps tuning into your sense of smell, sight and touch fully as you have your morning bath or shower; see what effect that has. That's better than just worrying about your day.

Dropping in with mini meditations

When you arrive at work you can easily be swept away by it all and forget to be mindful of what you're doing. The telephone rings, you get email after email, and get called into endless meetings. Whatever your work involves, your attention is sure to be sucked up.

This habitual loss of attention and going from activity to activity without really thinking about what you're doing is called *automatic pilot mode*. You simply need to change to mindful awareness mode and the most effective way of doing this is by one- to three-minute mini meditations, by feeling the sensation of your own breath as it enters and leaves your body. (Head to Chapter 5 for more about changing from automatic pilot.)

The breathing space meditation (a type of mini meditation) consists of three stages. In the first stage you become aware of your thoughts, emotions and bodily sensations. In the second stage you become aware of your own breathing. And in the third and final stage, you expand your awareness to the breath and the body as a whole. For lots more on how to do the breathing space meditation, check out Chapter 7.

When you're at work, give a mini meditation a go:

- ✔ **When?** You can do a mini meditation at set times or between activities. So when you've finished a certain task or job, you take time to practise a mini meditation before heading to the next one. In this way you increase the likelihood of being calm and centred, rather than flustered, by the time you get to the end of the day or working week. If you don't like the rigidity of planning your mini meditations ahead of time, just practise them whenever the thought crosses your mind and you feel you need to go into mindfulness mode.

  Additionally, you can use the meditation to cope with a difficult situation such as your boss irritating you. One way of coping with the wash of emotion that arises in such situations is to do a three-minute coping, breathing-space meditation (described in full in Chapter 7).

- ✔ **How?** Use any posture you like, as long as your spine is relaxed and upright. The simplest form of mini meditation is to feel your breathing. If you find feeling the breath too difficult, you can say to yourself 'in' as you breathe in, and 'out' as you breathe out. Alternatively, count each out-breath to yourself, going from one to ten. As always, when your mind drifts off, simply guide the attention gently and kindly back, even congratulating yourself for noticing that your mind had wandered off the breath.

> ✔ **Where?** You can do a mini meditation anywhere you feel comfortable. Usually, meditating is easier with your eyes closed, but that's not so easy at work! You can keep your eyes open and softly gaze at something while you focus your attention inwards. If you work outside, try going for a slow walk for a few minutes, feeling your breathing and noticing the sensations of your feet as they gently make contact with the earth.

You may dearly want to try out the mini meditation at work, but you simply keep forgetting. Well, why not make an appointment with yourself? Perhaps set a reminder to pop up on your computer, or a screen saver with a subtle reminder for you. One of my corporate clients popped a card on her desk with a picture of a beautiful flower. Each time she saw the picture, she took three conscious breaths. This helped to calm her and had a transformative effect on the day. Or, try a sticky note or a gentle alarm on your mobile phone – be creative in thinking of ways to remind yourself to be mindful.

Going from reacting to responding

A *reaction* is almost automatic thoughts, speech and behaviour from you following some sort of stimulus, such as your boss criticising you. A response to a situation is a more considered, balanced choice, often creative in reply to the criticism, and leads to solving your problems rather than compounding them.

You don't *have* to react when someone interrupts you in a meeting, takes away your project, or sends a rude email. Instead, having a balanced, considered *response* is most helpful for both you and your relationship with colleagues.

For example, say you hand in a piece of work to your manager and she doesn't even say thank you. Later on you ask what she thought of your work and she says it was okay, but nothing special. You've spent lots of time and effort to do a superb report, and you feel hurt and annoyed. You *react* by either automatically thinking negative thoughts about your manager, and avoiding eye contact with her for the rest of the week, or you lash out with an outburst of accusations and feel extremely tense and frustrated for hours afterwards. Here's how you can turn this into a mindful response.

Sit on your chair, gaze downwards and begin to feel the sensations of your breath. Notice if you're breathing in a shallow or rapid way, due to your frustration, but try not to judge yourself. Expand your awareness to a sense of your body as a whole. Become mindful of the processes taking place inside you. Feel the burning anger rising from the pit of your stomach up through your chest and throat, or the racing heart and dry mouth when you're nervous. Honour the feeling instead of criticising or blocking the emotion. Experiment. Notice what happens if you don't react as you normally do or feel like. Try breathing into the feeling. Bring kindness and curiosity to your emotions.

You may discover that the very act of being aware of your reaction changes the flavour of the sensation altogether. Your relationship to the reaction changes an outburst, for example, to a more considered response. Your tone of voice may subtly change from aggressive and demanding to being calmer and inquisitive. The point is not to try and change anything, but just to sit back and watch what's going on for a few moments.

To help you to bring a sense of curiosity when you're about to react to a situation at work, try asking yourself the following questions slowly, one at a time, and giving yourself time for reflection:

✔ What feeling am I experiencing at the moment, here at work? How familiar is this feeling? Where do I feel the feeling in my body?

✔ What thoughts are passing through my mind at the moment? How judgemental are my thoughts? How understanding are my thoughts? How are my thoughts affecting my actions at work?

✔ How does my body feel at the moment? How tired do I feel at work? What effect has the recent level of work had on my body? How much discomfort can I feel at the moment in my body, and where is the source of it?

✔ Can I acknowledge my experiences here at work, just as they are? Am I able to respect my own rights as well as responsibilities in the actions I choose? What would be a wise way of responding right now, instead of my usual reaction? If I do react, can I acknowledge that I'm not perfect, and make my next decision a more mindful response?

Perhaps you'd go back to your manager and calmly explain why you feel frustrated. You may become angry too, if you feel this is necessary, but without feeling out of control. Perhaps you'd choose not to say anything today, but wait for things to settle before discussing the next step. The idea is for you to be more creative in your *response* to this frustration rather than *reacting* in your usual way, if your usual way is unhelpful and leads to further problems.

The benefits of a considered, balanced response as opposed to an automatic reaction include:

✔ Lower levels of blood pressure, a cause of heart disease.

✔ Lower levels of stress hormones in your blood stream, leading to a healthier immune system.

✔ Improved relationships because you're less likely to break down communication between colleagues if you're in a calmer state of mind.

✔ A greater feeling of being in control, because you're able to choose how you respond to others rather than automatically reacting involuntarily.

Solving problems creatively

Your ideas need room. You need space for new perceptions and novel ways of meeting challenges, in the same way that plants need space to grow, or they begin to wither. For your ideas, the space can be in the form of a walk outside, a three-minute mini meditation or a cup of tea. Working harder is often not the best solution – working smarter is.

If your job involves dealing with issues and problems, whether that involves people or not, you can train yourself to see the problems differently. By seeing the problems as challenges, you're already changing how you meet this issue. A *challenge* is something you rise to, something energising and fulfilling. A *problem* is something that has to be dealt with, something draining, an irritation.

To meet your challenges in a creative way, find some space and time for yourself. Write down *exactly* what the challenge is – when you're sure what your challenge is, you find it much easier to solve. Try to see the challenge from a different person's perspective. Talk to other people and ask how they'd deal with the issue. Become mindful of your immediate reactive way of dealing with this challenge and question the validity of it.

Practising mindful working

Mindful working is simply being mindful of whatever you do when you work. Here are some examples of ways of being mindful at work:

✔ When typing, notice the sense of touch between your fingers and the keyboard. Notice how quickly your mind converts a thought into an action on keys. Are you striking the keys too hard? Are your shoulders tense, is your face screwing up unnecessarily? How's your posture?

✔ Before writing or checking an email, take a breath. Is this really important to do right now? Reflect for a few moments on the key message you need to get across and remember it's a human being receiving this message – not just a computer. After sending the message, take time to feel your breath and, if you can, enjoy it.

✔ When the telephone rings, let the sound of the ring be a reminder for you to be mindful. Let the telephone ring a few times before answering. Use this time to notice your breath and posture. When you pick it up, speak and listen with mindfulness. Notice both the tone of your own voice and the other person's. If you want to, experiment by gently smiling as you speak and listen, and become aware of the effect that has.

✔ No matter what your work involves, do it with awareness. Awareness helps your actions become clear and efficient. Connect your senses with whatever you're doing. Whenever you notice your mind drifting out of the present moment, just gently bring it back.

Using mindful leadership

If you're a leader in an organisation, responsibility goes with the job. Good leaders need to make effective decisions, manage emotions successfully and keep their attention on the big picture. In their book *Resonant Leadership* (Harvard Business School Press), Richard Boyatzis and Annie McKee highlight the need for mindfulness in order for leadership to be most effective. They found that the ability to manage your own emotions and the emotions of others, called emotional intelligence, is vitally important for an effective leader, and to achieve this, you need to find a way to renew yourself.

Renewal is a way of optimising your state of mind so you're able to work most effectively. The stress generated through leadership puts your body and mind on high alert and weakens your capacity for focus and creativity. Renewal is a necessary antidote for leadership stress, and one key way science has found to achieve this is through mindfulness.

Neuroscience has shown that optimistic, hopeful people are naturally in an *approach* mode of mind. They *approach* difficulties as challenges and see things in a positive light. Other people have more *avoidant* modes of mind, characterised by *avoiding* difficult situations, and denying problems rather than facing up to them. Mindfulness practised for just eight weeks has been shown to move people from unhelpful, *avoidant* modes to more helpful, creative, emotionally intelligent *approach* modes of mind, leading to a greater sense of meaning and purpose, healthy relationships, and an ability to work and lead effectively.

For example, one of my clients, a CEO of a medium-sized corporation, felt isolated and highly stressed. Through practising tailor-made mindfulness techniques, he began to renew himself, see the business more holistically, take greater time to make critical decisions and begin communicating more effectively with his team about the way forward. He now practises mindfulness on a daily basis for 10 minutes, as well as using other strategies during the day, to create renewal.

✔ Make use of the mini meditations to keep you aware and awake at work. The meditations are like lampposts, lighting wherever you go and making things clear.

Finishing by letting go

You may find letting go of your work at the end of the day very difficult. Perhaps you come home and all you can think about is work. You may spend the evening talking angrily about colleagues and bosses, or actually doing more work to try to catch up with what you should've finished during the day. This impacts on the quality and quantity of your sleep, lowering energy levels for the next day. This unfortunate negative cycle can spin out of control.

Reducing teacher stress

Teaching in schools in considered one of the most stressful jobs in the world. When I was a full-time schoolteacher, almost all my time was taken up in planning lessons and marking books. I'd work until the early hours of the morning and turn up the next day in a daze. The books were marked but I was of no real use to the children; I easily lost patience with them, and made mountains out of molehills. I was 'sweating the small stuff'.

By meditating for 20 minutes or so when I reached home, I was able to let go of all the worries and anxieties of the workplace and allow my evening to be that little bit more enjoyable. I prioritised my time and ensured that I found more time to exercise and socialise. The meditation gently drew me out of the undue stress, as well as helping me to organise my work and life more effectively.

You need to draw a line between work and home, especially if you're finding your stress levels are on the increase. Meditating as soon as you get home, or on your way home (see the following section), provides an empowering way of achieving this. You're saying 'enough'. You're taking a stand against the tidal wave of demands on your limited time and energy. You're doing something uplifting for your health and wellbeing, and ultimately for all those around you too. And you're letting go.

To let go at the end of the day most successfully, choose one of the formal mindfulness meditation practices in Chapter 6. Or take up a sport or hobby in which you're absorbed by gentle, focused attention; an activity that enables the energy of your body and mind to settle, and the mindfulness to indirectly calm you.

Using Mindfulness on the Move

I always find it amusing to see people from abroad on the Underground transport system in London, looking at the trains with awe, and taking plenty of photos. Other commuters look up, almost in disgust, before burying their heads back in a book, newspaper or their phone. When people are on holiday, they live in the moment and the present moment is always exciting. The new environment is a change from their routine. Travelling is another opportunity to bring mindfulness to the moment.

Meditating as you walk

Take a moment to consider this question: What do you find miraculous? Perhaps you find the vastness of space amazing; perhaps you find your favourite book or band a wonder. What about walking? Walking is a miracle too. Scientists have managed to design computers powerful enough to make the Internet work and for man to land on the moon, but no robot in the world can walk anywhere nearly as smoothly as a human being. If you're able to walk, you're lucky indeed. To contemplate the miracle called walking is the beginning of walking meditation.

Normally, in the formal walking meditation (as described in Chapter 6), you aren't trying to get anywhere. You simply walk back and forth slowly, being mindful of each step you take, with gratitude. However, when walking to work or wherever you're going, you have a goal. You're trying to get somewhere. This creates a challenge because your mind becomes drawn into thinking about when you're going to arrive, what you're going to do when you get there, and if you're on time. In other words, you're not in the moment. The focus on the goal puts you out of the present moment.

Practise letting the destination go. Be in the moment as you walk. Feel the breeze and enjoy your steps if you can. If you can't enjoy the walk, just feel the sensations in your feet – that's mindfulness. Keep bringing your mind back into the moment, again and again, and, hey presto, you're meditating as you walk.

Driving meditation

If everyone did driving meditation, the world would be a safer and happier place. Don't worry – it doesn't involve closing your eyes or going into a trance! Try this driving meditation, and feel free to be creative and adapt it as you like. Remember, don't read this book while you're driving – that would be dangerous.

1. **Set your intention by deciding to drive mindfully.** Commit to driving with care and attention. Set your attitude to be patient and kind to others on the road. Leave in plenty of time to get to where you're going so you can let go of overly focusing on your destination.

2. **Sit in the driver's seat and practise a minute or so of mindful breathing.** Feel your natural breath as it is, and come into the present moment.

3. **Start your car.** Get a sense of the weight and size of the car – a machine with tremendous power, whatever its size, and the potential to do much damage if you drive irresponsibly, or tremendously helpful if driven with mindful awareness and intelligence. Begin making your way to your destination.

4. **Be alert.** Don't switch on the radio or CD player. Instead, let your awareness be wide and perceptive. Be aware of what other vehicles and people are doing all around you. Let your awareness be gentle rather than forcing and straining.

5. **See how smoothly you can drive.** Brake gradually and accelerate without excessive revving. This type of driving is less stressful and more fuel-efficient.

6. **Every now and then, briefly check in with your body.** Notice any tension and let it go if you can, or become aware and accept it if you can't. You don't need to struggle or fight with the tension.

7. **Show a healthy courtesy to your fellow drivers.** Driving is all about trusting and co-operating with others.

8. **Stay within the speed limit.** If you can, drive more slowly than you normally would. You'll soon grow to enjoy that pace, and may be safer.

9. **Take advantage of red traffic lights, and traffic jams.** This is traffic meditation! These are opportunities to breathe. Look out of the window and notice the sky, the trees and other people. Let this be a time of rest for you, rather than a time to become anxious and frustrated. Remember that stress isn't caused by the situation but by the attitude you bring to the circumstance. Bring a mindful attitude, just as an experiment, and see what happens. You discover a different way of living altogether.

Travelling on public transport

If you travel on a bus, train or plane, you're not in active control of the transport itself, and so can sit back and be mindful. Most people plug themselves into headphones or read, but meditation is another option. Why not exercise your mind while travelling? If commuting is part of your daily routine, you can listen to a guided meditation, or just practise by yourself. If you think you'll go deeply into meditation, ensure that you don't miss your stop by setting the alarm on your watch or phone.

The disadvantage of meditating in this way is the distractions. You may find yourself being distracted by sudden braking or the person who keeps snoring right next to you. I suggest that you practise your core meditation in a relatively quiet and relaxed environment such as your bedroom, and use your meditation while travelling as a secondary meditation.

Here are some specific mindfulness experiments to try out while on the move:

1. **See if you can be mindful of your breath from one station to the next, just for fun.** Whether you manage or not isn't the issue – this is just an experiment to see what happens. Do you become more mindful or less? What happens if you put more or less effort into trying to be mindful?

2. **Hear the various announcements and other distractions as sounds to be mindful of.** Let the distractions be part of your meditative experience. Listen to the pitch, tone and volume of the sound, rather than thinking about the sound. Listen as you would listen to a piece of music.

3. **See if you can tolerate and even welcome unpleasant events.** For example, if two people are talking loudly to each other, or someone is listening to noisy music, notice your reaction. What is the particular thought that's stirring up emotion in you? Where can you feel the emotion? What happens when you imagine your breath going into and out of that part of your body?

4. **Allow your mindful awareness to spill into your walk to wherever you're going.** As you walk, feel your feet making contact with the ground. Notice how the rate of your breathing changes as you walk. Allow your body to get into the rhythm of the walk and enjoy the contact of the surrounding air with your skin as you move.

Using Mindfulness in the Home

Not only is doing mindfulness meditation and exercise at home convenient, but it also helps you to enjoy your everyday activities as well. Then, rather than seeing chores as a burden, you may begin to see them as opportunities to enjoy the present moment as it is.

Waking up mindfully

When you wake up, breathe three mindful breaths. Feel the whole of each in-breath and the whole of each out-breath. Try adding a smile to the equation if you like. Think of three things you're grateful for – a loved one, your home, your body, your next meal – anything. Then slowly get up. Enjoy a good stretch. Cats are masters of stretching – imagine you're a cat and feel your muscles elongate having been confined to the warmth of your bed all night. If you want to, do some mindful yoga or tai chi.

Then, if you can, do some formal mindful meditation. You can do five minutes of mindful breathing, a 45-minute sitting meditation, or a body scan meditation – choose what feels right for you.

Doing everyday tasks with awareness

The word *chore* makes routine housework unpleasant before you've even started. Give your chores a different name to help spice them up, such as dirt-bursting, vacuum-dancing, mopping 'n' bopping, or home sparkling!

The great thing about everyday jobs, including eating, is that they're slow, repetitive physical tasks, which makes them ideal for mindfulness. You're more easily able to be mindful of the task as you do it. Here are a couple of examples to get you started.

Washing dishes

Recently, one of my clients who works from home found mindful dishwashing a transformative experience. She realised that she used to wash dishes to have a break from work, but when washing up, she was still thinking about the work. By connecting with the process of dishwashing, she felt calmer and relaxed, renewed and ready to do a bit more creative work.

Have a go:

1. **Be aware of the situation.** Take a moment to look at the dishes. How dirty are they? Notice the stains. See how the dishes are placed. What colour are they? Now move into your body. How does your physical body feel at the moment? Become aware of any emotions you feel – annoyed or irritated? Consider what sort of thoughts are running through your mind, perhaps, 'When I finish this, then I can relax' or, 'This is stupid' or whatever.

2. **Begin cleaning, slowly to begin with.** Feel the warmth of the water. Notice the bubbles forming and the rainbow reflections in the light. Put slightly less effort into the scrubbing than you may normally, and let the washing-up liquid do the work of cleaning. When the dish looks completely clean, wash the bubbles off and see how clean the plate looks. Allow yourself to see how you've transformed a grimy, mucky plate into a spotless, sparkling one. Now let it go. Place the dish on the side to dry. Be childlike in your sense of wonder as you wash.

3. **Try to wash each dish as if for the first time.** Keep letting go of the idea of finishing the job or the other things you could be doing.

4. **When you've finished, look at what you've done.** Look at the dishes and how they've been transformed through your mindful awareness and gentle activity. Congratulate yourself on having taken the time to wash the dishes in a mindful way, thereby training your mind at the same time.

All meditation is like mindfully washing dishes. In meditation you're gently cleaning your mind. Each time your attention wanders into other thoughts and ideas, you become aware of the fact and gently step back. Each step you take back from your unruly thoughts is a cleansing process.

Vacuuming

Using the vacuum cleaner, another common activity in many people's lives, is usually done while your mind is thinking about other things – which isn't actually experiencing the process of vacuuming. Try these steps to experience mindfulness while vacuuming:

1. **Begin by noticing the area you want to clean.** What does it look like and how dirty is the floor? Notice any objects that may obstruct your vacuuming. Become mindful of your own physical body, your emotions, and thoughts running through your mind.

2. **Tidy up the area so you can use the vacuum cleaner in one go, without stopping, if you can.** This ensures you have time to get into the rhythm of the activity without stopping and starting, helping you to focus.

3. **Switch the vacuum cleaner on.** Notice the quality of the sound and feel the vibrations in your arm. Begin moving the vacuum cleaner, getting into a calm rhythm if possible, and continue to focus your mindful attention on your senses. Stay in the moment if you can, and when your mind takes your attention away, acknowledge that, and come back into the here and now.

4. **When you've finished, switch off and observe how you feel.** How was the process different to how you normally vacuum the floor? Look at what you've done and be proud of your achievement.

Mindful eating

Regular, daily mindfulness meditation practice is a key aspect of mindful eating. This acts as a foundation from which you can build a mindful-eating lifestyle. The discipline of mindfulness makes you aware of your emotions and thoughts. You begin to notice the kinds of situations, thoughts and emotions that lead you to eating particular foods.

Here's how to eat a meal mindfully:

1. **Remove distractions.** Turn off the television, radio and all other electronics. Put aside any newspapers, magazines and books. All you need is you, and your meal.

2. **Carry out three minutes of mindful breathing.** Sit with your back upright but not stiff, and feel the sensations of your breathing. Alternatively, try the three-minute breathing space detailed in Chapter 7.

3. **Become aware of your food.** Notice the range of colours on the plate. Inhale the smell. Remember how fortunate you are to have a meal today and be grateful for what you have.

4. **Observe your body.** Are you salivating? Do you feel hungry? Are you aware of any other emotions? What thoughts are going through your head right now? Can you see them as just thoughts rather than facts?

Second hunger: Overcoming problem eating

When you eat, you need to:

✔ Eat the right amount of food, neither too much nor too little, to maintain a healthy weight.

✔ Eat the right types of food for you to meet your daily nutritional needs.

However, you may not eat just to meet those needs. In reality you may eat to:

✔ Avoid feeling bored.

✔ Cope with a sense of anger.

✔ Fill a feeling of emptiness within you.

✔ Satisfy a desire for some taste in particular (such as sweet or fatty food).

✔ Help you cope with high levels of stress.

This 'comfort' eating, or *emotional eating* as it's sometimes called, tends to operate on an unconscious level, driving your cravings for food.

Emotional eating is like a second hunger, to satisfy the need for psychological wellbeing. *Your emotions are eating* rather than your stomach. You're using the food to calm your mind. This can lead to an unhealthy eating cycle. You experience a negative emotion, you eat food to cope with the emotion, which leads to a temporary feeling of satisfaction but, before long, the negative emotion returns. Mindful eating offers a way of becoming more aware of the inner thoughts and emotions driving your tendency to eat. Through a mindful awareness you begin naturally to untangle this web and begin to discover how to eat in a healthy and conscious way, making the right choices for you. Additionally you may like to try these strategies:

✔ **Hunger reality check.** Before eating, notice if your hunger is physical or emotional. If you've eaten recently and your tummy isn't rumbling, perhaps you can wait a little longer and see if the sensation passes.

✔ **Keep a food diary.** Simply writing down everything you eat for a few weeks is often an eye-opener. You may begin to see patterns emerging.

✔ **Manage boredom.** Rather than using boredom as a reason to eat, try doing an activity such as mindful walking, or calling a friend and being really aware of your conversation.

✔ **Avoid extreme dieting.** By depriving yourself of certain foods, you may end up fuelling your desire for the food. Instead, treat yourself occasionally and eat the food mindfully. Actually tasting the treat makes it even more tasty!

5. **Now slowly place a morsel of food into your mouth.** Be mindful of the taste, smell and texture of the food as you chew. Put your cutlery down as you chew. Don't eat the next mouthful until you've fully chewed this one. At what point do you swallow? Have you chewed the food fully?

6. **When you're ready, take the next mouthful in the same way.** As you continue to eat mindfully, be aware of your stomach and the feeling of being full. As soon as you feel you've had enough to eat, stop. As you've been eating slowly, you may find that you feel full up sooner than usual.

7. **If you feel full, but still have the desire to eat more, try doing another three minutes of mindful breathing.** Remember that the thought 'I need to eat' is just a thought. You don't have to obey the thought and eat if that's not the best thing for you.

Try eating in this way once a day for a week or two and become mindful of the effect it has.

Chapter 9

Establishing Your Own Mindfulness Routine

*L*earning a new language takes time, effort and patience. You need to dedicate yourself, and at the same time not expect rapid progress. You try to practise regularly, preferably daily. You can learn the language by using CDs, books, television programmes, videos, websites, or in person through a teacher – whatever way best suits your lifestyle and learning methods. Practising meditation has some similarities. You can begin in many different ways, as long as you practise regularly and with a certain commitment and the right attitude and intention (refer to Chapters 4 and 5 for more about nurturing your attitudes and intention). If you find committing yourself to a mindfulness practice difficult, you're not alone – you can try a different approach, adjust your practice method, explore possible barriers, and look for support as you discover the language of meditation.

Remember that when you learn a language, you can measure your progress – by, say, the number of new words you know. You can't measure progress in meditation so easily, if at all, because meditation invites you to stop searching for progress. Meditation is about being exactly where you are right now, and exploring the landscape, enjoying the scenery and being as you are, whatever that means for you. No matter how long you've been meditating, the present moment is always the same, and yet always fresh, new and full of possibilities.

In this chapter I introduce the eight-week, mindfulness-based stress reduction course, and explore how to choose which element of mindfulness is best for you to practise. I also give you some ideas you can use if you want to take your mindfulness meditation even deeper.

Trying the Evidence-Based Mindfulness Course

Perhaps the most well-proven stress reduction course is an eight-week programme called *mindfulness-based stress reduction* (MBSR), originally developed at the stress reduction clinic at the University of Massachusetts medical school by Jon Kabat-Zinn. The course has been researched many times with thousands of people, and proved to be effective at reducing stress, so the recommended practices are certainly worth a go. If, after the eight weeks, you've felt no change has happened and sense that mindfulness isn't for you, you can drop the practice. If you found the programme helpful, you can go on to develop your own practice, having experienced the range of meditative exercises.

Begin the programme by making a personal commitment to suspend your judgement and follow the recommended practices for eight weeks, and after that, decide whether mindfulness is something for you. You can ask others in your life to help support you over the next eight weeks, or at least to give you some space to engage in meditation daily for the next couple of months. Keep a journal on hand during the eight weeks to record your progress and any thoughts or emotions that arise.

Week One: Understanding automatic pilot

You operate on an automatic pilot far more than you may think. You may have experienced driving a car for a significant time before realising you were lost in thoughts, worries or daydreams. This may be okay for a little while, but if your whole life is run automatically, you miss the show. Your mind thinks the same old thoughts, you may react unnecessarily when things don't go your way, and your stress is compounded without you being fully aware of this process. Mindful awareness, as opposed to automatic pilot, allows for the possibility of responding to situations by offering you choice, a freedom from the mechanical, reactive habitual patterns of your mind. (Refer to Chapter 5 for more about overcoming living on automatic pilot.)

Making the mind–body connection

The root meaning of the phrase *to heal* is literally 'to make whole'. Meditation leads to a sense of being whole and complete, a sense of seeing the perfection of yourself, just the way you are, no matter what may be wrong with you.

One of the key ways modern medicine broke down the wholeness of being human was by splitting up the body and the mind as two distinct separate entities. Your attitudes, opinions and beliefs weren't thought to affect your physical health. Ample evidence now shows strong links between your inner attitudes and your physical health and wellbeing. In this context, healing means to make whole the connection between mind and body and see them as two parts of the same entity. Through practising meditation you see how your mind includes everything from breathing rate to the way you treat your colleagues at work, and how an emotional rollercoaster ride on a Monday may be influencing your flu-like symptoms on Wednesday. This doesn't mean that you're causing illness by thinking certain thoughts, but simply that the way your body functions is linked to the level of stress you experience.

This is the practice for Week One:

✔ Begin the week by engaging in the 'eating a raisin' meditation described in Chapter 6. Record in your journal what effect the exercise has on you. Reflect on the effect of operating on automatic pilot in your daily life. What are you missing out on? What effect is unawareness having on your thoughts, emotions and body, as well as your relationship with yourself, others and the world?

✔ Practise the body scan meditation (explained in Chapter 6) daily, using the CD provided with this book. Play the CD and follow the guidance as best you can. Each day, note whether you practised, and how you found the meditation. Don't worry if you don't enjoy it; persevere with it. Experiment with doing the body scan at different times of the day to see what works best for you.

✔ Choose a routine daily activity to practise mindfully. This can be brushing your teeth, showering, getting dressed, walking or driving to work, speaking with your partner, cooking, cleaning or anything you can think of. Bring a sense of curiosity to your experience. What matters is not what you choose, but your commitment to being aware of what you're doing, as you're doing it.

Week Two: Dealing with barriers

Daily meditation practice can be pretty challenging. Meditation provides the space for a whole range of trapped thoughts and emotions to rise to the surface; often the ones you want to avoid most. The tendency of the mind is to judge experiences as good or bad. The idea of mindfulness is to be aware of these judgements and let them go. The most important thing is to keep practising, no matter what your experience is.

The aim of the body scan or any other meditation isn't relaxation, so don't worry if you don't feel super-relaxed. The aim is simply to be aware of whatever your experience is, as far as you can. The experience may be unpleasant, and you may feel more tense by the end of the session, but that's still as good a meditation as any other – just keep practising.

This is the practice for Week Two:

- ✔ Continue to practise the body scan daily using the CD. You may now know when is the best time for you to practise meditation, and are able to stick with it. Make a short record in your journal, even just a sentence, of how the experience of the body scan is for you, on a daily basis.

- ✔ Choose another daily routine activity to do with mindfulness, in addition to the one you selected in Week One. Try pausing for a breath or two before starting the activity, and then connecting with your senses, noticing the thoughts and emotions playing in your mind.

- ✔ Practise being mindful of your breath for ten minutes a day by simply sitting comfortably straight and feeling the sensation of your breath. If your mind naturally wanders off, congratulate yourself for noticing, and guide your attention kindly back to the breath sensation. Avoid paying attention to self-criticism – if criticism does arise in your awareness, note the negative thought as just another thought, and turn your attention back to the breath. See Chapter 6 for how to practise mindfulness of breath in more detail.

- ✔ Complete a pleasant events diary in your journal (described in Chapter 11). Use the diary to become aware of your thoughts, feelings and bodily sensations when you experience something pleasant, in as much detail as you can.

Week Three: Being mindful in movement

One of the beauties of mindfulness is that you don't have to be sitting still to be mindfully aware. This week is an opportunity to explore mindfulness in movement. This is also an opportunity to reflect on the power of focusing on the breath. The breath can act like an anchor, a place always available, right under your nose, to draw you into the present moment. Being aware of your breath while focusing on something challenging can enable you to see the difficulty from a different angle, softening the tension a little.

Try this practice for Week Three:

- ✔ On days one, three and five, practise about 30 minutes of mindful walking or stretching. Many people enjoy developing mindfulness through yoga or tai chi and find the approach very powerful. (You can refer to *Yoga For Dummies* or *Tai Chi For Dummies* for ways to do this.)

- ✔ On days two, four and six, practise the body scan using the CD.

- ✔ Begin practising the mini meditation called the 'three-minute breathing space' three times a day (explained in Chapter 7). You may be more likely to remember to do the breathing space if you decide at the beginning of the week exactly when you want to practise.

- ✔ Complete an unpleasant events diary in your journal (see Chapter 13 for details) on a daily basis. This means writing down one thing each day that was unpleasant for you; and the sensations in your body, the thoughts going through your mind at the time, and how you felt emotionally.

Week Four: Staying present

This week, focus on the present moment. Reflect on the quality of this moment now. How does it compare with thinking about the past or the future? What effect does focusing on the here and now have on your thoughts and emotions?

You react to experience in one of three ways:

- ✔ Attachment to pleasant experiences
- ✔ Aversion to unpleasant experiences
- ✔ Indifference to everyday experiences

Grasping onto pleasant experiences leads to fear of what happens when you lose them. Aversion to unpleasant experiences leads to stress each time you have a bad time. Going into automatic pilot when facing a neutral event means you miss out on the mystery and wonder of being alive.

This week, focus on your aversion to unpleasant experiences. You, like everyone on the planet, have to face difficulties from time to time. The question is *how* you meet the challenge – do you run away from, suppress or fight the feelings? Is there another way? However you meet difficulties, by becoming more mindful of the process, your reactions begin very slowly to untangle themselves. You begin to consider the possibility of responding in a way that reduces rather than compounds your stress.

Here's your practice for Week Four:

- ✔ On days one, three and five, practise 30 minutes of mindful movement: stretching or walking, followed by 15 minutes of mindful breathing.

- ✔ On days two, four and six, practise the 30-minute guided sitting meditation explained in Chapter 6, using the CD provided.

- ✔ Practise the three-minute breathing space meditation three times a day at times predetermined by you.

- ✔ Additionally, practise the three-minute breathing space when something unpleasant happens. Write in your journal what effect the meditation has on your experiences.

- ✔ Become aware of times of stress. How do you react to the stress? Do you create a block, resist or suppress the stress, or shut down? Become aware of what's happening in your body. When you react in a certain way to the stress, what's going on for you? What effect does staying present with a difficulty have on your response? Allow yourself to be deeply curious about your relationship to stress.

Week Five: Embracing acceptance

This week, try allowing things to be as they are, rather than immediately wanting to change them. For example, if someone irritates you, rather than reacting immediately, just stay with the feeling of irritation. Feel it in your body and notice your automatic thoughts. If you feel a headache coming on, observe what happens if you let the pain be just as it is, and watch it rise and fall. What effect does allowing, accepting and acknowledging have on unpleasant and pleasant sensations?

If you want to become more relaxed, the first step is to allow things to be as they are, however they are. If you feel frustrated, the feeling is already there, so rather than getting frustrated about that too, try to begin accepting the frustration. Notice the thoughts, feelings and bodily sensations that go along with it. You can try saying to yourself, 'It's okay, whatever it is, it's okay. It's already here. Let me feel it.'

Acceptance isn't resignation – you're facing up to the difficulty rather than running away. Mindfulness involves accepting awareness and using it as a way to change, not resigning yourself to a situation in which change will never happen.

Try this practice for Week Five:

- ✔ Practise the guided sitting meditation using the CD, noticing how you react to thoughts, emotions and bodily sensations. Record any observations in your journal.

✔ Do the three-minute breathing space meditation three times a day. Try to connect it with everyday activities such as meal times, after waking up and just before going to sleep.

✔ Practise the three-minute breathing space when you're going through a difficulty. Use the practice to explore your thoughts and feelings rather than trying to get rid of them, if you can.

✔ Explore the difference in responding in a controlled way to more challenging situations, whether they occur during meditation or not, rather than reacting uncontrollably to your experience. Become more aware of your reactions and the thoughts and emotions that drive them.

Week Six: Realising that thoughts aren't facts

Usually, when you think of something, like 'he hates me' or 'I can't do this', you accept it as a fact, a reality. You may believe that almost any thought that pops up into your awareness is an absolute truth. If your mind habitually pops up with negative or unhelpful thoughts, seeing the thoughts and images as facts has stressful consequences. However, you can free yourself of this burden. Switch things round and try seeing thoughts as automatic, conditioned reactions rather than facts. Question the validity of thoughts and images. Step back from the thoughts if you can and don't take them to be you, or reality. Just watch them come and go and observe the effect of this.

Thoughts are just thoughts, not facts. Thoughts are mental events. You're not your thoughts.

When you're feeling challenged, read Chapters 13 and 18, and see if you can identify what types of thoughts are taking place.

Practice for Week Six:

✔ Now you can begin to mix and match as you wish. Combine the sitting meditation, the body scan and mindful movement for 45 minutes a day. You can split the time into two or three parts, and spread them out through the day. Some days you may choose not to use the CD.

✔ Practise the three-minute breathing space three times a day, and additionally practise when a difficulty or challenge arises for you. Notice any recurring patterns, notice the effect of mindful breathing on your body, and let the mindfulness spread into whatever you're facing next.

✔ If you can make time, practise a day of silent mindfulness meditation. See the section 'Setting aside a day for mindfulness' later in this chapter for how you can plan and do this meditation day.

Week Seven: Taking care of yourself

The activities you choose to do, from moment to moment and from day to day, strongly influence how you feel. By becoming aware of the activities that uplift you and the activities that deplete you, you may be able to adjust the choices you make to best take care of yourself.

Here's your practice for Week Seven:

- ✔ Choose any formal mindfulness meditation you like, such as the body scan, or sitting meditation, or a combination of the meditations, and practise it daily, with or without the CD.

- ✔ Continue to practise the three-minute breathing space three times a day and when a difficulty arises. Try making a wise choice after or during a difficulty.

- ✔ Design a stress warning system in your journal by writing down all the *warning signs* you have when under excessive stress, like feeling hot or behaving impatiently, and then write down an *action plan* you can take to reduce the stress, such as a mini meditation, going for a walk or talking to a friend. Refer to your action plan when you next feel overly stressed and notice what effect it has.

Week Eight: Reflection and change

Sometimes, when faced with a problem, no matter how hard you try, no matter how much effort you put into solving the problem, you're still stuck with the difficulty. Nothing seems to work. If you keep trying, you may become more and more tired, and perhaps move farther from a solution rather than nearer. In such circumstances, stop trying to solve the issue, and accept the circumstance for now. In this act of kindness to yourself, a solution may or may not arise. However, you're likely to feel less angry, frustrated, stressed or depressed. The feeling of helplessness arises when you keep trying and no benefit seems to manifest itself. Acceptance is a change in itself.

You may already know the serenity prayer, which seeks for:

The serenity to accept the things I cannot change;

The courage to change the things I can; and

The wisdom to know the difference.

Sticking to your decisions

How long you decide to practise meditation each day depends on your motivation for meditating in the first place. So far, research has found that the longer you meditate, the greater the benefit. Experiments have also shown that even short bouts of mindfulness, even a few minutes, or a few mindful breaths, have positive effects on your wellbeing. Deciding how long to meditate for depends on:

✔ Your intentions.

✔ Your past experience with meditation or prayer.

✔ How committed you are to reaping the long-term benefits of meditation.

✔ Your level of discipline.

The important thing is: *once you've decided how long you're going to meditate, stick to your decision.* This is *very* important for training your mind. If you practise for as long as you feel like, and then get up, you're acting on a feeling. You stop being mindful if your mind says so. However, if you've decided to meditate for ten minutes and after five minutes feel like getting up, you still stay put. This makes you experience feelings of restlessness or boredom, frustration or agitation. What's the benefit of this? Well, you're taking a stand. *You* are saying to *your mind,* 'I'm in charge here. I've decided to sit still for ten minutes and feel the sensations of my breathing to help me to focus and stay calm.' The mind eventually calms down. You're no longer a slave to what your mind throws at you. This is the *freedom* of meditation – you're free to choose what you do and how you act, rather than your mind choosing.

In this last week of the course, reflect on how the experience has been for you. What have you found most helpful? What aspects would you like to integrate into your daily practice? Write your thoughts in your journal.

And finally, your practice for Week Eight:

✔ Decide which formal mindfulness practice you would like to do for the next week, and carry out your decision as best you can.

✔ At the end of Week Eight, reflect on how the eight weeks of the course went for you, recording your thoughts in your journal. Consider some of these questions to help with your journal entries. How did your level of stress change over the course of the eight weeks? How did you meet difficulties in your life, whilst engaging in this course? How can you adapt the mindfulness practices to integrate them into your life?

✔ Congratulate yourself for reaching this point, no matter how much or how little mindfulness you actually managed to do. The practice of mindfulness on a daily basis isn't an easy one to do – any mindfulness you managed is better than none at all.

Choosing What to Practise for Quick Stress Reduction

How do you decide what you're going to eat for dinner tonight? Your decision probably depends on how hungry you or your family are, who's cooking, the food in the fridge, the day of the week, the meal you ate yesterday and so on. Many factors come into account. How do you decide which mindfulness meditation to practise today when establishing your own mindfulness routine? I give you some options in this section.

Many people come to mindfulness for stress reduction. Stress impacts everyone. If you're alive, you're going to experience stress. The question is, how do you handle the stress?

 Trying to get rid of your stress only increases it. You're trying to pull open a door that has a sign saying push. No matter how hard you pull, the door won't open! If you pull hard enough, the door handle may fall off, which won't help. Stress comes from doing, doing and more doing. You can't 'do' stress reduction. Stress reduction requires you to stop doing – or non-doing. This is what mindfulness offers. So, let go of the idea of stress reduction, practise the following tips daily over a period of a few weeks, and see what happens. Also, write down all the events in your day that caused you stress. What was going through your mind? What fixed ideas did you have? Do you notice any patterns? Watch out for these patterns the next time you're in a stressful situation and notice what effect being aware of the repeating pattern has.

✔ For quick stress reduction, try the three-minute breathing space meditation (covered in Chapter 7 and on the CD). This meditation cleverly includes a little bit of all the different types of mindfulness meditations in one neat, bite-size package. You don't have to use the CD once you've got the hang of it, and you don't even have to close your eyes. If you're at work, you can softly gaze at the bottom of the computer screen, or pop to the lavatory and practise there – why not?! It's quiet (hopefully!), you can lock the door, lower the lid and sit with your spine straight. Your boss may wonder why you look so serene every time you step out of the toilet!

✔ Try ten minutes of mindful breathing, using the CD track or practising on your own. Ideally, do this meditation in the morning to set you up for the day, but if you don't like that, do it any time of the day that suits you, or whenever you feel stressed.

✔ Walking meditation is a wonderful practice to integrate into your day. You're then combining some gentle exercise with mindfulness – a powerful combination for stress reduction. Head to Chapter 6 for the walking meditation.

Using mindfulness for self-discovery

Many people use mindfulness as a way to *self-discovery*. This is about deepening your own understanding of who you are and your relationship with yourself, others and the wider environment. In meditation, your conceptual mind with its thoughts and ideas stops being the only reference point for you.

You discover the concept of being separate from everything else as you grow up. Babies don't identify with their own bodies. The baby looks in wonder at its own foot just as it may look at a bunch of keys. There's no sense of me and not me. Humans have a deep-seated need to feel part of a bigger whole, whether socially or spiritually. Albert Einstein is attributed with the following striking observation:

A human being is a part of the whole, called by us 'Universe', a part limited in time and space. He experiences himself, his thoughts and feelings as something separated from the rest – a kind of optical delusion of his consciousness. This delusion is a kind of prison for us, restricting us to our personal desires and to affection for a few persons nearest to us. Our task must be to free ourselves from this prison by widening our circle of compassion to embrace all living creatures and the whole of nature in its beauty.

This is the 'task' of mindfulness. You're seeing this 'optical delusion' as Einstein puts it, as the self-limiting thoughts and beliefs about who you are and your place in the world. Through mindfulness comes insight and you begin to see this prison of separation and in doing so, are released, even if only momentarily. But each moment of freedom is nourishing and uplifting, and energises and motivates you to keep walking the journey towards healing, wholeness, health and self-discovery. Remember, you don't need to travel far – the present moment is right here, right now.

✔ Spend ten minutes or more stretching your body in a mindful way. Use any stretching movements you prefer. The stimulation of the body as you stretch draws your attention out of your mind and into the physical sensations. If you have time during the day, you can also engage in the odd gentle stretch now and then. Remember, the most important thing is to be aware of the feelings in the body and mind as you stretch, in a kind and gentle way. Keep breathing mindfully as you move – let go of any tendency to hold your breath if you can.

✔ Spend some time seeing a stressful situation from the other person's perspective or just a different perspective to help you relieve stress.

✔ Before you go to sleep, think of three things you're grateful for. Doing so relieves stress and has a beneficial long-term effect. See Chapter 4 for more on gratitude.

Going Even Deeper

So, you've established a mindfulness routine. You feel you're ready for the next step. You can progress in your practice by meditating for more extended periods of time. This section offers ways for you to step beyond your routine and find further support in your journey.

Setting aside a day for mindfulness

In this day and age, people work very hard. You're working hard for your employers, your own business or perhaps at home, looking after your parents or children. Even looking after yourself requires time, energy and effort. Meditation offers some respite, a chance to stop doing, to stop fulfilling your endless needs and desires to help others or yourself, and to simply *be*. Have you ever treated yourself to a whole day of non-doing? This doesn't mean watching TV all day, or just sleeping all day – even when you sleep, your mind can be in overdrive, going from one dream to another. By non-doing, I mean using the time to let go of excessively thinking about the past or worrying about the future – to softly reside in the here and now.

A day of mindfulness is a beautiful gift you can give to yourself. The idea is to spend a whole day in mindful awareness. Here are some instructions on practising this exercise:

1. The evening before, place a reminder next to your bed and around the house that you're going to spend the day mindfully. Be clear in your mind that you're going to keep the phone, computer, television and other electronics switched off. Drift off into sleep by feeling your breathing as you lie in bed.

2. When you wake up on your day of mindfulness, begin the day with some mindful breathing as you lie in bed. Feel each in-breath and each out-breath mindfully. If you like, smile gently. Spend some time reflecting on what you're grateful for – your home, your relationships, your income, your family, your body, your senses or whatever you feel you have that perhaps others don't.

3. Slowly and mindfully step out of bed. If you have a pleasant view from your window, spend some time looking outside. Enjoy looking at the trees, or grass, or the people walking purposefully to fulfil their needs. Look, if you can, without encouraging judgements and reactions. Your mind is bound to wander off into other thoughts and worries – just gently bring your attention back as soon as you realise.

4. Practise some formal mindfulness meditation. You can do the body scan meditation for example.

5. Have a bath or shower. Do this at a leisurely pace. Take your time, even if you feel like rushing for no apparent reason. Feel the sensations of the water on your body – in many places throughout the world people have to walk for hours to collect water so be grateful for the easy access you have to water.

6. Take your time making your breakfast and preparing tea. Connect with your senses and keep bringing your attention into the here and now. Pause for a few moments before you start eating your breakfast. Ensure that you've tasted and fully chewed each mouthful before you start the next one. This is mindful eating.

7. You may choose to spend the mid-morning going for some walking meditation or doing some mindful yoga or perhaps a little gardening. Whatever you choose to do, do it with a gentle, kindly awareness. Avoid spending more than a few minutes reading a book or a magazine. The idea is to connect with your senses rather than encouraging the mind to think too much.

8. Spend some time preparing and eating lunch. Again, allow the process to unfold leisurely. You don't need to rush. If feelings of boredom, restlessness or frustration arise, see if you can offer them the space to come to pass, to surface and diminish again. Eat your meal with gratitude and attention; chew each morsel unhurriedly.

9. Engage with a gentle physical activity after lunch, or perhaps have a siesta. Why not! Connect your senses with another hobby of your choice. Every now and then, practise the breathing space meditation for a few minutes to help bring you into the present moment. You may even choose to do another extended meditative practice, such as a sitting meditation or some mindful yoga or tai chi. Don't be surprised if you begin to find the whole process challenging or emotional. You may not be used to giving yourself so much room to simply be present, and this can allow unprocessed thoughts and emotions to release themselves into your consciousness. Be as kind and patient with yourself as you're able to.

10. Continue to allow the day to unfold in this way, eating, resting, walking and practising meditation. If you can't help cleaning out a cupboard, or organising your paperwork, really take your time with the actions, doing things one step at a time.

11. Having prepared and eaten your evening meal, which is ideally the lightest of the meals you've had during the day, you can rest and relax before going to bed. Lie in bed and ride on the waves of your own breathing, allowing yourself to doze naturally into a slumber.

Joining a group

Why would anyone want to meditate in a group? Meditation is often spent sitting down with your eyes closed, in silence. Not much banter goes on; nobody's cracking open the beers. So, why on earth would you need to bother joining a meditation group? Here are some reasons:

- ✔ **By attending a regular group, you commit to practising frequently.** Without such a commitment, you may lose momentum and end up not meditating even though you really want to and find it valuable.

- ✔ **Your meditation is deeper when practising in a group.** Many of my clients say this when they attend a class. You're less likely to fidget unnecessarily when sitting with others; if the body remains still, the mind also becomes still. You're also more likely to make a little more effort in your sitting posture, sitting straighter and with dignity. People who are spiritually inclined believe that by meditating together you create a certain positive energy in the room that generates a favourable atmosphere, intensifying the quality of the meditation.

- ✔ **You often end up making friends with people who enjoy meditation.** This can create a 'positive feedback system' within your social circle, because the more time you spend with other fellow meditators, the more you think and remember to practise and the more you're likely to hear about the latest and greatest book, teacher or retreat. You begin to support each other in other areas of life too, which is always a nice thing.

How do you go about choosing a group? You may be able to find a mindfulness meditation group in your area by searching on the Internet. You don't have to join a mindfulness group, however. You can join any type of meditation group and, through trial and error, find one you feel comfortable with. Most Buddhist organisations practise some form of mindfulness meditation.

If you can't find a group for you, consider setting up one yourself. I know one couple who started a weekly group that grew naturally by itself until they had about 15 regular members, just by word of mouth. In each session, you just need a period of silence for meditation, perhaps 30 minutes or so, and then a period of time to explore and share how the practice and week has gone. You may want to read a paragraph of text from a book on mindfulness. After that, I would suggest some time simply to socialise over a cup of tea and a few delicious biscuits. In the summer, I organise mindful walks and picnics in parks or along the river – perhaps these are the kind of events you too can set up.

Finding an appropriate retreat

When you've been practising meditation for at least a few months, you may be ready to attend a meditation retreat. This is a magnificent opportunity for you to develop your meditation practice and discover more about yourself. Retreats can be any length from one day to several years! I strongly recommend you begin with the one-day retreat, then gradually extend to a weekend, then a week, and if you're very serious in your practice, you can go for even longer.

Retreats cost between £20 and £200 for a day, or £150 and £2000 for a week, which includes all food and accommodation. Buddhist retreats usually invite an additional donation for the teachers and organisers who sometimes work voluntarily.

Some of the questions to ask before booking yourself on a meditation retreat include:

✔ **Is the retreat in silence?** Silence offers a powerful way of intensifying your meditative discipline. When you talk, you unconsciously stir up thoughts in your mind, and weaken your quality of attention. Through an extended period of silence, your mind quite naturally begins to calm down, and you find your meditation has a different quality altogether. You may feel going on a silent retreat is a little too much, especially to begin with; you can try and find a mindfulness holiday, combining meditation with free time to relax and socialise too.

✔ **Is the teacher experienced?** In most retreats, the person leading is normally quite experienced, but this is worth checking, especially if you're attending for an extended period of time.

✔ **What's a typical schedule for the day?** Find out the time you're expected to wake up, so you know what you're letting yourself in for. And check how much time is spent in the day meditating too. Waking up at 4 a.m. and meditating in two-hour stretches throughout the day may be too much for you, and could put you off meditation altogether. You can find many retreats with far gentler schedules if you look around.

✔ **Is it a cult?!** If the organisation says things like 'our way is the best/only way' or 'if you stop following us, you'll derail/die/suffer/never be happy', then say thank you and walk away. Many wise organisations run meditation retreats but, as with everything, a few suspect ones do too. If the organisation says 'you're free to walk away at any time', or 'our way is one way of practising meditation but there are many other ways that you're welcome to investigate if you wish', or 'ultimately, only you can discover what is the best way for you to meditate through your own observation and experience', you're probably in a good organisation. Good luck with the search.

The best place to find a retreat is to search online. I have put together a recommended selection on www.learn-mindfulness.com/retreats based on locations all over the world. Some are Buddhist and others are secular. Even if they're not in your area, they may lead you to find a suitable retreat within easy reach. Some are silent retreats and others combine mindfulness with a holiday/vacation, so you can do some mindfulness together with a group, and have some time to relax and unwind in your own way too, exploring your surroundings – they can be great fun.

Chapter 10

Dealing with Setbacks and Avoiding Distractions

● ●

In This Chapter

▶ Dealing with setbacks in meditation

▶ Overcoming common problems

▶ Avoiding distractions

● ●

*W*hen you first learnt to walk you must have fallen over hundreds, if not thousands of times before you could balance on two legs. But you didn't give up. You probably giggled, got up, and tried again. Learning meditation, a powerful way of deepening mindfulness, is a similar process. When you first try to meditate, you're going to fall over (well, not literally I hope, unless you're trying the lesser-known hopping-on-one-leg meditation). But setbacks are part of the process of meditation. The question is how you deal with them. If you see setbacks as learning opportunities rather than failures, you're bound to succeed. Each time a problem occurs, you simply need to get up and try again, with a smile if possible. In the end you may realise that meditation isn't about achieving a certain state of mind, but about meeting each experience in a warm, accepting way. This chapter shows you how.

Getting the Most out of Meditation

Mindfulness meditation means setting aside time to intentionally pay attention to a certain aspect of your experience with a kindly acceptance from moment to moment, as best you can. So, for example, you can pay attention to your breathing as it enters and leaves your body, accepting the rate of the breathing just as it is.

Ultimately, *you have nothing to get out of meditation*. I know that sounds pretty crazy but it's an important point. Meditation isn't a way of *getting* something, because you already have everything you need to be whole and complete. Rather, meditation is about letting go. All the benefits of meditation (which I cover in Chapter 2) are best seen as side effects. Meditation is about being with whatever your experience is, whether pleasant or unpleasant, and seeing what unfolds. Meditating is a bit like doing your favourite hobby. If you like painting, you paint. If you paint for the love of painting, rather than looking for an outcome, you paint in an effortless and joyful way. Meditation is like painting – if you spend your time looking for the benefits you kind of spoil the fun.

Making time

If you're interested in developing the art of meditation, try engaging in some form of meditation every day, called *formal practice*. Whether you choose to meditate for five minutes or one hour is up to you, but making a daily connection with meditation has a profound effect.

Too busy to meditate daily? I know the feeling. Life is full of so many things to do that finding time to practise meditation can be hard. But you find time to brush your teeth, get dressed and sleep. You find the time for chores because you have to. You don't feel right if you fail to do these things. Meditation is like that too. Once you get into the rhythm of daily meditation, you don't feel right if you haven't had your daily fix of it. That's when you find the time to meditate.

The great thing about mindfulness is that you can practise it at any time. Right now, you can become aware of the fact that you're reading. You can feel the position of your body as you're reading this sentence. That's mindfulness. When you put this book down and walk somewhere, you can feel the sensations of your feet on the floor, or the tension in your shoulder or the smile on your face. When you're aware of what you're doing, that's mindfulness.

Practising mindfulness actually saves time. Research has found that meditators work more efficiently than others. Or, you may say that meditation makes time.

Rising above boredom and restlessness

Boredom and restlessness are like opposite poles of an energy scale. Boredom is associated with a lack of enthusiasm and connection, whereas restlessness implies energy that's pumping through the body, itching to burst out. Mindfulness is designed to observe both of these states and find a balance between the two.

Sharpening your tools

Once upon a time there was a woodcutter. He had lots of trees to cut down and was working frantically, puffing and sweating away to complete his work on time. A wise person happened to be passing through (they always do in these stories) and asked, 'Why are you working so hard trying to cut that tree down? Wouldn't it be easier and faster if you took the time to sharpen your axe?' The woodcutter looked up at the wise man and said, 'Can't you see how many trees I need to cut down today? I don't have time to sharpen the axe!'

Our own lives can be a bit like that. If you find the time to meditate, to sharpen the axe of your mind, you can save much time and energy in your life. Yet a common reaction to meditation is, 'I'm too busy!'. If you ever have that thought, think about the woodcutter and the time he'd have saved by sharpening his tools.

Boredom

Meditation can sound like the ultimate boring activity. Sit there and do nothing. What could be more boring? Even watching paint dry may sound a more exciting prospect. Society seems geared up to help you avoid boredom. Television adverts are short and snappy to grab your attention, and mobile phones help to distract you at any moment that a hint of boredom arises. These continual forms of distraction make you bored more quickly and more easily. Meditation is a courageous step against the tide.

If you feel bored during meditation, you're not really being mindful. Boredom generally implies a lack of connection, or that you're thinking about the past or future instead of the present. If you're finding attending to your breathing boring, imagine if your head was plunged into water – you'd suddenly become very interested in breathing! Each breath is unique and different. Noticing feelings of boredom and moving your focus back to your breathing is all part of the process of mindfulness and quite natural.

The following techniques can help you work with the feelings of boredom during meditation:

- ✔ **Acknowledge the feeling of boredom.** Boredom is the feeling that has arisen, so accept it in this moment.

- ✔ **Notice the thoughts running through your mind.** Perhaps, 'Ohhhh, I can't be bothered!' or 'What is the point of doing this?'

- ✔ **Get interested in boredom.** Allow yourself to become curious. Where did the boredom come from? Where's it going? Can you feel boredom in certain parts of your body? Notice the desire to sleep or do something else other than continuing to practise.

✓ **Connect your attention to the sensations of breathing and see what happens to boredom.**

✓ **Take a step back from the emotion of boredom.** If you're aware of the boredom, you're not the boredom itself. Observe the boredom from this stance of a decentred, detached awareness, as if the boredom is separate from you.

Observing boredom can be very interesting. When boredom arises you get to see the thoughts and feelings that run through you every time you get bored. These feelings can rule your life without you noticing. By becoming aware of them, they begin to loosen and let go. Your mental programmes are shadows and through the light of mindfulness the programmes lose their apparent reality and disappear, without you doing anything much.

Restlessness

Restlessness is similar to boredom, but is associated with excessive levels of energy and a common mental state. You run around all day doing a million and one things and then when you sit down to meditate, your mind is still racing.

Try these two ways of coping with restlessness:

✓ **Begin your meditation practice with some mindful movements.** You may choose to go mindful walking or perhaps do some mindful yoga (both talked about in Chapter 6). This helps to slowly calm your mind so that you're able to practise some sitting or lying down meditations.

✓ **Observe your restlessness without reacting to it.** Feel the restlessness in your body. What is your mind telling you to do? Continue to sit despite what the mind says. This is a powerful meditation, a discipline that trains the mind to do what you tell it to do rather than the other way round. You're in control. Just because your mind is restless you don't have to run around like a headless chicken doing what it tells you. The mind can say things like, 'Oh, I can't stand this. I need to get up and do something.' You can watch this show going on in the mind, breathe into it, and guide your attention back to the inhalation and exhalation.

Staying awake during meditation

Sleep and mindfulness are opposites, as shown in Figure 10-1. When you fall asleep you're at a low level of consciousness; lower than during normal everyday life. Meditation is designed to heighten your state of awareness, so that it's greater than your normal daily existence.

Figure 10-1:
The different levels of consciousness.

Increasing Awareness

Higher states of awareness

Ordinary wakefulness

Half Awake

Dreamy sleep

Deep Sleep

Sometimes your mind makes you feel sleepy in order to avoid the meditation practice. Sleepiness during meditation is very common and you're certainly not alone if you experience it. Don't beat yourself up about it. Becoming sleepy is a clever trick your mind plays to prevent you from facing up to difficult thoughts or emotions (see the later section 'Getting over difficult emotions'). If you start to feel sleepy, begin to recognise the feeling.

Try these suggestions to cope with or avoid sleepiness:

- ✔ **Ensure that you get enough sleep.** If you don't get enough sleep, you're likely to fall asleep in your next meditation.

- ✔ **Take a few deep, slow breaths.** Repeat a few times until you feel more awake.

- ✔ **Don't eat a big meal before meditating.** If you feel hungry before a meditation, eat a small snack beforehand rather than a three-course meal.

- ✔ **Stand up and do some mindful stretching, yoga, tai chi or walking.** Then go back to your sitting- or lying-down meditation.

- ✔ **Experiment with meditating at different times of day.** Some people feel wide awake in the mornings, others in the afternoon or evening. Find the right time for you.

- ✔ Open your eyes and let some light in. In some meditation traditions, all meditations are done with eyes half or fully open for the duration of the practice. Experiment to see what works for you. When doing this, continue to focus on your breath, body, sounds, sights, thoughts or emotions – whatever you've decided to make the focus of your mindful awareness.

There's a time and a place!

I had a meditation student who, when we meditated together, kept bowing his head and then jolting it up. At the end of the meditation, I asked him if he was feeling sleepy. He said, 'Not at all. When I learnt meditation, my teacher kept doing that, so I thought that was part of the meditation practice and copied him!' His teacher was of course falling asleep when teaching this student, and the student innocently imitated him.

✔ **Become aware of the state of mind called sleepiness.** This is difficult but worth a try. Before you feel too sleepy, notice and get curious about how your body, mind and emotions feel. This can sometimes dissipate the sleepiness and enable you to cope with it next time it happens.

Ironically, one of the first benefits of meditation that many of my students report is better sleep. Through practising meditation, people seem to be able to allow difficult thoughts to be released from the brain, enabling the state of sleep to arise more naturally when necessary.

If you do find yourself falling asleep despite your best efforts, don't worry about it too much. I find many of my students overly criticising themselves for falling asleep. If you fall asleep, you fall asleep – nobody's perfect.

Finding a focus

When you sit for meditation, how do you decide what to focus on?

Think of your breathing as your anchor. Whenever you want to practise mindfulness, begin by focusing on a few breaths. These breaths bring your body and mind together. Breathing can be conscious or unconscious and focusing on breathing seems to have a wonderful way of creating a state of relaxed awareness. Your breathing also changes with your thoughts and emotions, so by developing a greater awareness of it you can regulate erratic feelings on a daily basis. The simple sensations of your breath as it enters and leaves your body can be like drinking an ice-cool refreshing drink on a hot, stuffy day. So, don't forget to breathe.

After you feel you've established your attention on breathing, you can go on to focus on bodily sensations, thoughts, feelings or the different parts of the body, as I describe in Chapter 6.

Re-charging enthusiasm

When you've established yourself in a mindfulness meditation practice, getting into a routine is easy. The habit of practising mindfulness regularly is certainly helpful, but not if you do so in a mechanical way. If you get the feeling that you're doing the same thing every day and keep falling asleep, or you just sit there with no real purpose, then it's time to re-charge your enthusiasm.

Here are some ideas for firing up your enthusiasm:

✔ Do a different meditation practice. Look through this book or refer to the resources in Part III for ideas.

✔ Join a meditation group or go on a retreat. One or other is almost certain to shift something in you.

✔ Try doing your practice in a different position. If you normally sit, try lying down, or walking very slowly.

✔ Change the time that you practise meditation.

✔ Treat yourself to a day of mindfulness. Spend the whole day right from the moment you open your eyes in the morning to the time you go to bed at night doing nothing in particular apart from being mindful. Let the day unfold naturally rather than controlling it too much.

✔ Get in touch with a mindfulness meditation teacher or try attending a course or workshop. From time to time I invite to my classes experienced meditators who love getting back in touch with beginners and discussing their practice.

Practice is important, whether you feel enthusiasm or not. Keep going and see what benefits you gain from your practice in the long term.

Dealing with Common Distractions

Distractions – whether internal or external – are a part of meditation in the same way as these words are part of this book. They go hand in hand. If you find yourself frustrated, criticising the distraction and getting annoyed, feel it, let it be part of the mindfulness practice, and gently guide your attention back to the breathing or the focus of your meditation.

Getting frustrated can be a mind pattern and watching and noticing the frustration, rather than reacting to it, may gradually change the pattern. Being distracted during meditation is a very common experience, a part of the learning process. Expect some frustration and then see how to cope with it rather than trying to run away from it.

Reduce external distractions to a minimum. Here are a few precautions to take:

- ✔ Switch off or unplug all your phones.
- ✔ Turn off all televisions, computers and pretty much anything electronic.
- ✔ Ask anyone else in your home to give you some quiet time if possible.

The very effort you make to reduce distractions can have a beneficial effect on your practice. If you still get distracted, remember that everyday events always get in the way of the practice – listen to the sounds and let them become part of the practice rather than blocking them out.

You can manage internal distractions in the following ways:

- ✔ If you need to deal with something particularly urgent or important, do it before you start meditating. Your mind can then be at rest during the meditation.
- ✔ Watch the stream of thoughts that arise in your mind like clouds that pass across the sky. See the thoughts as separate from you and note what effect that separation has.
- ✔ Welcome your thoughts for a while. Notice how you feel.
- ✔ Be patient. Remember that it's natural for the mind to think. Label each thought with a word such as 'thinking' or 'planning' and then gently invite the attention back to your breathing.

Handling unusual experiences

Meditation isn't about getting a certain experience but about experiencing whatever is happening right now. Blissful experiences come and go. Painful experiences come and go. You just need to keep watching without holding on to either. The practice itself does the rest. Meditation is far, far simpler than people think.

In meditation you may sometimes experience floating (just imaginary, I'm not talking about levitating yet!), flashing lights, flying pigs or pretty much anything the mind can imagine. Whatever unusual feelings arise, remember that these are just experiences and come back to the focus of the meditation. In mindfulness you don't need to judge or analyse these experiences – simply let them go, as far as you can, and then come back to the senses. If you find yourself really struggling or feeling unwell, gently come out of the meditation and try again later – take things slowly, step by step.

Learning to relax

The word *relax* originally comes from the Latin word to loosen or open again. Relax is such a common word. 'Just relax', people say. If only it were so simple. How do you relax during meditation? Essentially by learning to accept the tension you're currently experiencing, rather than fighting with it. Consider this scenario:

You feel tense. Your shoulders are hunched up and you can't let go. What do you do? Try the following steps if tension arises during your meditation:

1. **Become aware of the tension.** Get a sense of its location in your body.

2. **Notice whether the tension has an associated colour, shape, size or texture.** Allow yourself to be curious about it rather than trying to get rid of the tension.

3. **Feel right into the centre of the tension and breathe into it.** Feel the tense part of the body as you simultaneously feel your natural breathing. Just be with the tension as it is.

4. **Notice if you have any feeling or desire to get rid of the tension.** As best you can, let go of that too and see if you can accept the sense of tension a little bit more than you already do.

Fighting to let go of tension just leads to more stress and tension. That's because trying implies effort and if the tension doesn't disappear, you can end up more frustrated and angry. A warm, gentle acceptance of the feeling is far more effective.

Meditation can lead to very deep relaxation. However, relaxation is not the aim of meditation – meditation is ultimately an aimless activity.

Developing patience

Whenever I'm at a party and I'm asked what I do, I explain that I'm a teacher of mindfulness meditation. One of the comments I often get back is along the lines of: 'Oh, you must be patient. I don't have the patience for teaching anything, let alone meditation.' I don't think patience is something that you have – or don't have; you can develop it. You can train your brain to become more patient. And it's a muscle worth building.

Meditation is patience training. To commit to connect with the breath or the senses requires patience. If you feel impatient in your meditation practice but continue to sit there, you're beginning to train the patience muscle. Observe the feeling of discomfort. See if your impatience stays the same or changes. Just as your muscles hurt when you're training in the gym, sitting through impatience is painful, but gradually the feelings of impatience and discomfort diminish. Keep pumping that iron!

You may be impatient for results if you're a beginner to mindfulness. You've heard of all the benefits of meditation and so you want some. That's fair enough. However, because meditation requires patience, when you begin to practise regularly, you'll see that the more impatient you are, the fewer 'results' you get.

Decide how long you're going to practise mindfulness meditation and stick to it. Take the meditation moment by moment and see what unfolds. You spend all your life trying to get somewhere and achieve something. Meditation is a special time for you to let go of all that and just be in the moment. As well as requiring patience, meditation develops it.

If you can't cope with being still and feeling your breath for ten minutes, try five minutes. If that's too much, try two minutes. If that's too much, try ten seconds. *Begin with however long you can manage*, and build it up, step by step. The most important thing is to keep at it, practise as regularly as you can, and gradually increase the time you can practise for. Eventually you'll become a super-patient person. Think of those huge bodybuilders who started off skinny but by taking small steps achieved Olympic weightlifting standards. Believe you can develop patience, and take the next step.

Learning from Negative Experiences

Think back to the first time you met a dog. If your first encounter with a dog was pleasant, you're likely to think that dogs are wonderful. If, as a child, the first thing a dog did was to bite you or bark excessively, you probably think dogs are aggressive. Your early experiences have a big impact on your attitudes and ways of coping later in life. By learning to see that a negative experience is just a momentary thing rather than something that lasts forever, you can begin to move forward.

Meditation is similar. If you happen to get lucky and have a few positive experiences to start with, you'll stick to it. But if you don't, please don't give up. You've only just begun the journey, and you have a lot more to discover. Stay with it and work through any negative experiences you encounter.

Dealing with physical discomfort

In the beginning, sitting meditation will probably be uncomfortable. Learning to cope with that discomfort is an important hurdle to jump in your meditation adventure. When the muscles in your body get used to sitting meditation, the discomfort will probably diminish.

To reduce physical discomfort when meditating, here are several things you can try:

✔ Sitting on a cushion on the floor:

- • Experiment with using cushions of different sizes.

- • Slowly and mindfully stand up, stretch with awareness, and sit back down.

✔ Sitting on a chair:

- • Try raising the back two legs of the chair using books or wooden blocks, and see if that helps.

- • You may be sitting at an angle. Gently lean forwards and backwards and to the left and right to find the middle point.

- • Ask a friend to look at your posture to check that you look straight.

- • Ensure that you're sitting with a sense of dignity and uprightness but not straining too much.

Getting over difficult emotions

Many of my clients come to mindfulness with difficult emotions. They suffer from depression, anxiety, or are stressed at work. They're trying to cope with anger, lack of confidence, or are 'burnt out'. Often they feel as if they've been fighting their emotions all their lives and are now just too tired to keep fighting. Mindfulness is the final resort – the answer to coping with their difficulties. What mindfulness asks of people (to stop running away from themselves and to transcend difficulties as they arise in awareness, moment by moment) is both very simple and very challenging. As soon as you get a glimmer of the effect mindfulness has, your trust in the process grows and a new way of living emerges.

The next time you're faced with difficult emotions, whether you're meditating or not, try the following exercise:

1. Sit with your back straight but not straining.

2. Feel the emotion present in the here and now.

3. Label the emotion in your mind, and repeat it (perhaps 'fear, fear').

4. Notice the desire to get rid of the emotion, and as far as you can, gently be with it.

5. Be mindful of where you feel the emotion in your body (most emotions create a physical sensation in the body).

6. Observe the thoughts running through the mind.

7. Breathe into the emotion, allowing your breathing to help you observe what you're feeling with warmth and friendliness.

8. Become aware of the effect of this exercise on the emotion for a few moments.

Try to get a sense of the gentleness of this exercise. Look at the emotion as you would a flower – examine the petals, smell its fragrance and be gentle with it. Think of the emotion as wanting to talk to you, and listen to it. This is the opposite of the normal way people meet emotion, by bottling it up and running away.

If this all sounds too overwhelming, take it step by step. Make the tiniest step you can manage towards the feeling. Don't worry about how small the step is – it's the intention to move towards the difficult emotion rather than run away that counts. A very small step makes a massive difference, because it begins to change the pattern. This is the positive snowball effect of mindfulness.

When you first move towards difficult emotions, they may grow bigger and feel more intense because you're giving them your attention. This is absolutely normal. Try not to get frightened and run away from these emotions. Give yourself some time and you'll find that your emotions flux and change and aren't as fixed as you've always believed.

Accepting your progress

Mindfulness meditation is a long-term process – the more time and right effort you put in, the more you get out of it. Mindfulness isn't just a set technique that you do to see what you get immediately – it's a way of living. Be as patient as you can. Keep practising, little and often, and see what happens. Most of the time your mind may wander all over the place and you may feel you're not achieving anything. This isn't true – just sitting down and making a commitment to practise daily for a certain period of time has a tremendous effect; you just can't see its effect in the short-term.

Think of meditation as planting a seed. You plant the seed in the most nourishing soil you can find, you water it daily, and you allow it to grow in a sunny spot. What happens if you poke around in the soil to see how it's doing? You disturb the progress of course. Germinating a seed takes time. But there's no other way. You just need to regularly water your seed and wait.

Be patient about your progress. You can't see a plant growing if you watch it, even though it's actually growing all the time. Every time you practise meditation you're growing more mindful, though it may seem very difficult to see from day to day. Trust in the process and enjoy watering your seed of mindfulness.

Going beyond unhelpful thoughts

'I can't do meditation' or 'It's not for me' were some comments I heard when I was last at a Health and Wellbeing Conference. These attitudes are unhelpful because they make you feel as if you won't be able to meditate, no matter what. I believe everyone can learn meditation. 'I can't do meditation' actually means 'I don't like what happens when I look at my mind'.

Here are some common thoughts with useful antidotes to remember:

- ✔ **'I can't stop my thoughts.'** Mindfulness meditation isn't about stopping your thoughts. It's about becoming aware of them from a detached perspective.

- ✔ **'I can't sit still.'** How long can you sit still for? A minute? Ten seconds? Take small steps and gradually build up your practice. Alternatively, try moving meditations detailed in Chapter 6.

- ✔ **'I don't have the patience.'** Then meditation is perfect for you! Patience is something you can build up step by step too. Start with short meditations and increase them to increase your patience.

- ✔ **'It's not for me.'** How do you know that if you haven't tried meditating? Even if you've tried it once or twice, is that enough? Commit to practising for several weeks or a few months before deciding whether mindfulness meditation is suitable for you.

- ✔ **'This isn't helping me.'** This is a common thought in meditation. If you think this, just make a mental note and gently guide your attention back to your breathing.

- ✔ **'This is a waste of time.'** How do you know that for sure? Thousands of scientific studies and millions of practitioners are unlikely to be wrong. Mindfulness meditation is beneficial if you stick to it.

Failure thoughts have an effect only if you approach meditation with the wrong attitude. With the right attitude, there's no failure, only feedback. By feedback, I mean if you think your meditation didn't work for some reason, you now know what doesn't work and can adjust your approach next time. Think of when you were a child learning to talk. Imagine how difficult that must have been! You had never spoken in your life and yet you learnt how to talk at only a few years old. As a young child you didn't know what failure meant so you kept trying. Most of the time what came out was 'ga-ga' and 'goo-goo' but that was okay. Step by step, before you knew it, you were speaking fluently.

There's no such thing as a good or bad meditation. You sit down to practise meditation – or you don't. It doesn't matter how many thoughts you have or how bad you feel in the meditation. What matters is trying to meditate and making the effort to cultivate the right attitude.

Finding a Personal Path

The journey of mindfulness is a personal one, though it affects every person you meet as you interact with her in a mindful way. Many people have walked the path before, but each journey is unique and special. In the end you learn from your own experience and do what feels right for you. If meditation doesn't feel appropriate, you probably won't do it. However, if some quiet, calm voice or feeling underneath all the chatter seems to resonate with the idea of mindfulness, you begin taking steps. You decide in each moment the next course of action that can best deal with setbacks and distractions. These choices shape your personal mindfulness journey.

Approaching difficulties with kindness

When you're faced with a difficulty in life, how do you meet it? How you relate to your difficulty plays a big role in the outcome. Your difficulties offer you a chance to put mindfulness into practice and see these difficulties in a different way. How do you meet problems? You can turn towards them or away from them. Mindfulness is about turning towards them with a sense of kindness rather than avoidance.

Difficulties are like ugly, scary shadows. If you don't look at them properly they continue to frighten you and make you think they're very real. However, if you look towards them, even though the difficulties scare you, you begin to understand what they are. The more light you shine on them the more they seem to lose their power. The light is mindfulness or a kindly awareness.

People can be very unkind to themselves through self-criticism, often learnt at a young age. The learnt behavioural pattern of self-criticism can become like an automatic reaction any time you're faced with difficulties or you make mistakes. The question is, how do you change this harsh, critical inner voice that keeps attacking you? The mindful approach is to listen to it. To give it space to say what it wants to say and listen, but in a gentle, friendly way, as you may listen to a young child or a piece of beautiful music. This ends up breaking down the repetitive, aggressive tone and ends up calming and soothing the self-criticism a little. Just a tiny shift in your attitude towards these thoughts makes all the difference in dealing with difficulties.

Meditation maestro

Meditation is similar to training to be a musician. You may love playing music, but you need to put in the practice every day. Some days are great and wonderful sounds emerge from your instrument – you feel at one with the harmony of the piece. Other days are tough. You don't want to practise, you can't see the point, you feel like giving up. But the musician still perseveres. Deep down you know the magic of music and trust that your practising will pay off. You play music because you love music. Meditation is the same. You have good and bad days, but if you know deep down that it's important for you, you keep putting in the time. That depth of motivation and vision is the secret to making the most of meditation.

If a strong memory or worry of a past or present difficulty comes up in your practice of meditation, try taking the following steps:

1. Become aware of the fact that something challenging has come up for you that keeps drawing your attention.

2. Observe what effect this difficulty is having on your physical body and emotions at the moment.

3. Listen to the difficulty as you would listen to a friend's problems, with a warm sense of empathy rather than criticism.

4. Say to yourself, 'It's okay. Whatever the difficulty is, it's okay. Let me feel it.'

5. Accept the difficulty just as it is for the time being.

6. Breathe into it and stay with the sensations, even if they seem to grow larger at first. With practice, stay with the feeling of the difficulty for longer.

7. When you're ready, gently go back to the focus of the meditation.

Everyone experiences difficulties of varying degrees from time to time. Mindfulness is here to help you to be with it if you can't change the circumstances that are causing the problem.

Understanding why you're bothering

In the middle of your mindfulness meditation practice, you may start thinking, 'Why am I bothering to do this?' and 'I'm wasting my time'. This is quite normal and part of the process of learning to meditate. Simply notice the thought, gently say to yourself 'thinking, thinking', and turn your attention back to the breath or other focus of meditation. When you practise for a while and begin to see the benefits of meditation, your trust in the process grows, and your doubts diminish.

If you feel you've forgotten why you're practising meditation in the first place and are lacking in motivation, refer to Chapter 3.

Realising that setbacks are inevitable

When I first learnt to meditate, I tried too hard. I thought I had to *get* something. I sat up extremely straight in a stiff way, rather than naturally upright. Each time my mind wandered away from the breath I hauled it back instead of kindly guiding it back to the breathing. I waited for an experience. I kept trying to clear my mind completely. Sometimes it felt wonderfully blissful and I thought I had got it! But then it went away. So, there I was again, trying to *get* it. I felt I was going through setback after setback.

In fact, I was going through a learning process; beginning to understand what meditation was all about. You can only have a setback if you're trying to get something or go somewhere. If you have no goal, you can't really have a setback. Ultimately, meditation is about letting go of goals and being in the here and now.

Imagine you're sitting at home and you decide you're going to go home. What do you need to do? You guessed it – nothing! You're already there. The journey of mindfulness is like that. You feel you're getting closer to true meditation but really, *each moment you practise* is true meditation, no matter what your experience.

Setting realistic expectations

If you think that mindfulness meditation is going to make you feel calm and relaxed and free of all problems straight away, you're going to have a hard time. When you first learn to drive, you don't expect to be an expert after one lesson. Even after you pass the test, it takes years to become a good driver. Meditation, like any other learning experience, takes time too. Have realistic expectations about meditation.

Here are ten realistic expectations to reflect on:

- ✔ 'My mind will wander around. This is what happens in meditation, even if it's for a few breaths.'

- ✔ 'There's no such thing as a good or bad meditation. It's like when a small child does a scribble for drawing. It just is what it is.'

✔ 'Mindfulness isn't about getting certain experiences. It's about being with whatever arises moment to moment with acceptance.'

✔ 'I'll sometimes feel calm and sometimes feel agitated and tense in meditation. With time, the calmness will increase.'

✔ 'Meditation is a long-term practice. I'll gradually learn to let go of my expectations as I practise.'

✔ 'It may be difficult to motivate myself to practise every day, especially at the beginning. Some days I may forget to practise. That doesn't mean I should immediately give up.'

✔ 'Sometimes I may feel worse after the meditation than before. This is part of the learning process that I need to understand.'

✔ 'I can never know how I've benefited from meditation. I can only practise every day and see what happens.'

✔ 'Even after years of meditation, I may sometimes feel I haven't progressed. This isn't a fact but an idea. Meditation works below conscious awareness and so I can't know what's happening there.'

✔ 'The more I practise, the easier it gets.'

Looking at change

Humans are creatures of habit. Once you get into a habit, you effortlessly do it day after day without a second thought. So, for change to last and become effortless, it needs to become a new habit – in this case, the habit of mindfulness. When you establish a pattern of mindfulness, your brain immediately begins to change, gradually transforming your experience of life for the better.

Creating a new habit pattern results in new neurons firing in your brain. And neurons that fire together, wire together. As you practise regularly, the neural pathways in your brain involved in being mindful begin to link up, thereby creating a healthy habit.

To create a habit of mindfulness meditation try the following:

1. Decide on a plan of action – how long you'll meditate every day and at what time.

2. Stick to the plan whether you feel like it or not.

3. If you forget to meditate on the odd day, don't give up. Slipping up is natural. Pick up and start again.

4. Assess your progress after four or eight weeks. Make changes if necessary and make a new plan, perhaps meditating for a longer duration.

Creating a habit of mindfulness meditation sounds so simple. However, the difficult bit is Step 2. You listen to thoughts saying things like 'don't bother today' or you give in to feelings of tiredness or restlessness. This is your moment to challenge the usual way you behave. You can practise what you committed to, or you can follow the old habit pattern. Listen to what you decided to do in the first place and stick to the discipline as best you can. As soon as you've established the habit of mindfulness you find yourself becoming mindful without even thinking about it – the neurons in your brain have wired together. Step by step you can change.

Part IV
Reaping the Rewards of Mindfulness

The 5th Wave   By Rich Tennant

MENU
Fish Chips
$700
Inc. 5

"I _am_ being mindful about food and my eating.
That's how I know you've got 3 more chips
on your plate than I do."

In this part . . .

You find out the wonderful ways in which mindfulness can help you, from boosting your happiness to dealing with anxiety. Try some of the techniques used in mindfulness therapy to combat depression. You even discover ways of teaching mindfulness to children and pick up some useful tips for mindful parenting.

Chapter 11

Discovering Greater Happiness

I'd just started my career. I had a job with a proper salary going straight into my bank account – much more money than any pocket money or student loan I'd received. The feeling was exhilarating: I'd made it! All those years at school, all those exams at University, slogging away, and now I'd made it. Now what? Spend it of course, I thought. So, I went out and spent it. A new car, clothes, the latest gadgets and gizmos – and yet the pleasure was short-lived. Before long that sense of emptiness I'd been running from returned. Something was missing. Chasing after stuff wasn't the way to happiness, even though the whole of society seemed to advertise that it was. My search for real and lasting happiness began.

This chapter explores the relationship between the science of wellbeing (positive psychology) and the art of mindfulness. By applying the findings of what makes a happy life with the contemplative exercises of mindfulness, you can explore ways to be more content and peaceful in your life.

Discovering the Way to Happiness

The Dalai Lama, often giggling or smiling with others, says: 'I believe that the very *purpose* of our life is to seek happiness.' That's a huge statement. Imagine living as if your very purpose was to seek happiness. A life where your decisions and choices were based on whether your wellbeing would be increased or decreased. What would your life be like? How would it be different? Is it even possible? If the sole purpose of life is to seek happiness, then you need to find the best way to greater wellbeing.

Whether happiness is the key purpose of life or not, happiness has scientifically proven benefits. Through achieving greater wellbeing, you can:

- ✔ **Do better in social relationships.** You have more friends and get on better with them.

- ✔ **Use your intelligence more efficiently.** No matter how smart you are, you use those brain cells well.

- ✔ **Be more optimistic.** You see the bright side in most situations.

- ✔ **Live longer and more healthily.** You have lower blood pressure and fight off diseases more effectively.

- ✔ **Be more creative.** You're capable of coming up with new and innovative ideas for home and work.

Exploring your ideas about wellbeing

Some people describe themselves as extremely happy, whereas others claim to be unhappy. Happiness seems to be at different levels, from person to person, and from moment to moment.

Ask yourself the following question:

> Considering everything, how would you say things are these days – would you say you're very happy, pretty happy, or not too happy?

If you rated yourself not too happy, don't despair! This chapter is designed to help you begin working towards greater wellbeing. You can begin using a whole range of well-researched approaches right away.

An interesting way of finding out your ideas about happiness is a technique called sentence completion. Complete the following sentences quickly with five or six different answers, without thinking too much.

The things that truly make me happy are . . .

To be 5 per cent more mindful in my life, I need to . . .

To be 5 per cent happier in my life I need to . . .

Keep your answers handy. Practise this exercise daily for a few weeks to see what kind of answers you get. You may need to act on them, or you may not. Just by becoming aware of your responses, you naturally begin to move towards becoming happier.

Challenging assumptions about happiness

The most common assumption about happiness is that *pleasure equals happiness*. By maximising the number of positive feelings and minimising the number of negative, a happy life is created. It turns out that this is a very small part of the picture. Research shows that pleasure alone doesn't lead to any greater sense of life satisfaction at all. So, although nothing's wrong with luxurious hotels and enjoying your favourite food, they just result in a fleeting feel-good effect.

That money equals happiness is another popular belief. The relationship between happiness and money is really interesting because society gears itself towards acquiring more money and therefore hoping for more happiness. One experiment compared the happiness of big lottery winners to the happiness of people who had been in a serious accident and become paralysed. That's a serious test – what a comparison! The results showed that after two years, the people who won the lottery went back to the happiness level they had been at before. The same happened with the paralysed accident victims. Isn't that amazing? Whether you become paralysed or win the lottery, you end up with the same level of happiness in the long term. I think that's incredible!

Imagine that you were able to sell your happiness. Once you'd sold it, you'd never be happy again. Your happiness would be gone. How much would you sell your happiness for? £1,000? Most people say no. How about £50,000? That gets people thinking, but usually the answer is no. How about a million pounds in cash, crisp £50 notes, in exchange for your happiness? Think about that for a moment. A million pounds. Would you sell it? A million pounds can buy you a lot of stuff, but you'd get no happiness in return. How about a billion pounds?

I find the question of selling happiness an interesting one because it really gets you to reflect on how much you value happiness. But you sell your happiness very easily in the short term. You sell your happiness when you can't find a parking space, if your partner irritates you or a demanding manager is rude to you. It's easy to forget how much your happiness is worth. Perhaps it's priceless?

In his book *Happiness*, Buddhist monk Matthieu Ricard, states that wellbeing is a deep sense of serenity that *underlies and permeates all emotion states*, including joy and sorrow. This sense of being, or well-*being*, is cultivated through 'mind training' (meditation). Mind training involves becoming aware of destructive emotions like jealousy and anger, and rather than acting on them, which just reinforces the self-perpetuating process, watching them arise in your awareness, without judgement. As you watch the negative feelings rise up in you, and refrain from acting, or reacting, these feelings naturally subside in their own time. This doesn't mean you spend all day trying to force a grin on your face (though apparently that's no bad thing), but you see different emotional states as opportunities to find out about them and create an emotional balance between them. You're not pushing them away, or grabbing hold of them – just dispassionately observing them, from moment to moment.

A happiness recipe

I've found a sense of wellbeing through the following 'recipe':

✔ A **daily practice** of mindfulness meditation and being mindful from moment to moment in what I do.

✔ An attitude of **gratitude** for what I have.

✔ **Valuing social relationships** and practising forgiveness when things go wrong.

✔ **Letting go** of anything outside my control and accepting life as it is in the present moment.

✔ Having **meaningful goals** in my life that are in line with what I believe is important and enjoying the journey towards achieving them rather than getting fixated on results.

✔ Seeing things in a **positive light**.

✔ Having a light-hearted approach – **laughing** uncontrollably from time to time!

✔ Working with a **sense of service** to the community.

I'm not perfect and have good and bad days, of course. However, the practice of mindfulness is always available to me, and helps me to access my deep inner resources for healing, wellness and peace. Consider what your happiness recipe is, and write it down. Which ingredients do you need?

Applying Mindfulness with Positive Psychology

Positive psychology is the science of wellbeing – it's concerned with people's strengths, improving normal lives, and building healthy organisations. Mindfulness is one of the most powerful tools in the positive psychology toolkit because evidence demonstrates a link between mindfulness practice and levels of wellbeing.

Psychology has traditionally studied people's problems. Psychologists were interested in conditions like depression, anxiety, schizophrenia and psychosis. This is certainly not a bad thing and has resulted in a number of mental illnesses now being treatable. Through talking treatments and drugs, psychology has helped people to reduce their sadness. The problem is that in their rush to help suffering people, psychologists forgot about how to make relatively normal human beings happier. So psychologists can move people from unhappy to neutral but they haven't considered how to go from neutral to happy. If you drive a car, you know that you can't get very far in neutral! Positive psychologists focus on moving people towards greater wellbeing.

Understanding the three ways to happiness

Positive psychology describes three different ways to happiness. You can use all three interchangeably.

Pleasure

Maximising the amount of pleasure you experience leads to feelings of happiness. Eating your favourite chocolate, going out to watch a film, or going shopping are all examples of seeking pleasure. They make you feel happy temporarily, but if you keep repeating them, they become unpleasant. For example, eating one bar of chocolate is delicious, but not 100 bars of chocolate!

Engagement or flow

With flow, you give complete 100 per cent attention and are one with whatever you're doing, whether pleasurable or not. Flow usually requires some effort on your part. The activity involved is just challenging enough to hold your relaxed attention. Refer to Chapter 5 for a complete description of flow.

You can develop engagement in anything you do, if you give it your full attention. This is where mindfulness comes in: developing a relaxed, calm, focused awareness with whatever you're doing, whenever you remember, from moment to moment. Even washing the dishes or walking the dog is an opportunity to live in this state of flow, a condition of wellbeing. Give 100 per cent attention to whatever you're doing, whenever you remember.

Meaning

Living a meaningful life involves knowing your strengths and using them in the service of something larger than yourself. We live in an individualistic society and the word 'service' isn't often thought to be attractive. However, helping others is the core ingredient for a happy life. Don't worry, you don't have to change your job. You just need to make a genuine attitude shift. If you're a lawyer who wants to make as much money as possible, that severely limits your overall sense of wellbeing. The same work can offer more with the right motivation. Justice, equality, the inner desire to help others all give you a much greater sense of meaning and purpose in such a career. Other ways of creating greater meaning include volunteer work or joining a religious or spiritual group. Simply performing acts of kindness wherever you can gives life greater meaning.

Using your personal strengths mindfully

Positive psychologists carefully analysed a range of strengths and virtues, and found 24 of them to be universally significant across cultures. By discovering and using your strengths in your work and home life you achieve a greater sense of wellbeing because you're doing something you're good at, and that you love doing.

Table 11-1 shows the 24 key signature strengths under six key categories. Scan through the list and reflect on what you think are your five main strengths or virtues.

Table 11-1			The 24 Signature Strengths		
Wisdom	*Courage*	*Love*	*Justice*	*Temperance*	*Transcendence*
Creativity	Bravery	Intimacy	Responsibility	Forgiveness	Appreciation
Judgement	Perseverance	Kindness	Fairness	Self-control	Gratitude
Curiosity	Integrity	Sociability	Leadership	Humility	Optimism
Love of learning	Enthusiasm			Caution	Humour
Perspective					Spirituality

The great thing about discovering your signature strengths is finding a strength you never knew you had. I found out that one of my strengths was kindness. I never thought of that as a strength, but it is. And it makes me happy to offer kindness to others. You too can dust down your undiscovered strengths and apply them to your life.

Link your strengths with your mindfulness practice by becoming more aware of when you do and don't use your strengths. Also, notice what effect mindfulness meditation has on your signature strengths – for example, you may find you become better at leadership as your confidence grows, or your general level of curiosity increases.

Looking on the funny side of life

One of my top five signature strengths turns out to be humour. Now, let me make it clear, that doesn't mean I'm going to be the next big hit on the comedy circuit. It means I love laughing and making others laugh. I never thought of it as a strength until I discovered that I rated highly for it in the signature strengths test I did online. Now I know that, I value time to be with friends and colleagues who like to see the funny side of life. I also use it to see life in a light-hearted way when things aren't going my way, and let myself clown around from time to time. Mindfulness is an important practice, but if you take it too seriously, you miss out on an important attitude. By discovering your own signature strengths, you can spend more time developing them in a mindful way. When I'm coaching clients in mindful living, I sometimes recommend identifying strengths as an beneficial approach.

For example, say one of your undiscovered strengths is 'love of learning' but your job is boring and seems to involve repeating the same thing every day. How can you use your love of learning? Well, you do an evening course, start a masters degree or make time to read more. Or you can integrate your strength into your work in a mindful way. Become aware of each of the tasks you do and think about what makes that task boring. Look at co-workers and discover what attitudes others have that make them feel differently about the job. Discover something new about the work every day, or research ways of moving on to a more suitable career. By doing so you use your strength, and feel a bit better every day.

To increase your day-to-day feelings of happiness, try this:

- ✔ Discover your signature strengths. You can discover your own strengths for free at www.authentichappiness.org.
- ✔ Use your signature strengths in your daily life wherever you can and with a mindful awareness.
- ✔ Enjoy the process and let go of the outcome.

Writing a gratitude journal

The human brain is designed to remember things that go wrong rather than right. This is a survival mechanism and ensures that you don't make the same mistake again and again, which may be life-threatening if you live out in the jungle and need to remember to avoid the tigers. If you don't live in the jungle, focusing on the negative is a problem. The antidote for the human brain's tendency to look for what's going wrong is gratitude. And gratitude has been found to be very effective.

A gratitude journal is a powerful and simple way of boosting your wellbeing. The journal is simply a daily record of things in your life that you're grateful for. By reflecting on what made you grateful at the end of each day, research has found that levels of gratitude increase and people feel significantly happier. It works!

Here's how to write an effective gratitude journal:

1. **Get a book or diary in which you can make a daily record.** As long as it has sufficient space for you to write three sentences every day, that's fine.

2. **Every evening, before you go to bed, write down three things that you're grateful for.** Try to vary choosing what you're grateful for. Writing that you're grateful for your cat, apartment and car every single day isn't as effective as varying it unless you really mean it and feel it. You don't have to choose huge things – anything small, even if you feel only slightly grateful about it, will do. Examples include having a partner, enjoying a conversation at work, a relaxing drive home, a roof over your head. You're training the gratitude muscle. The more you practise, the better you get at it.

3. **Notice what effect your gratitude diary has on the quality and quantity of your sleep and how you generally feel throughout the day.** By checking in on how you're feeling and what effect the exercise is having, you're able to fine tune it to work for you. Noticing the benefits of gratitude also helps to motivate your practice.

4. **Continue to practise regularly if you find it beneficial.** After a while, gratitude will become a pleasant habit.

Through practising mindfulness meditation, you may naturally find that you're grateful for the simpler things in life and feel happier as a result. Writing a gratitude journal complements your daily mindfulness practice very well (refer to Chapter 9 for a daily routine). Both are proven to boost your levels of wellbeing, so you're sure to feel more emotionally resilient over time. You can even write the journal together with a loved one, to deepen your relationship.

The *gratitude visit* is a very popular experiment among positive psychologists because it's so powerful. Think of someone who made a big difference to your life who you haven't properly thanked. Write a letter to express your gratitude to that person. If you can, arrange to visit and read the testimonial out to him. Even three months later, people who express their gratitude in this way feel happier and less depressed. Add mindfulness to this exercise by simply being aware of your thoughts and feelings that arise as you do the exercise. See what happens.

Savouring the moment

Savouring the moment means becoming aware of the pleasure in the present time by deliberately focusing attention on it. Here are some ways of developing this skill:

- **Mindfulness.** Being aware of what you're doing in the moment is the only way of ultimately savouring the moment. If your mind and heart are in two different places, you miss the joy of the moment – the breeze that passes through the trees or the flower on the side of the pavement. Most of the exercises in this book help you to grow your inner muscle of mindfulness.

- **Sharing with others.** Expressing your pleasure to those around you turns out to be a powerful way of savouring the moment. If you notice a sunset or beautiful sky, share your pleasure with others. Letting someone know about the pleasure it gave you helps to raise the positive feeling for both of you. However, don't forget to look at it fully first – sometimes it is easy to get carried away talking and miss the beauty of the moment itself.

- **Seeking new experiences.** Vary your pleasurable experiences rather than repeating the same ones over and over again – it's a happier experience. And if you like ice cream, eat it once in a while and mindfully rather than eating lots at the same time. I know, it's easier said than done!

Painting joy

Last year I decided to paint the walls my living room. Now, you may see this as a boring task with no particular opportunity apart from getting the room painted, or you can see it as a fantastic chance to be absolutely 100 per cent mindful of the task. So I felt the bristles on the brush as I dipped it into the thick paint, connected with the sensations in my arm as I moved it over to the edge of the wall, and enjoyed watching the colour magically release itself from the brush and onto the surface. As I got into a calm rhythmic movement, I gradually lost my usual sense of self and was at one with the painting. By the time I had finished, I felt energised and uplifted. I'd been fortunate enough to enter the state of flow, or mindful awareness.

Serving others mindfully

Of the three ways of achieving satisfaction in life (pleasure, engagement and meaning), engagement and meaning are by far the most effective, and of the two, *meaning has been found to have the most effect.*

To achieve deeper meaning, you work towards something that's greater than yourself. This involves doing something for others, or in other words, serving others. A meaningful life is about meeting a need in the world through your unique strengths and virtues. By serving a greater need, you create a win-win situation – the people you help feel better, and you feel better for helping them.

 Doing things just for your own happiness doesn't really work. Imagine cooking a meal for the whole family, and then just eating it yourself and watching the rest of the family go hungry. Where's the fun in that? The food may taste good, but without sharing, you're missing something really important. Happiness is the same. If you practise mindfulness just for your own happiness and no one else, the meditation has a limited effect. Expand your vision and allow your mindfulness to expand to benefit all and you'll find it far more fulfilling. Each time before you practise, recall the positive effect mindfulness has on both yourself and those around you, ultimately making the world a better place to live in. (Refer to Chapter 6 for an exercise in metta meditation, which encourages kind feelings for yourself and others.)

Testing selfish and selfless happiness

In positive psychology classes, students are sometimes given the task of doing something for their own happiness followed by doing something to make someone else happy. Students who did something for their own pleasure like watching a film, eating out in a restaurant or surfing on the Internet found the happiness to be short-lived and lacking in depth. They then had to do something that would make someone else happy, such as giving their partner a massage or complimenting a friend. Students always found making others happy far more enriching and fulfilling, with the sense of well-being lasting for much longer. Why not try this out today?

Generating Positive Emotions with Mindfulness

Mindfulness is about offering a warm, kind, friendly, accepting awareness to your moment-by-moment experience, whatever that may be. For this reason, any practice of mindfulness, in the long term, develops your ability to generate positive feeling towards your inner (thoughts, emotions) and outer (world) experience. To develop this further, try the exercises in this section.

Mindfulness practice is like training in the gym. You may feel uncomfortable at first, but through regular practice you get better at being mindful in each moment. As it's such a gradual process, you may not notice any change at all at first, but just trust in the process and give it a decent try. Keep going to the brain gym!

Breathing and smiling

Research has found a connection between the muscles you use to smile, and your mood. You smile when you feel good, but interestingly, simply smiling makes you feel good. It works both ways.

You can test this out for yourself. Try smiling right now and simultaneously think a negative thought. Can you? I find that smiling certainly has an effect over negative mood.

Smiling is contagious – have you noticed how infectious a smile is? If you see someone smiling, you can't help but do the same. It also reduces stress – by deliberately becoming aware of your breathing and smiling, you act against the body's automatic defence mechanism and allow a more restful and calm state to occur.

Thich Nhat Hanh, a world-famous meditation teacher, has dedicated his life to the practice of mindfulness. One of his recommended practices is breathing and smiling. He offers the following meditation. Try reciting these lines as you breathe in and out:

> *Breathing in, I calm body and mind.*
>
> *Breathing out, I smile.*
>
> *Dwelling in the present moment*
>
> *I know this is the only moment.*

He goes on to say:

> *'Breathing in, I calm body and mind.' This line is like drinking a glass of ice water – you feel the cold, the freshness permeate your body. When I breathe in and recite this line, I actually feel the breathing calming my body, calming my mind.*

> *'Breathing out, I smile.' You know the effect of a smile. A smile can relax hundreds of muscles in your face, and relax your nervous system. A smile makes you master of yourself . . . When you smile, you realise the wonder of the smile.*

Smile, especially when you don't feel like it or it feels unnatural. Even though you don't feel great, it has a small effect. You're planting the seeds of happiness. With time, the seeds are sure to grow.

Mindfulness increases happiness: The proof

Jon Kabat-Zinn of the University of Massachusetts Medical School, and Richard Davidson, Professor of Psychology and Psychiatry of University of Wisconsin-Madison, and their colleagues have proved that mindfulness increases happiness.

The researchers randomly split a group of employees at a biotech company into two groups. The first group did an eight-week course in mindfulness-based stress reduction (MBSR) and the others did nothing. The electrical activity of their brains was studied before and after the training.

After eight weeks, the people who did the mindfulness training had greater activation in a part of the brain called the left prefrontal cortex. This part of the brain is associated with positive emotions, wellbeing and acceptance of experience. Left prefrontal cortex-activated people normally describe themselves as interested, excited, strong, active, alert and enthusiastic. In comparison, right prefrontal cortex-activated people describe themselves as afraid, nervous, scared, upset and distressed.

The experiment showed that just eight weeks of mindfulness meditation training in a busy workplace environment can have positive effect on wellbeing. Other studies with more experienced meditators suggest these changes in the brain become a permanent feature – explaining the mild grin on the faces of experienced meditation practitioners.

Releasing Your Creativity

What is creativity? Where does creativity come from? How can you become happier and more creative? Good questions! The act of creativity is a deep mystery. If creativity is a mechanical process in which you do such and such, it ceases to have its intrinsic uniqueness.

For example, I'm being creative by writing this book. I simply type the words that come to my mind. I don't know where the thoughts are coming from; they seem to arise into awareness, and vanish again in the same mysterious way. Creativity is a beautifully magic process that seems to be a natural part of the Universe. By using ways to calm your mind, you find the creative process naturally unfolds itself, which increases your happiness.

Exploring creativity

Play is an important aspect of creativity. If you're willing to play and have fun, creativity is sure to follow on. When you play, you engage the more creative right side of the brain. You let go of the usual rules. If you stick to the normal rules, you can't come up with something new. The new is born from transforming the way you see things.

Let's say for example, you're trying to think of something different to do with the family for a weekend. Here's one way to get the creative juices flowing:

1. Write down what you want to achieve. For example, I'm looking for an exciting weekend getaway with the whole family, to cheer us all up and have fun together.

2. Let go of the problem. Allow the mind to slow down and connect with the breath for five minutes or more.

3. Write down several things you've done before at weekends for fun. For example, staying over at your sister's place, going to the nearest beach, staying over at your friend's house, going to local museums, playing different sports.

4. Change your perspective. Imagine you're very rich or you don't have a family or you live in a forest. What would you do then? For example, if you were very wealthy you might fly to a bigger city for the weekend, if you didn't have children you might book a romantic weekend getaway, if you lived in the forest, you might start building a tree house.

5. Now see what ideas can be used from that. For example, you can travel by train or budget airline to a relatively cheap hotel in a city you haven't been before, you can ask your neighbours if you can stay at their country home for the weekend, or you can find a hotel that caters for children while you spend some quality time with your partner.

To be highly creative, you need to calm the mind completely. Many research papers show that a calm and relaxed mind is far more creative than an anxious and stressed one. When you're calm, your thoughts aren't firing off too often, so you have space for creative ideas to rise to the surface. Creativity is a bit like looking for treasure at the bottom of a lake. If the water is choppy and murky, you can never see the treasure below. But if the lake is clear and calm, you can easily see it. Mindfulness gives space for the mind to become calm and at the same time raises your level of awareness. You're not forcing calmness, you're just allowing the right conditions for it to happen.

I often get new ideas when practising informal mindfulness. I can be going for a stroll through my local park, looking at the trees, or enjoying the blueness of the sky when a new idea pops into my head. I usually carry around a small notebook in which to jot ideas down. I don't do this when I'm doing formal mindfulness meditation, however, as that would be a distraction. I don't *try* to get ideas or force them to come up.

Keep your mind engaged in the moment, and ideas naturally arise. Imagine you're trying to remember where you left your keys, and no matter how hard you try, you can't recall where they are. Then you forget about it, and whoosh – the location shoots into your head.

Look at the picture in Figure 11-1.

Moments of genius

Arguably one of the greatest scientific creative thoughts in the last hundred years didn't occur in a lecture theatre or seminar with top scientists. It arose in the relaxed, curious, open and questioning mind of a teenager. Einstein's greatest moment of genius occurred to him when he was 16 years old, strolling along and dreaming what it would feel like to ride on a beam of light – which led to his famous theory of relativity. I'd call that state of mind 'mindfulness of thought', where Einstein allowed the mind to wander but was aware of thoughts and ideas arising.

Inventors need to be aware to spot everyday problems that need a new invention. James Dyson was vacuuming in his home when he realised the top-of-the-range vacuum cleaner was losing suction and getting clogged up. He became aware of this (mindfulness) and then went on to design over 5000 different prototypes before coming up with his famous bagless vacuum cleaner.

Another inventor, George de Mestral, embodies the mindful attitude of curiosity. He was walking his dog on a beautiful summer's day in Switzerland and returned home to find burrs – plant seed sacs – stuck to his dog and his own trousers. With his burning curiosity he examined the burrs under a microscope to discover that they were covered in tiny hooks which clung onto the loops in his trousers. In that moment, he had the idea to invent Velcro, made of hooks on one side and loops on the other. Genius!

Figure 11-1:
Optical
illusion.

If you haven't seen this illusion before, you probably see a series of random dots. Now try feeling your breath, becoming aware of the feelings and sensations in your body for a few moments, and then look again in a more relaxed way. As best you can, let go of any frustrations or desires to 'get it'. Spend a few minutes doing this. Look at the image just as it is. Has it changed? Can you see it in a different perspective? Be patient and see what unfolds. I'm going to tell you now, are you ready . . . it's a Dalmatian. If you still can't see the dog, what can you do? You can ask someone else, come back to it later, or try looking at different angles – in other words, you look for creative alternative ideas. Can you see how getting frustrated may be a natural reaction, but isn't helpful?

This shows how the same thing (that picture) can be seen in two different ways. One seems random, and the other a fairly clear image of a dog. We create our reality. By letting go and looking deeply, other realities can unfold. The interesting thing is, once you've 'seen it', you can't forget it! Sometimes you may do this with problems too – seeing the same problem instead of new and innovative approaches to a solution. Try letting go of the obvious answer – walk away, meditate, do something else and come back to the challenge later on with a refreshed, and therefore more creative and happier mind.

Creating conditions for originality

Here are a few ways of creating the right conditions for mindfully allowing originality to arise:

1. **Eliminate any potential distractions if possible.** This helps you to calm your mind a little, making creative thought more likely.

2. **Find a space where you're sufficiently warm and comfortable**, and if you can, loosen any tight clothing. If your body is happy, your mind will be happy, and a happy mind is a creative mind.

3. **Become aware of each in-breath and each out-breath, as best you can.** Awareness of the breath is a powerful way of immediately centring yourself, bringing you to the here and now.

4. **Become aware of thoughts as they arise and pass like clouds in the sky.** By seeing thoughts like clouds, you stop holding on to them, and clear out the old ideas to make way for the new ideas.

5. **Notice the gap or space between thoughts.** Creative ideas come from a place of silence and calm, which is always available to you between thoughts. Noticing the gap tunes you into a more creative state.

6. **Continue for at least ten minutes, and more if you can.** You need to give yourself time to tune into this creative space. When you feel you've finished, come out of the meditation slowly and see what new ideas spring up.

Through this exercise you begin to allow your inner creative space to fill with fresh, new ideas. You're clearing out the old, limiting ideas to make space for the brand new ones. Feel free to interrupt the meditation any time to write your ideas down, as this isn't a formal meditation practice but a creativity exercise – allow yourself to have fun with it and experiment.

Chapter 12

Reducing Stress,
Anger and Fatigue

· ·

· ·

Difficulties are part and parcel of life – you can't stop them unfortunately. What you *can* stop is the way you meet and relate to challenges.
Perhaps you habitually go into denial, or maybe you throw yourself in head
first and end up overly tired. If you can face the difficulty in the right way,
you can take heat out of the problem, and even use the energy generated by
the issue to manage your emotions and activities.

Mindfulness offers you the opportunity to become more intimate with the
working of your own habitual patterns of operation. If you haven't really
noticed how you currently meet challenges, you're bound to have a hard
time accessing whether your approach is useful or not. Whether the way you
react is helpful or not depends on what effect your reaction has. If you have
no clear idea of the effects, you're not benefiting from experience – you're
just replaying a record again and again. As this chapter shows, by becoming even slightly more mindful, your awareness grows and something can
shift – and the smallest shift can make the biggest difference. As astronaut
Neil Armstrong said (sort of): One small step for you, one giant leap for your
wellbeing!

Using Mindfulness to Reduce Stress

Research shows mindfulness reduces stress, in the short and long term, even
well after people have completed a training in mindfulness. This is because
many people choose to continue to practise some form of mindfulness as
part of their daily routine years later because they found it so helpful. In this

section you explore the various ways stress creeps up on you, and how mindfulness can help you say goodbye to unmanageable levels of stress.

Understanding your stress

Stress is a natural and everyday occurrence. Whenever you have a challenge to meet, doing so triggers the physiological reaction of stress. Stress isn't an illness but a state of body and mind. However, if your stress level is very high, or goes on for too long, then you can suffer from both physical and mental ill health.

Stress isn't always a bad thing – when you or someone near you faces a physical danger, stress is helpful. For example, if you see a child running out in the street, the stress response provides you with the energy and focus you need to run and stop her. However, if you're lying in bed, worrying about your tax bill, stress isn't helpful – the result is that you don't sleep. If this stress goes on for too long, your health is likely to suffer.

Stress researcher Richard Lazarus found that stress begins with you *interpreting* the situation as dangerous or difficult, and rapidly deciding what resources you have to cope with the challenge. If you interpret an event as dangerous or difficult, and you don't have the resources to cope, you experience a stress reaction. This is why one person loves going on a rollercoaster, whereas for another the experience is a living nightmare.

When you interpret a situation as challenging, your body's primitive nervous system is hard-wired to automatically begin a chain of reactions in your body. This includes stress hormones being released into the bloodstream, your pupils enlarging, perception of pain diminishing, attention becoming focused, blood moving from the skin and digestive organs into the muscles, breath and heart rate rising, blood pressure increasing, and more sugars being released into your system, providing you with an immediate source of energy.

In this state of body and mind, called the *fight or flight response*, you see almost everything as a potential threat. You're in an attack mode, and see things from a survival, short-term point of view, instead of the long-term impact of your words and actions.

Imagine that your boss tells you how poor your last presentation was, and that you're not working hard enough. If you *interpret* this as a personal attack, your blood pressure rises, your pupils dilate, you sweat and feel anxious. Your body is behaving as if you're about to be attacked by a life-threatening bear, and you're ready to fight or flee. However, if you interpret the situation as 'the boss is in a bad mood' or 'he says the same to everyone – it's no big deal', you're less likely to trigger so great a stress reaction. The interpretation is far more important than the 'reality' of the situation, from a stress point of view.

Research shows that everyone has an optimum level of stress. Think of stress levels like the pressure of a pencil on a piece of paper. If you push too hard (high levels of stress), you tear the paper or snap the pencil. If you push too lightly (too little stress), nothing you draw can be seen, which is dissatisfying. The optimum balance is between the two. Then a beautiful drawing can emerge. Too little stress leads to a lack of motivation and too much leads to over stimulation and ill health. Mindfulness can help you cope with higher levels of pressure before your stress reaction becomes too highly activated.

Noticing the early signs of stress

How do you know when you're *beginning* to get stressed about something? What are your early warning signs? Does your eye start twitching, or do you begin to get a headache? Perhaps you lose patience easily, or begin worrying. By becoming more aware of your early reactions to stress, you can begin to take appropriate action before the stress spirals out of control.

Regular mindfulness meditation and doing your daily activities with a mindful awareness makes you more aware of your own thoughts, feelings and bodily sensations. You're more likely to be aware when stress levels begin to rise and you can then take appropriate action.

Take a few moments to reflect on the last time you were stressed. What did you notice happening to your body? Which parts became tense? How did your behaviour change? What sorts of emotions did you feel? What thoughts were going through your mind? Bear them in mind and look out for these changes when facing your next challenge. Then, you can use mindfulness to reduce your stress levels to more acceptable levels.

Assessing your stress

You may find using a stress diary a useful way of assessing your level of stress from day to day. Stress diaries make you more mindful of the areas in your life that cause you stress in the short term, as well as your own reaction to the stress. This knowledge makes you more aware of the onset of stress and your response to it, allowing you to make more helpful choices to lower your stress levels if they're too high.

Designate a notebook as your stress diary and try the following. Write down:

✔ How stressed you feel on a scale of one to ten, with ten being extremely stressed.

✔ What caused the stress.

✔ The thoughts going through your mind, your emotions, and bodily sensations like headache or tense shoulders.

✔ How you're responding to, and handling, the stress.

Moving from reacting to responding to stress

When experiencing stress, I call the things that you do automatically, without even thinking about it, stress *reactions*. If you're lucky, some of your reactions may be helpful and therefore dissipate the stress. More often than not though, reactions to stress are unhealthy and lead to further stress. A *response* is more mindful, includes some time for reflection, is aware rather than automatic, and tends to be more helpful.

Your reactions to stress are partly based on what you assimilated in childhood, partly genetic, and partly based on your own experiences with stress. If whoever brought you up reacted in a certain way to stress, you have a greater chance of behaving in a similar way. Your own experience of ways of dealing with stress also comes into the equation. Perhaps you've always drunk several cups of coffee when you're feeling stressed, and find the caffeine helps you to get your work done. Although you may feel this is effective, caffeine is a stimulant and the more you drink, the *more* stressed you'll probably become.

Reacting automatically implies a lack of choice. Through practising mindfulness, you begin to have a greater choice of ways to respond, and can thereby achieve a more satisfactory outcome.

Make a list of the unhelpful and helpful ways you deal with stress:

✔ Unhelpful reactions may include drinking too much alcohol or caffeine, negative thinking, zoning out, working even harder, or eating too much or too little food.

✔ Helpful responses may include going for a walk, exercising, meeting up with friends, meditating, or listening to music.

✔ Become more aware of the choices you make following a stressful event, and begin choosing small, helpful strategies such as going for a walk. Make use of mindfulness skills to help you to make wiser choices.

Here's the two-step mindfulness process for responding rather than reacting when you feel your stress levels rising:

1. **Notice your current reactions.** What are your body, mind and emotions doing? Are they showing the signs of stress? Acknowledge the fact that you're suffering from stress. Observe how you're reacting to the stress. Your *body* may be tense in certain places. Perhaps you're suffering from indigestion or have had a cold for weeks. Your *behaviour* may be different to usual. You may be snapping with anger for the smallest thing. You may not be making time to meet up with friends. Your *emotions* may be fluctuating. You may feel tired or out of control. Your *thoughts* may be predominantly negative. You may have trouble concentrating. At this stage, you just need to become aware of what's happening, without judging the situation as bad or wrong – just be aware, without the judgement if you can. By becoming aware of what's happening within you, *the experience is already transforming.* This is because you're *observing* the stress, rather than *being* the stress. As the *observer* of experience, you're no longer tangled up in the emotions themselves. You can't be what you observe.

2. **Choose a mindful response.** Now, from an awareness of the level of stress you're experiencing and how you're currently coping with that stress, you can make a wise, mindful choice as to the best way to cope. You know yourself better than anyone else – you need to decide how best to cope with the stress. As you become aware of your own inner reactions, you make space for creative action to arise rather than habitual, well-worn paths you've chosen many times before.

Here are some suggestions for a mindful response to your stress:

- Take as many mindful breaths as you have time for.

- Do a three-minute mini meditation (refer to Chapter 7), or practise a formal mindfulness meditation for a more extended period.

- Go for a walk, perhaps in the park, or do some yoga, tai chi or stretching exercises.

- Avoid excessive alcohol, caffeine, drugs, and sugary or fatty foods.

- Talk to someone or socialise.

- Watch a hilarious comedy.

- Observe the stress rise up in your body-mind, and fall away. Consider yourself as the witness of stress – whole, complete and free just as you are.

- Do some vigorous but mindful exercise such as running, swimming or cycling.

Breathing out your stress

Your breath is a particularly helpful ally in coping with stress. Many relaxation programmes are well aware of the power of the breath in regulating stress and recommend deep breathing to manage stress.

Usually, in mindfulness, you simply need to be aware of your breath and don't have to change your breathing rate. However, here are some different techniques you can use to help to relieve stress.

- ✓ **Diaphragmatic or belly breathing.** You can do this lying down, sitting up with your back straight, or in whatever position suits you. Take a natural breath and allow your belly to fill up with air. Allow the breath to release as you normally do. Repeat for as long as you feel necessary. Feel each breath coming in and going out of your body. (See Chapter 6 for more about diaphragmatic or belly breathing.)

- ✓ **Counting your breaths.** Adopt a comfortable posture and close your eyes if you want to. Feel your breath coming in and out. Each time you breathe out, count. Begin with one, and work your way up to ten. When you reach ten, start again from one. If at any point you lose count, begin again at one. You may find it difficult to get past the number two or three before your mind goes off into worries or dreams – no problem. All that matters is that as soon as you notice that your mind has drifted off, you start again at one, *without criticising yourself if you can.*

- ✓ **Deep mindful breathing.** Take a deep breath and allow your belly to fill up with air. Hold your breath for a few moments and then slowly release the breath. Repeat for as long as you feel comfortable. As you breathe out, allow yourself to let go of all tension and stress as best you can. If you can't, you don't need to worry – just try again later.

- ✓ **Mindful breathing with other activities.** Mindful breathing while engaging in day-to-day activities provides a calming and nourishing antidote to stress. If you're doing a simple or repetitive activity, become aware of your breathing as you do it. For example, as you walk, feel your breath and notice how your breathing rate changes. If you're waiting for your computer to start up, or in a queue, or hanging up the clothes on the washing line, simply allow some of your awareness to go to the feeling of your breath.

As you practise, you may become great friends with your own breath. You look forward to being with the breath, and with noticing its calming, rhythmic flow.

Using your mind to manage stress

Stressors don't cause stress on their own. First, you need to interpret the stress as a problem that may have a negative impact on you. Then the stress reaction occurs. This simple but fundamental process can be seen in Figure 12-1 below. Remembering that you're the observer of your stress rather than the stress itself helps you to become free, and stress becomes less of a problem.

Figure 12-1:
Stress,
interpreta-
tion and the
observer

Use the following tips to lower your level of stress by becoming aware of how you interpret challenges:

✔ **Write down the thoughts that are causing you stress.** For example, if you've just suffered a relationship breakdown, just keep writing whatever comes to your head. Nobody else needs to see what you write but you, so be totally honest. The process of writing helps to slow your mind down, and enables you to tackle the stressful thoughts one at a time. Having written them, remember that thoughts are just thoughts – not necessarily facts. Your stress is caused not so much by the thoughts, but because you *believe them to be true.* Seeing thoughts as just sounds and images that pop in and out of consciousness reduces their impact significantly.

✔ **See the big picture.** What effect does seeing things from a different angle have on the situation? How would you feel if you were in someone else's shoes? This may be the person who seems to be causing the stress, or someone else – you choose! Or, imagine you're zooming up into the sky, away from your life. See your own town, your region, your country. Keep imagining you're zooming out of the planet to the solar system and beyond! Is your stress still such a big issue?

✔ **Consider what's the worst that could happen.** Sometimes you may imagine the situation to be worse than it actually is. By considering the worst, you may realise things aren't that bad.

✔ **Break down the problem.** If you have a big problem and can't face up to the issues, try splitting up the problem into small steps. Then take things one step at a time. For example, if you've lost your job and are short of cash, the first step to getting a new job may be to rewrite your

CV (résumé). You can even break that down to phoning a friend to help you write one, or getting a book from your local library on writing CVs.

✔ **See problems in a different way.** If you see difficulties in life as challenges, your mind may automatically begin to start searching for helpful solutions. If all you see is problems, you're more likely to feel drained and stressed by their weight on your shoulders. See challenges as opportunities to discover new things about yourself and your resilience, rather than problems to be avoided or coped with.

✔ **Discuss the cause of the stress with someone.** The process of talking about your issue is likely to help you to see aspects you never even thought of. And even if you don't, the very act of talking about the issues you're facing helps to dissipate their potency.

✔ **Let go of perfectionism.** Perfectionism is a common reason for high levels of stress. Understand that being perfect is impossible to reach. Adjust your standards by lowering them a little. You can try aiming for 80 per cent perfection and see if that helps.

✔ **Appreciate what's going well.** Think of all the things that are going well for you at the moment, and write them down. They don't need to be big things – anything you're even slightly grateful for will suffice. Doing so encourages you to feel less stress.

Life is the way you see

How often you experience high levels of stress is at least partly, if not completely, dependent on the way you see things. This old Sufi story illustrates the point beautifully:

A young traveller from another country entered a new territory. She saw an old man sitting under a tree and asked the man, 'What are the people like in this country?' The old man looked up and asked, 'How do you find the people in your own country?' The young woman enthusiastically replied, 'Oh, they are kind, hospitable and generous.' 'Well,' replied the old man with a gentle smile, 'you'll find the people of this country to be kind and friendly too.'

A little later on in the afternoon, another traveller was passing through into the country. He too spotted the old man under the tree, and asked, 'Hey, what are the people like in your country?' The old man asked, 'What are they like in your own country?' 'Terrible,' he sighed. 'They're always fighting, often inhospitable, and sly.' The old man answered, 'I'm afraid you'll find the people of this country to be the same as yours.'

The secret to transforming the level of stress you experience is to change the way you see life.

Cooling Down Your Anger

Anger can be healthy if the emotion is controlled and used sparingly. For example, if you're being treated unfairly, you may need to become angry to ensure you're treated justly and with respect. However, being out of control when you're angry can cause tremendous harm both to yourself and to your relationships with others. Cooling down anger isn't an easy process, and requires a clear decision, effort, and support from others. Mindfulness can help, as this section shows.

Understanding anger

Anger is a normal human emotion. If you're mistreated, feeling angry is perfectly natural. The problem is what you do with the emotion if you hurt yourself or others with the anger.

Anger arises when you feel something *should* happen but it doesn't. For example, if you receive bad customer support for something you've bought, or you see how much crime has gone up in your city and feel angry because the government *should* be taking more action.

Different situations make different people angry. Like all emotions, anger depends on the *interpretation* of the situation, rather than the situation itself. If someone at a checkout gives you the wrong amount of change and you see this as a mistake, you probably forgive her straight away and think nothing of the oversight. However, if you think that she did this to you on purpose, you're more likely to become annoyed, frustrated or angry. So, it's *your interpretation* that causes the anger, not the situation itself.

Anger arises from a thought or series of thoughts. Anger doesn't just come up on its own. You may not be aware of the thought causing the anger you feel, but a thought must have arisen for the emotion to surface. For example, if you think 'that cashier is out to rip me off' you feel anger surging through your body almost instantly afterwards.

You experience certain physical sensations when angry such as tensing your shoulders, tightening your stomach, headache, clenching your hands or jaw, poor concentration, feeling sweaty, increasing your breathing rate, restlessness, and a fast heart rate.

Anger in the aisles

A manager at a supermarket overheard an employee who was helping a customer pack her bags with groceries. The customer said, 'Do you know when you'll get some?' The bagger replied 'No, I don't know. We may not have any all week, or maybe even longer.' The customer said, 'Oh. Okay, thanks. Bye,' and walked off. The manager glared at the bagger and chased after the customer saying, 'We'll have some in tomorrow. Don't worry, I'll guarantee we'll get it for you.' He then turned back to the bagger and was furious. 'Don't ever, ever say that we don't have something. And if we don't have it, say we'll have it in by tomorrow. That's the policy. You're useless! What did she want anyway?' 'She wanted rain,' replied the bagger.

When you're stressed out, you're more likely to see things the wrong way.

Coping when the fire rises up

You arrive home and your partner hasn't cooked any food. You were working late and you begin to feel anger rising up in you. What do you do? You know that logically you're far better off talking calmly about the issue and resolving the conflict rather than spoiling the evening with an argument. Here's how:

1. **Become aware of the physical sensation of anger in your body.** Notice the sensations in your stomach, chest and face. Become aware of your rapid heart and breathing rate. Observe if your fists or jaw are clenched. Witness the tension in the rest of your body.

2. **Breathe.** Breathe into the physical sensations of your body. Close your eyes if you want to. You may find counting out ten breaths helpful. Imagine the breath entering your nose into your belly, and as you breathe out, imagine the breath going out of your fingers and toes, if you find this useful.

3. **Continue to stay with the sensations as best you can.** Bring a sense of kindness and gentleness to your feelings of anger. Look at the discomfort in the way you would look at scenery – taking your time and being with the landscape of your inner self. Try to see the anger as an opportunity to understand about the feeling, how the burning rises up in your being, and how the breath may or may not have a cooling effect on the flame within you.

4. **Notice your thoughts.** Thoughts like 'it's not fair' or 'I'm not having this' feed the fire of anger. Notice what effect you have by letting go of these thoughts, for your own health and wellbeing more than anything else. If you can't let go of the thoughts, which is common, just continue to

watch the way thoughts and feelings feed into each other, creating and recreating the experience of anger as well as other feelings, like guilt, frustration and sadness. If you have lots of energy pumping through your body, try walking around the room and feeling the contact between your feet and the ground. Alternatively, instead of walking, you can try slow, mindful stretching, feeling the body as you extend your various muscle groups.

5. **Step back.** Take a step back from your internal experiences. Notice that you're the observer of your thoughts and emotions and not the thoughts and emotions themselves. Just as images are projected onto a screen, but the screen itself is unaffected, so thoughts, emotions and sensations arise in awareness, but you, as awareness, are untouched.

6. **Communicate.** As soon as the main force of your anger has dissipated, you may need to communicate your feelings with the other person. Begin with 'I' statements instead of 'you' accusations. If you blame the other person for your feelings, you're more likely to make her act defensively. If you say, 'I felt angry when you didn't cook dinner' rather than, 'You made me angry when you didn't cook dinner', you're taking responsibility for your feelings. As you continue to communicate, stay aware and awake to your own feelings, and let go of any aggression if you can – less aggression and more honesty are more likely to lead to a harmonious and productive conversation and result.

Coping with anger is a challenging task, and nobody can follow these steps perfectly. The idea is to keep these steps in mind, and follow them with small levels of frustration rather than outright anger. When you do, you become more adept at cooling the flames of anger.

Here are some other ways of managing your feelings of anger:

✔ **Be mindful of the thought patterns that feed your anger.** These include:

- **Over-generalising** by using sentences like 'You *always* ignore me' or 'You *never* respect me'. Be specific instead.

- **Mind-reading** by thinking you *know* what the other person is thinking, and often predicting the thoughts as negative, such as 'I know you think I nag you too much'. Try to avoid making assumptions like this.

- **Blaming** others for your own anger with thoughts like 'You always make me angry' or 'It's all their fault'. Instead, take responsibility for your anger.

✔ **Mindful physical exercise.** By exercising regularly, you build up a greater resilience to stress and this may dissipate some of your anger. By exercising mindfully, paying attention to all the physical sensations as you perform an exercise, you simultaneously build up your mindfulness muscles too, leading to greater levels of awareness and less reactive, automatic-pilot behaviour.

✔ **Connect with your senses.** Listen to the sounds around you or listen mindfully to some music. Smell some of your favourite, calming scents. Eat a snack as slowly as you can, chewing and tasting with as much awareness you can muster. Have a shower or bath and connect with the sensations on your skin. Look out of your window and enjoy the sky, clouds, trees or rain.

✔ **Question your reaction.** Ask yourself questions like 'Is this worth it?', 'Is this important in the big picture?', 'How else can I respond in this situation?', 'What is a more helpful thing to do now?'.

Figure 12-2 shows how mindfulness can be used to dissipate the anger cycle.

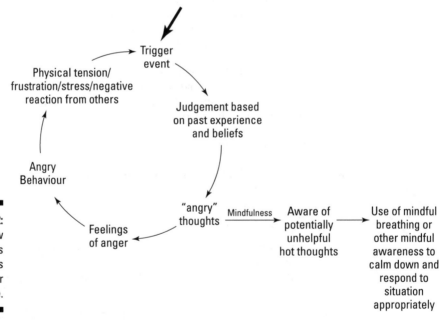

Figure 12-2: Seeing how mindfulness dissipates the anger cycle.

Dealing with the roots of anger

If you have a short fuse, you may wonder why you get angry so easily. For many people, the reason is a difficult upbringing. If those who cared for you were often angry, being angry is the only way in which you understood how to react to situations. If your parents or carer treated you badly, you're bound to have feelings of anger trapped inside. Highly stressful and traumatic events can also lead to anger.

If you easily react with anger, you may be using the anger to cover up other, deeper feelings. The anger acts as a protection, to prevent you from becoming aware of more subtle feelings of fear, shame, guilt or embarrassment. By becoming mindful of the feelings behind your anger you can begin to unlock the emotional chains that may be controlling you. One way of doing this is by feeling the emotion as you notice it arising, and being aware when it manifests itself in your body. By feeling this with openness and kindness, rather than criticising yourself, you begin the healing process within yourself.

Coping with your anger as the emotion arises is a bit like fire-fighting. Dealing with the cause of the anger when you're not in the midst of the emotion is like fitting a smoke alarm, and acting before things become out of hand.

Powerful ways of dealing with the roots of anger include meditation and forgiveness meditations. Loving kindness, or metta meditation can also be very effective (covered in Chapter 7).

Adopting mindful attitudes to cool the flame of anger

Cultivating a mindful attitude can reduce the frequency, duration and level of anger you experience from day to day.

Mindfulness groups sometimes take an approach with the acronym RAIN for a mindful way of dealing with emotions. Just as rain falls equally on everyone, and provides for your body, so can RAIN help to transform your inner world:

✔ **R**ecognise that a strong emotion is present.

> Often, you can easily be swept up by the emotion itself, and immediately begin acting on it. Emotions can be such an integrated part of who you are that you don't give the feeling due credit. Begin with recognition of the emotion.

✔ **A**ccept that the emotion is there.

> With strong emotions, sometimes the natural reaction is to pretend the feeling isn't really present. In this step you accept that in this precise moment, you're experiencing anger. You can even

say to yourself, 'I am experiencing a strong feeling of anger at the moment.' You aren't being passive and giving in to the feeling. If you don't accept what's here now, you can't hope to manage the emotion in any way.

✔ **Investigate thoughts, feelings and bodily sensations.**

In this third step, you're not trying to analyse, but instead observe what's going on in your mind, heart and body. What thoughts are running through your head? What feelings are you mindful of? What areas of your body feel tense, or burning, or warm, or relaxed? How does your body feel as a whole? Do you have a burning, throbbing, unpleasant sensation, or is the physical expression of the emotion quite pleasant? Where is the core of the emotion located exactly, and what effect does a sustained mindful awareness have on the physical aspect of your experience? Simply observe the sensations.

✔ **Non-identification with the passing emotion.**

E*motion* has the word motion in it. Emotions are always moving, fluxing and changing. No emotion stays completely fixed forever. This final step is to try to distance yourself and create a space between you and your emotion. By offering a space, the emotion is more likely to do what emotions do quite naturally, which is to keep moving. Remember that you are not your anger. Anger comes and goes, but you don't come and go – you're always here. Another way of seeing this is like clouds in the sky. The clouds come and go; some are black, some are white and fluffy. No matter what happens to the clouds, the sky itself remains unaffected. In the same way, emotions come and go, but your awareness, like the sky, is free.

For an entire book's worth of tips and strategies on coping with anger, see *Anger Management For Dummies* by Gillian Bloxham and W. Doyle Gentry (Wiley).

Reducing Fatigue

If you're full of energy, getting your daily tasks done is a doddle – you may come home from work brimming with energy, able to cook, clean, go out with your friends, socialise and generally have a good time. If you're lacking in the energy department, everything becomes a drag – right from getting out of bed in the morning, to getting back into bed at the end of the day. You can find some helpful tips to reduce your fatigue in this section.

Assessing your energy levels

Begin by assessing your energy levels in a typical week or month. You can do this by simply making a note in your diary or journal. You'll find several benefits of doing this:

✔ You discover how your energy levels change from one day to the next.

✔ You see what times of the day you have most energy available to tackle your more challenging tasks.

✔ You may begin to see patterns – certain foods or certain physical activities may be boosting or draining your energy levels.

Practise some mindfulness meditation on a daily basis, just to see what effect the exercise has on your energy levels. Mindfulness isn't a short-term fix, but a long-term way of meeting life in a healthy way – any improvements in energy may take some time but be long-lasting, so persevere with your practice.

Discovering energy drainers

Some activities are similar to energy leeches – they suck energy out of your system. By discovering and mindfully reflecting on what takes energy out of you, you can begin to reschedule your lifestyle, or reduce your intake of energy drainers. Energy drainers include:

✔ **Too much stress.** If you allow yourself to become overly stressed out, and don't take steps to manage the stress, you stand to burn lots of your energy. This is because the stress reaction, or fight or flight response, pushes all your energy reserves out of your digestive and immune system and into your muscles. If you keep engaging the stress reaction again and again, your energy reserves gradually become more and more depleted. Use the mindfulness tips earlier in this chapter to help combat stress.

✔ **Too much thinking.** If you take your thoughts too seriously, you give your mind undue attention. This tends to feed the mind and encourages you to think more and more. The brain uses a massive 20 per cent of all your energy – if you give thoughts too much attention, they spiral out of control, zapping your energy. Take a step back from thoughts, and don't let thoughts become your master.

✔ **Too much sugar.** Although sugar may seem to uplift your energy in the short term, your energy levels soon plummet. Reduce your intake of refined sugar and watch out for low-fat foods that contain high levels of sugar to make them taste good. Read *The GL Diet For Dummies* by Nigel Denby and Sue Baic (Wiley) for delicious meals that deliver slow-releasing energy.

✔ **Skipping breakfast.** Lots of research shows the benefits of eating a healthy breakfast. In fact people who don't eat breakfast not only lack energy but are also more likely to put on weight due to overeating later on in the day.

Finding what uplifts you

You can take control of your energy levels by making active, healthy steps to raise your liveliness. Keep in mind that you want the kind of energy that's revitalising rather than getting you overly excited! Too much of a 'high' eventually results in you crashing out as you burn your energy rapidly. That's okay from time to time when you want to have fun, but not all the time. Do the following suggestions with a mindful, gentle awareness:

✔ **Engage in mindful physical exercise.** Rather than draining your energy, regular exercise actually gives you a boost. This may be due to the release into your brain of a chemical called serotonin that helps you feel better and less frustrated or stressed. Health organisations recommend 30 minutes of vigorous physical exercise on a daily basis, which can include a brisk walk to the shops and back. Anything that gets your heart beating, your breathing rate up and makes you a bit sweaty and out of breath is classified as a vigorous exercise. Read Chapter 7 for more about mindful physical exercise.

✔ **Enjoy mindful, regular meals.** Eating smaller portions on a regular basis, rather than having a few big meals, is healthier and helps to maintain your energy levels. Wholegrain rye bread, porridge, pasta, beans, lentils and noodles all contain energy that releases slowly into your body, helping to sustain you throughout the day. Eat mindfully too, by looking at your food, tasting as you eat, eating one mouthful at a time, and not doing anything else when eating.

✔ **Drink plenty of water.** Aim to drink six to eight glasses of water a day, and more if you're exercising. Become more aware of your feeling of thirst, or better still, drink before the feeling arises in case you're already dehydrated. As you drink, remember how lucky you are to have water available to you, and feel the water in your mouth and how it has a cooling effect as it goes down into your stomach.

✔ **Meditate.** Both informal mindfulness and a formal meditation on a daily basis help to increase your energy levels. This is because mindful awareness helps ultimately to lower the stress you experience. As you continue to practise on a daily basis, your tendency to become stressed in the first place diminishes and therefore your energy levels increase to a healthy level. As your ability to be calm and focused increases, your energy becomes calm and focused too.

Using meditations to rise and sparkle

Here's a meditation you can practise whenever you want to focus on increasing your energy levels:

1. Sit or lie down in a suitable posture for you in this moment. You may choose to sit up straight in a chair, or lie down on your bed.

2. Adjust your intention of this meditation to simply be with whatever arises without trying to push things away or grab hold of experiences. Let your attitude be one of curiosity and kindness.

3. Feel the gentle rhythmic sensations of your own breathing. Feel the sensations of the breath from moment to moment, non-judgementally. Just allow the breathing to happen by itself. As you breathe in, imagine you're breathing in nourishing, fresh, energising oxygen into your body. Get a sense of this nutritious oxygen permeating your whole body, feeding each cell generously. As you breathe out, imagine any toxins being released out of your system. Breathe out anything that's troubling you, and let go of unhelpful thoughts, emotions, ideas or sensations.

4. With each breath you take, feel more energised and uplifted. Essentially you're a container of energy, interchanging with the energy all around. Get a sense of this as you continue to breathe. Feel the exchange of energy with your surroundings – both a give and take process, a cycle.

5. Now come back to a sense of awareness of the breath: breathing itself. Enjoy the in-breaths and out-breaths with a spirit of acceptance, caring and empathy.

6. As you come towards the end of this meditation, notice your transition into a normal, wakeful state. Continue to be mindful of this exchange of energy taking place with your surroundings as you go about your daily activities.

Here are a couple of other helpful meditations to provide an energy boost:

   ✔ **Body scan.** You can do this practice no matter how tired you feel. You simply need to listen to the *Mindfulness For Dummies* CD and lie down on the floor, mat or bed. Even if you're unable to concentrate for much of the time, something will shift. You may drop a stressful idea, you may drift into a restful sleep, or you may feel immediately energised by the end of the practice. (See Chapter 6 for a full description of the body scan.)

   ✔ **Three-minute breathing space.** This is an ideal meditation if you don't have much time available. If you can find the time and discipline to practise this exercise several times a day, you begin to become aware of the kinds of thoughts and emotions running through your system, tapping off your vital energy. (Refer to Chapter 7 for a description of the breathing space.)

Chapter 13

Using Mindfulness to Combat Anxiety and Depression

. . . .

In This Chapter

▶ Finding out about depression and anxiety

▶ Discovering ways in which mindfulness reduces depression and anxiety

▶ Exploring specific techniques

. . . .

Depression and anxiety are both serious illnesses. According to the World Health Organisation, depression is the planet's leading cause of disability, affecting 121 million people worldwide. About one in six people suffer from clinical depression at some point in their lives. About one in fifty people experience *generalised anxiety* at some point in their lives – feeling anxious all day.

Medical evidence suggests that mindfulness is very powerful in helping people with recurrent depression, and studies with anxiety sufferers look extremely promising too. If you suffer from either of these conditions, following the mindfulness advice in this chapter can really help you.

If you think that you suffer from a medical condition, please ensure that you visit your doctor before following any advice here. If you currently suffer from depression as diagnosed by a health professional, wait until the worst of the illness is over and you're in a stronger position to digest and practise the mindfulness exercises in this chapter. Often mindfulness can work well together with other therapy or medication – again check with your doctor before you begin, so he can best advise and support you.

Dealing Mindfully with Depression

Of all mental health conditions, recurring depression has most clearly been shown to respond to mindfulness. If the body of evidence continues to grow, mindfulness may go on to become the standard treatment for managing depression all over the world. This section explains what depression is and why mindfulness seems to be so effective for those who have suffered from several bouts of depression.

Understanding depression

Depression is different to sadness. Sadness is a natural and healthy emotion everyone experiences from time to time. If something doesn't go the way you expected, you may feel sad. The low mood may linger for a time and affect your thoughts, words and actions, but not to a huge extent.

Depression is very different. When you're depressed, you just can't seem to feel better, no matter what you try. Unfortunately, some people still believe that depression isn't a real illness. Depression *is* a real illness with very *real symptoms*.

According to the National Health Service, if you have an ongoing low mood for most of the day, everyday for two weeks, you're experiencing depression and you need to visit your doctor. The symptoms of depression can include:

- ✔ A low depressed mood
- ✔ Feelings of guilt or low self-worth
- ✔ Disturbed sleep
- ✔ A loss of interest or pleasure
- ✔ Poor concentration
- ✔ Changes to your appetite
- ✔ Low energy

Understanding why depression recurs

Depression has a good chance of being a recurring condition, and to understand why, you need to understand the two key factors that cause mild feelings of sadness to turn into depression. They are:

✔ **Constant negative thinking (rumination).** This is the constant, repetitive use of self-critical, negative thinking to try to change an emotional state. You have an idea of how things are (you're feeling sad) and how you want things to be (feeling happy/relaxed/peaceful). You keep thinking about your goal and how far you are from your desired state. The more you think about this gap the more negative your situation seems, and the further you move away from your desired emotion. Unfortunately, thinking in this way – trying to fix the problem of an emotion – only worsens the problem and leads to a sense of failure as depression sets in. Rumination doesn't work, the reason being that emotions are part of being human. To try to fix or change emotions by simply thinking about what you want doesn't work. Rumination is a hallmark of the *doing mode* of mind, explained in Chapter 5.

✔ **Intensely avoiding negative thoughts, emotions and sensations (experiential avoidance).** This is the desire to avoid unpleasant sensations. But the process of experiential avoidance feeds the emotional flame rather than reducing or diminishing the emotion. Running away from your emotions makes them stronger.

When you first suffer from depression, you experience negative thoughts, a negative mood and sluggishness. When this occurs, you create a connection between these thoughts, feelings and bodily sensations. Even when you feel better, the underlying connections are still there, lying dormant. Then, when by chance you feel a little sad, as everyone does, you begin to think, 'Here we go again. Why is this happening to me? I've failed,' and so on. The negative thoughts recur. This triggers the negative moods and low levels of energy in the body, which create more negative thinking. The more you try to avoid your negative thoughts, emotions and sensations, the more powerful they become. This is called the downward mood spiral, as shown in Figure 13-1.

Using mindfulness to change your relationship to mood

One of the key ways in which depressive relapse occurs and is sustained is through actively trying to avoid a negative mood. Mindfulness invites you to take a different attitude towards your emotion. Depression is unpleasant, but you see what happens if you approach the sensation with kindness, curiosity, compassion and acceptance. This method is likely to be radically different to your usual way of meeting a challenging emotion. Here are some ways of changing your relationship with your mood, and thereby transforming the mood itself.

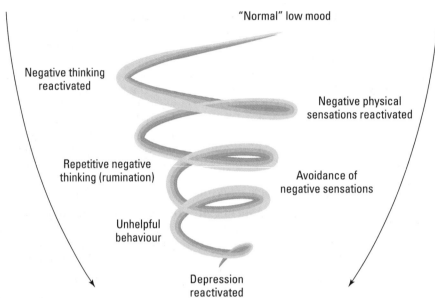

"Normal" low mood

Negative thinking
reactivated

Negative physical
sensations reactivated

Repetitive negative
thinking (rumination)

Avoidance of
negative sensations

Unhelpful
behaviour

Depression
reactivated

Figure 13-1:
Downward
mood spiral.

When you experience a low mood, try one of these exercises as an experiment and see what happens:

- ✔ **Identify where in your body you feel the emotion.** Is your stomach or chest tight for example? What happens if you approach that bodily sensation, whatever the sensation is, with kindness and curiosity? Can you go right into the centre of the bodily sensation and imagine the breath going in and out of the sensation? What effect does that have? If you feel too uncomfortable doing that, how close can you get to the unpleasant feeling in your body? Try playing with the edge of where you're able to maintain your attention in your body, neither pushing too hard, nor retreating away. Try saying to yourself, 'It's okay, whatever I feel, it's okay, let me feel it'.

- ✔ **See yourself as separate from the mood, thought or feeling.** You're the observer of the sensation, not the sensation itself. Try stepping back and looking at the sensation. When you watch a film, you have a space between you and the screen. When you watch the clouds going by, a space separates you from the clouds. A space also exists between you and your emotions. Notice what effect this has, if any.

✔ **Notice the kinds of thoughts you're thinking.** Are they self-critical, negative thoughts, predicting the worst, jumping to conclusions? Are the thoughts repeating themselves again and again? Bring a sense of curiosity to the patterns of thought in your mind.

✔ **Notice your tendency to want to get rid of the emotion.** See if you can move from this avoidance strategy towards a more accepting strategy and observe what effect this has. See if you can increase your acceptance of your feelings by 1 per cent – just a tiny amount. Accept that this is your experience now, but won't be forever, so you can temporarily let go of the struggle, even slightly, and see what happens.

✔ **Try doing a three-minute breathing space as described in Chapter 7.** What effect does that have? Following the breathing space, make a wise choice as to what is the most helpful thing for you to do at the present moment to look after yourself.

✔ **Recognise that recurring ruminative thinking and having a low mood are a part of your experience and *not part of your core being*.** An emotion arises in your consciousness and at some point diminishes again. Adopting a de-centred, detached perspective means you recognise that your low mood isn't a central aspect of your self – of who you are.

Understanding avoidance and approach modes

The more you try to avoid emotions, the greater the emotion grasps hold of you and strengthens. However, by approaching the emotion you begin to open up the possibility of releasing yourself from its hold. By approaching the sensations with a sense of kindliness, compassion and gentleness, you create the possibility of allowing and accepting your present-moment experience as it is. You let go of the possibility of a downward mood spiral, created by an avoidance mode of mind.

Professor Richard Davidson, top neuroscience professor at the University of Wisconsin-Madison and friend of the Dalai Lama, has shown that the avoidance mode of mind is associated with activation of the right prefrontal cortex part of the brain (commonly seen in those in depression), and the approach mode of mind is associated with greater activation in the left prefrontal cortex part of the brain (commonly seen in more positive people). He's also shown that mindfulness helps to move people's brain activation from right to left; in other words from avoidance mode to approach mode. This creates a healthier, more open, detached stance towards emotions, thereby allowing them to operate in a more natural way. In a nutshell, mindfulness can train your brain to become healthier!

Discovering Mindfulness-Based Cognitive Therapy (MBCT)

Mindfulness-based cognitive therapy (MBCT) is an eight-week group pro-gramme, based on the mindfulness-based stress reduction (MBSR) course described in Chapter 9. The MBSR course has been found to be very helpful for people with a range of physical and psychological problems. MBCT was spe-cifically adapted for those who've suffered repeated episodes of depression. Research so far has proven that MBCT is 50 per cent more effective than the usual treatment for those suffering from three or more episodes of depression.

MBCT is a branch of a more general form of therapy called cognitive behav-ioural therapy (CBT), which holds that thoughts, feelings and actions are intimately connected. The way you think affects the way you feel and the activities you engage in. Conversely the way you feel, or the activities you undertake, affects the way you think, as shown in Figure 13-2.

Figure 13-2:
The rela-
tionship
between
thoughts,
feelings and
activities.

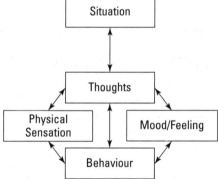

Traditional CBT encourages you to challenge unrealistic, negative thoughts about yourself, others or the world (discover more in *Cognitive Behavioural Therapy For Dummies* by Rob Willson and Rhena Branch). Mindfulness-based cognitive therapy takes a slightly different approach. Rather than deliber-ately considering alternative thoughts, you move towards your unpleasant thoughts, emotions and physical sensations in a more de-centred, kind, curi-ous and compassionate way – in other words, mindfully. The emphasis isn't on changing the experience, but on being with the experience in a different way. You develop the ability to do this through mindfulness meditation.

If you want to do the MBCT course on your own using this book, you can follow the eight-week MBSR course described in Chapter 9, and in addition do the activities in this chapter. This isn't the same as doing a course with a group and a professional teacher, but gives you an idea of what to expect and certainly may help you.

Seeing the scientific basis of mindfulness

A recent survey in the United States found that more than 40 per cent of mental health professionals do some form of mindfulness therapy to encourage healing in both the body and mind. In group clinical settings, mindfulness is applied mainly through two programmes:

✔ Mindfulness-Based Stress Reduction (MBSR): An eight-week training in mindfulness meditation for reducing stress in those with a wide range of medical conditions.

✔ Mindfulness-Based Cognitive Therapy (MBCT): Based on the eight-week MBSR course with added elements of Cognitive Behavioural Therapy, developed to address the problem of relapse in clinical depression, and now being tested and used for a wide variety of ailments.

Mindfulness-Based Stress Reduction was developed by Dr Jon Kabat-Zinn and colleagues in a hospital setting at University of Massachusetts Medical School more than 20 years ago.

The scientific evidence proving the medical benefits of mindfulness is impressive.

Here's a small sample of the research on mindfulness so far:

✔ More than 200 patients with chronic pain were referred for mindfulness treatment, and large overall improvements in physical and psychological wellbeing following MBSR were observed for the majority.

✔ A study on the use of MBSR for patients with anxiety disorders showed significant reductions in anxiety and depression scores for more than 90 per cent of the patients.

✔ In an experiment, some patients with psoriasis were given a guided mindfulness meditation to listen to while in a light box. Those patients healed four times faster than the patients without the mindfulness audio in the light box. This shows that mindfulness itself seems to accelerate the healing effect.

✔ Two trials have shown that MBCT is effective in preventing relapse in depression, showing that in patients with three or more previous episodes of depression, MBCT reduced the recurrence rate by 55 per cent.

Chapter 9 explores MBSR.

Pleasant and Unpleasant Experiences

In everyday life you experience a whole range of different experiences. They can all be grouped into pleasant, unpleasant and neutral experiences. Pleasant experiences are the ones you enjoy, like listening to the birds singing or watching your favourite television programme. Unpleasant experiences can be like having to sit in a traffic jam or dealing with a difficult customer at work. Neutral experiences are the ones you just don't even notice, like the different object in the room you're in at the moment, or the taste of the tea or coffee you're drinking. Mindfulness encourages you to become curious about all aspects of these experiences. This can be done through the following exercise, which is normally done over two weeks:

Take a sheet of paper, or use your journal, and create four columns. Label them 'Experience', 'thoughts', 'feelings', 'bodily sensations'. Under each column heading, write down one experience each day that you found to be pleasant. Write down the thoughts that were going through your head, the feelings you experienced at the time, and how your body felt under the appropriate columns. Continue this each day for a whole week.

In the following week, repeat the exercises, but this time for an unpleasant experience each day. Remember, you don't need to have very pleasant or unpleasant experiences – even a small, seemingly insignificant experience will suffice.

The purpose of this exercise is to:

✔ Help you to see that experiences aren't one big blob. Your experiences can be broken down into thoughts, feelings and bodily sensations. This makes difficult experiences more manageable rather than overwhelming.

✔ Notice your automatic, habitual patterns which operate without you even knowing about them normally. You learn how you habitually grasp onto pleasant experiences with a desire for them to continue, and how you push away unpleasant experiences, called experiential avoidance, which can end up perpetuating them.

✔ Learn to become more curious about experience instead of just judging experiences as good or bad, or like or dislike.

✔ Encourage you to understand and acknowledge your unpleasant experiences rather than just avoid them.

Interpreting thoughts and feelings

You can do this visualisation exercise sitting or lying in a comfortable position.

1. Imagine you're walking on one side of a familiar road. On the other side of the road you see a friend. You call out his name and wave, but he doesn't respond. Your friend just keeps on walking into the distance.

2. Write down your answers to the following questions:

What did you feel in this exercise?

What thoughts did you have?

What physical sensations did you experience in your body?

If you think, 'Oh, he's ignored me. I don't have any friends,' you're more likely to feel down and perhaps your body may slump. If you think, 'He couldn't hear me. Oh well, I'll catch up with him later,' you're unlikely to feel affected by the situation. The main purpose of the exercise is to show that your *interpretation* of a situation generates a particular feeling, rather than the situation itself.

Almost all people have a different response to this exercise because they have a different *interpretation* of the imagined event. If you're already in a low mood, you're more likely to interpret the situation negatively. Remember: *Thoughts are interpretations of reality, influenced by your current mood.* Don't consider your thoughts to be facts, especially if you're in a low mood. *Thoughts are just thoughts, not facts.*

Combating automatic thoughts

Mindfulness encourages you to recognise and deal with negative automatic thoughts that can prolong depression or cause it to worsen.

Consider the following statements (adapted from Kendall and Hollon's 'Automatic Thoughts Questionnaire').

- ✔ I feel as if I'm up against the world.
- ✔ I'm no good.
- ✔ I'll never succeed.
- ✔ No one understands me.
- ✔ I've let people down.
- ✔ I don't think that I can go on.
- ✔ I wish I were a better person.
- ✔ I'm so weak.
- ✔ My life's not going the way I want it to.
- ✔ I'm so disappointed in myself.
- ✔ Nothing feels good anymore.
- ✔ I can't stand this anymore.
- ✔ I can't get started.
- ✔ Something's really wrong with me.
- ✔ I wish I were somewhere else.
- ✔ I can't get things together.

✔ I hate myself.

✔ I'm worthless.

✔ I wish I could just disappear.

✔ I'm a loser.

✔ My life is a mess.

✔ I'm a failure.

✔ I'll never make it.

✔ I feel so helpless.

✔ My future is bleak.

✔ It's just not worth it.

✔ I can't finish anything.

How much would you believe these thoughts right now if any one of them popped into your head? How much would you believe them if any one of them popped into your head when you were in your lowest mood? *These thoughts are attributes of the illness called depression, and aren't to do with your true self.*

By considering depression in a detached way you become more detached from the illness. You see depression as a human condition rather than something that affects you personally and almost no one else. You see depression as a condition that's treatable through taking appropriate steps.

Alternative viewpoints

Alternative viewpoints are the different ways in which you can interpret a particular situation or experience.

This exercise from MBCT shows how feelings affect thoughts, and thoughts affect feelings. The exercise is similar to the 'Interpreting thoughts and feelings' exercise earlier in the chapter, but focuses more on how you interpret situations depending on how you're already feeling.

Consider the following scenario: You've just been *criticised* by your boss for your work and you feel low. You walk past one of your colleagues and are about to say something to him, and he says he's really busy and can't stop. Write down your thoughts and feelings.

Now consider a different scenario: Your boss has just *praised* you for doing an excellent job. You walk past one of your colleagues and are about to say something to him, and he says he's really busy and can't stop. Write down your thoughts and feelings.

You probably found very different thoughts and feelings in the two different circumstances. By understanding that your thoughts and feelings are influenced by your interpretation of a situation, you're less likely to react negatively. Mindfulness allows you to become more aware of your thoughts and feelings from moment to moment, and offers you the choice to respond to a situation in a different way, knowing that your thoughts are just thoughts, or interpretations, rather than facts.

De-centring from difficult thoughts

Practise the three-minute breathing space meditation (explained in Chapter 7), and then ask yourself some or all the following questions. Doing so helps you to de-centre or step back from your more difficult thoughts and helps you to become more aware of your own patterns of mind.

- ✔ Am I confusing a thought with a fact?
- ✔ Am I thinking in black and white terms?
- ✔ Am I jumping to conclusions?
- ✔ Am I focusing on the negative and ignoring the positive?
- ✔ Am I being perfectionist?
- ✔ Am I guessing what other people are thinking?
- ✔ Am I predicting the worst?
- ✔ Am I judging myself or others overly harshly?
- ✔ What are the advantages and disadvantages of thinking in this way?
- ✔ Am I taking things too personally?

Listing your activities

Make a list of all the typical activities you do in a day, such as preparing food, getting dressed, travelling to work, interacting with others, hobbies, sports, evening classes and so on. Then label each activity as nourishing or depleting. Nourishing activities make you feel uplifted and enthusiastic, giving you energy and joy. Depleting activities drain your energy, making you feel low in vitality and dull in attention. Consider what you can do to increase the number of nourishing activities and decrease the number of depleting activities in your daily routine.

Now list activities that give you a sense of mastery or pleasure. Activities that offer a sense of mastery are those that are quite challenging for you, such as tidying up a cupboard, making a phone call you've been avoiding, or forcing yourself to get out of the house to meet a friend or relative. Activities that offer pleasure may include having a hot bath, watching a film or going for a gentle stroll.

When you feel stressed or low in mood, choose a 'mastery' or 'pleasure' activity. Prior to making your choice, carry out the three-minute breathing space meditation to help bring mindfulness to the experience.

Making wise choices

When experiencing a low mood, a depressing thought, a painful sensation or a stressful situation, practise the three-minute breathing space and choose what to do next, which may be:

- ✔ **Mindful action.** Go back to doing what you were doing before, but in this wider, more spacious, being mode of mind (Chapter 5 explains a being mode of mind). Do each action mindfully, perhaps breaking the activity into small, bite-size chunks. The shift may be very small and subtle in your mind, but following the breathing space, you'll probably feel different.

- ✔ **Being mindful of your body.** Emotions manifest in your physical body, perhaps in the form of a tightness in your jaw or shoulders. Mindfulness of body invites you to go to the tension and feel the sensations with an open, friendly, warm awareness, as best you can. You can breathe into the sensation, or say, 'Opening, acknowledging, embracing', as you feel the uncomfortable area. You're not trying to get rid of the sensations, but discovering how to be okay with them when the sensations are difficult or unpleasant.

- ✔ **Being mindful of your thoughts.** If thoughts are still predominant following the breathing space, focus your mindful awareness onto what you're thinking. Try to step back, seeing thoughts as mental events rather than facts. Try writing down the thoughts, which helps to slow them down and offers you the chance to have a clear look at them. Reflect on the questions listed in the section 'De-centring from difficult thoughts'. Bring a sense of curiosity and gentleness to the process if you can. In this way, you're trying to create a different relationship to your thoughts other than accepting them as 100 per cent reality, no matter what pops up in your head.

- ✔ **A pleasant activity.** Do something pleasant like reading a novel or listening to your favourite music. Whilst engaging in this activity, primarily engage your attention on the activity itself. Check in to notice how you're feeling emotionally and how your body feels, and be mindful of your thoughts from time to time. Try not to do the activity to force any change in mood, but instead do your best to acknowledge whatever you're experiencing.

- ✔ **A mastery activity.** Choose to do something that gives *you* a sense of mastery no matter how small, such as washing the car, going for a swim or baking a cake. Again, give the activity itself your full attention. Notice if you're trying to push your feelings out, going back to habitual doing mode (Chapter 5), and instead allow yourself to accept your feelings and sensations as best you can, which is being mode (Chapter 5). Bring a genuine sense of curiosity to your experience as you go about your activity.

Using a depression warning system

Writing out a depression warning system is a good way of nipping depression in the bud rather than letting it spiral downwards. Write down:

1. **The warning signs** you need to look out for when depression may be arising in you, such as negative thinking, oversleeping or avoiding meeting friends. You may want to ask someone close to you to help you to do this.

2. **An action plan** of the kind of things you can do that are helpful, such as meditation, yoga, walking or watching a comedy, and make a note of the kind of things that would be unhelpful too that you need to try to avoid if you can (perhaps changing eating habits, negative self-talk or working late).

Calming Anxiety

Anxiety is a natural human emotion characterised by feelings of tension, worried thoughts, and physical changes like increased blood pressure. You feel anxious when you think that you're being threatened. Fear is part of your survival mechanism – without feeling any fear at all, you're likely to take big risks with no concern about dangerous consequences. Without fear, walking right on the edge of a cliff would feel no different to walking in the park – not a safe position to be in!

Anxiety and panic can be due to a combination of factors, including your genes, the past life experiences you've had, the current situation you're in, and if you're under the influence of drugs, including caffeine.

This section looks at how mindfulness can help with managing your anxiety and fear, whether the feelings appear from time to time, or if you have a clinical condition such as generalised anxiety disorder (GAD) where you feel anxious all the time.

Feel the fear . . . and make friends with it

Eliminating fearful thoughts isn't easy. The thoughts are sticky and the more you try and push them out, the stronger the worries and anxieties seem to cling on. In this way, you can easily get into a negative cycle in which the harder you try to block out the negatives, the stronger they come back.

Mindfulness encourages you to face up and experience all your experiences, including the unpleasant ones. In this way, rather than avoid anxious thoughts and feelings, which just makes them stronger and causes them to control your life, you begin to slowly but surely open up to them, in a kind and gentle way, preventing them building up out of proportion.

Perhaps this analogy may help. Imagine a room filling up with water. You're outside the room trying to keep the door closed. As more and more water builds up inside the room, you need to push harder and harder to keep the door shut. Eventually you're knocked over, the door flings open and the water comes pouring out. Alternatively, you can try opening the door very slowly at first, instead of pushing the door shut. As you keep opening the door, you give the water a chance to leave the room in a trickle rather than a deluge. Then you can stop struggling to keep the door shut. The water represents your inner, anxious thoughts and feelings, and the opening of the door is turning towards the difficult thoughts and feelings with a sense of kindliness, gentleness and care, as best you can.

Using mindfulness to cope with anxiety

If you worry a lot, the reason for this is probably to block yourself from more emotionally distressing topics. For example, you may be worrying whether or not your son will pass his exams, but actually your worry-type thoughts are blocking out the actual feeling of fear. Although the worry is unpleasant and creates anxiety, the thoughts keep you from feeling deeper emotions. However, until you open up to those deeper emotions, the worry continues. Worry is an example of experiential avoidance, described earlier in the chapter. Mindfulness trains you to become more open and accepting of your more challenging emotions, with acknowledgement, curiosity and kindness. Mindfulness also allows you to see how you're not your emotions, and that your feelings are transient, and so it helps you to reduce anxiety. Mindfulness encourages you to let go of worries by focusing your attention on the present moment.

Welcoming the noisy neighbours

Your anxious thoughts are like the music from a noisy neighbour. Mindfulness isn't so much about forcing the neighbour to stop, which may or may not work, but about listening to the noise in a different way. When you're listening to your favourite piece of music, you let the sounds come into you, you open yourself fully to the rhythm. In the same way, you need to open up and listen to your thoughts and feel the underlying emotions without trying to fix or change them – just acknowledging them as they are. Training your mind like this isn't an easy process and takes practice. The 'music' (your anxious thoughts) may or may not change – all you can control is your attitude towards them. Let the attitude be one of curiosity and kindness as far as you can.

Here's a mindful exercise for anxiety.

1. **Get comfortable and sit with a sense of dignity and poise on a chair or sofa.** Ask yourself, 'What am I experiencing now, in the present moment?' Reflect on the thoughts flowing through your mind, emotions arising in your being, and physical sensations in your body. As best you can, open up to the experiences in the here and now for a few minutes.

2. **Place your hand on your belly and feel your belly rising and falling with your breath.** Sustain your attention in this area. If anxious thoughts grasp your attention, acknowledge them but come back to the present moment and, without self-criticism if possible, focus back on the in- and out- breath. Continue for a few minutes.

3. **When you're ready, expand your awareness to get a sense of your whole body breathing, with wide and spacious attention, as opposed to the focused attention on the breath alone.** If you like, imagine the contours of your body breathing in and out, which the body does, through the skin. Continue for as long as you want.

4. **Note your transition from this mindfulness exercise back to your everyday life.** Continue to suffuse your everyday activities with this gentle, welcoming awareness, just to see what effect mindful attention has, if any. If you find the practice supportive, come back to this meditation to find some solace whenever you experience intrusive thoughts or worries.

 Mindfulness isn't about trying to get rid of your anxiety, or any other difficult experience. Mindfulness offers the possibility of developing a healthy stance towards your unpleasant experience. The unpleasant experience is here, whether you want it or not. You can try distracting yourself in the short term, but this is tiring and tends not to work in the long term. The invitation of mindfulness is a radical one – to take a courageous, challenging step towards the difficulty, whatever the difficulty is, and see what unfolds. This act of acknowledgement changes your relationship with the anxiety and therefore gives freedom for that emotion to move on, when you're ready.

Being with anxious feelings

If you want to change anxiety, you need to begin with the right relationship with the anxiety, so you can be with the emotion. Within this safe relationship, you can allow the anxiety to be there, neither suppressing nor reacting to it. Imagine sitting as calmly as you can while a child is having a tantrum. No tantrum lasts forever, and no tantrum stays at exactly the same level. By maintaining a mindful, calm, gentle awareness, eventually and very gradually the anxiety may begin to settle. And even if it doesn't go away, by sitting calmly next to it, your experience isn't quite such a struggle.

You don't need to face anxiety head-on straight away – here are the steps you can take over a period of days, weeks or months.

1. Observe how you normally react when anxiety arises, or if you're always anxious, notice your current attitude towards the emotion.

2. Consider the possibility of a more mindful attitude to take towards the anxiety.

3. Feel the anxiety for about a minute with as much kindness and warmth as you can, breathing into it.

4. Notice the colour, shape and texture of the feeling. What part of your body does it manifest in? Does the intensity of the sensation increase or decrease with your mindful awareness? Explore the area somewhere between retreating away from and diving into the anxiety and allow yourself to be fascinated by what happens on this edge with your kindly, compassionate awareness.

5. Watch the feeling as you may look at a beautiful tree or flower, with a sense of warmth and curiosity. Breathe into the various sensations and see the sensations as your teacher. Welcome the emotion as you may welcome a guest with open arms.

This isn't a competition to go from Steps 1 to 5 but is a process, a journey you take at your own pace. Step 1 is just as important, significant and deep as Step 5. Remember that these steps are a guide – move into the anxiety, or whatever the emotion is, as you see fit. *Trust in your own innate wisdom to guide your inner journey.*

Chapter 14

Getting Physical: Healing the Body

. . . .

In This Chapter

▶ Understanding the real connections between mind and body

▶ Discovering ways to manage pain mindfully

▶ Exploring how to cope with your illness using mindfulness

. . . .

Mindfulness for people with serious medical problems was initially adopted in the United States and is becoming increasingly popular in the UK. Doctors who'd exhausted all traditional medical routes referred patients to a stress-reduction clinic that used mindfulness to help people cope with pain, anxiety and stress.

As the patients engaged in mindfulness, they began to discover a different way of relating to their challenging experiences. They began to feel better, despite their medical problems. The symptoms didn't necessarily disappear, and the aim of mindfulness wasn't to make them go away. The patients found a different way of coping with the illness, from a state of wholeness and wisdom, rather than fear and disharmony.

This chapter explores why mindfulness may be beneficial for those suffering from a chronic health condition, and offers a variety of different ways of beginning that journey. You certainly don't have to be ill to benefit from mindfulness, but thousands suffering from serious medical conditions have found relief through the mindfulness meditation.

Contemplating Wholeness: Healing from Within

The word *heal* is related to the Old English word for 'whole' (*hal*). The word 'health' originally meant 'wholeness'.

Get a sense of what being whole means for you, and as you read this chapter, continue to reflect. Meditation is about going to that capacity you have to be aware, whole and free, no matter how broken you feel your body to be. This is a totally different way of seeing what healing truly means, but seems to lead to a peace of mind conducive to feeling better.

Physical disease, or dis-ease, isn't just a problem with the body, but a problem for the mind too. As I explore in this section, your mind and body are inseparable, a whole. When you suffer from a disease, you need to look after both your body and mind to best manage your difficulties. You also need to consider how a sense of being whole can come about whatever happens to your body. Everyone's physical body perishes in the end – how can you live so that this process is dignified rather than full of stress, anxiety and the feeling of being broken?

When you practise mindfulness, you practise an act of love. You're befriending yourself, slowly but surely. You're engaging in an activity for yourself, to look after, care and nurture your own health and wellbeing.

In mindfulness meditation you may at some point connect with your own deep, innate sense of wholeness. You begin to touch a depth of relaxation, of peace, of calm that you may not have been aware of beforehand. This encounter with your own wholeness is profoundly healing in the sense of feeling at peace with yourself and with an inner conviction that things are going to be okay, however they work out. Your ill heath, your body, your thoughts, the emotions that arise and pass away, aren't everything. They're a part of the whole. The thought, 'It's all my fault; I'm completely useless,' is just thought, not facts. When you begin to touch this inner wholeness, your illness becomes less threatening. You become more optimistic in both the present moment and the future. From your more detached, free and light-hearted stance, your perception of your predicament shifts, and you allow more space for your body to heal as best it can, while taking all the medical treatment as appropriate.

Mindfulness helps you to see things from a bigger perspective. If, due to your disease, you feel low and down, out of control, and that you just can't dig yourself out of the hole that you're in, you probably feel depressed, isolated, lonely and afraid. However, consider the same situation from a bigger perspective; remember that you're suffering in the same way as many others. You can become aware of both the suffering you feel and those aspects of you that are healthy and well. Although you may have a bad back, what about the parts of your body that are functionally well? Mindfulness shifts the fixed patterns of the mind and enables you to see from eyes of wholeness. Then perhaps you can forgive yourself for feeling down – you're human after all.

Seeing the Connection between Mind and Body

Imagine you're scared of spiders. As you walk downstairs before dawn, you can see a shape on the floor in the gloom. 'It's a spider!', you think. Your heart starts pounding and you begin to sweat. You're not sure if you should even move, in case you disturb the spider. Your thoughts go wild. Then you look again to notice the shape doesn't look quite right. You switch on the light to discover it's only a mark on the carpet! You feel relieved.

When you saw the mark as a spider, a whole series of changes took place in your body. You experienced the changes because of what you thought and interpreted the mark to be – in other words, because of your mind. When you realised it was just a stain on the carpet, a set of calming reactions took place. The object remained exactly the same. The way you changed your bodily reaction was by bringing curiosity to your experience, and then switching on the light. Through awareness and curiosity, you begin to interpret things differently, to see them as they actually are rather than what you *think* they are.

By becoming more skilful in the way you use your mind, you can create the conditions to help rather than hinder the healing process. High levels of stress reduce the strength of your immune system, so any creative ways of reducing stress are bound to have some positive effect.

Here's a very short exercise you can try that clearly demonstrates the link between your mind and body.

1. Make yourself comfortable sitting or lying down and close your eyes if you want.

2. Imagine you're hungry and are about to eat your favourite food. You can smell the food and see it on your plate. Take a few minutes to imagine what the food looks and smells like. You take a piece of the food, and begin eating. Imagine the taste of the delicious food in your mouth.

3. Notice any changes happening in your body. Are you salivating? Do you feel the desire to have this food now? Do you feel certain emotions manifesting in your body? Are some parts of your body becoming tense or relaxed?

This short exercise (or form of torture with all this talk about food!) again shows how your mind can directly have an effect on your body. All you did in this exercise was use your mind to create images in your head. And yet all sorts of physical changes took place in your body. You may now even go off to cook this food you've been imagining. In the same way, using your mind in the right way can go on to create positive, healing effects in your body.

Appreciating the power of placebos

A *placebo* pill is a non-active substance, usually made of sugar, which has no actual medicine in it. Whenever scientists want to test a new drug, they compare the drug to a placebo. Amazingly, many studies show that patients feel better after taking a placebo, rather than the real medicine. How? The answer lies in your belief system. If you believe that a pill is going to help you, the positive belief seems to accelerate the healing process.

Here are some interesting facts about placebos:

✔ Placebos seem to release natural painkillers from your body into the bloodstream, if you *believe* that the pill is a painkiller. This can have the equivalent effect of a moderate dose of morphine!

✔ Expensive placebos work better than cheap ones. I love this fact! In one experiment, researchers gave half the patients a placebo saying it cost $2.50, and half a placebo saying it cost 10 cents. The group that thought they had the more expensive placebos experienced less pain when given a mild electric shock in their hands.

✔ Placebo surgery is where the patients think that they've had surgery but no actual surgery has taken place. For ethical reasons placebo surgery has only been done about five times, according to the literature. In the latest study in 2002, 180 patients with osteoarthritis of the knee were randomly assigned to have either actual surgery or placebo surgery. After 24 months, at no point did the actual surgery group report less pain or better function than the placebo surgery group.

The 'placebo effect' is powerful, and proves how the mind can actually affect the healing process.

Acknowledging Your Limits

You have a certain amount of time and energy on this planet. If you didn't have any limits on time, you'd live forever. If you didn't have any limits on your energy, you'd never need to sleep. So, how can you best use the time and energy you do have? If you try to do more and more, you eventually break down. You're better off becoming aware of your limits and acknowledging them, but continuing to push those boundaries every now and then, in a healthy and mindful way.

At one point in my career, I believed that I could do anything and everything. I took on more and more jobs and responsibilities. In the end I was doing more but achieving less. By the end of the day I was exhausted, my energy levels were very low and I was just about finding time to meditate, just to keep going. One day I woke up and thought 'enough is enough' – why sacrifice my health and wellbeing for the sake of a bit of extra cash? I began to reduce the responsibilities that I could reduce, and looked for more efficient and creative ways of doing the things I had to do. In this way, I enjoy challenging myself, and testing my limits, but I don't overdo it.

Don't confuse accepting or acknowledging your limits with feeling defeated. If you suffer from a long-term health condition for example, you don't have to give up and curl up in the corner for the rest of your life. Accepting your limits means accepting that your body isn't well and you need to start taking small steps to begin improving your condition, as your doctor advises. You may need support of a group, or from your own friends or family. You also need to remember that you won't magically transform and that therefore you need to work at accepting your limits slowly but surely.

Accepting limits reminds me of what bees do. When a bee is stuck in a room, it continues to fly into the closed window thinking that it can go through. If the bee could see that the window is a limit, and it's not possible to get out that way, it wouldn't keep knocking into the window until it died. If you find yourself hitting limits again and again, and getting frustrated, be imaginative and try a different approach – don't keep flying into the window just because the view looks great outside.

Rising above Your Illness

To rise above your illness means to separate yourself from your illness rather than to identify yourself with the disease. In this way, you may become less overwhelmed by your condition.

Dana Jennings, who suffered from cancer, wrote in a *New York Times* blog:

> *Being able to laugh in the face of cancer lets you continue to own yourself, as hard as that might be, rather than ceding ownership to the disease. A good laugh reminds you that you are not your cancer.*

You are not your illness. Laughter may be one way of reminding you of that fact, and meditation is another. Some days are better than others. Some days may be dark and you may need just to hang on until things lighten up a bit. Remembering 'I am not my illness' may help.

Recently, when I was practising meditation, my body felt lighter and lighter, in a pleasant way. I felt completely calm and at ease. Everything was okay with the world. At that point in time, I didn't identify with my body and yet I felt completely at ease and fine with the experience. In fact, I felt as if I was truly myself. Experiences such as this remind me that my body isn't as solid and real as I normally think. I am not my body but I am aware of my body.

I am the awareness – aware of thoughts, feelings, my body and the world around me. In this sense of wholeness, you experience a freedom from the chains of thinking 'I'm ill' or, 'I'm incomplete' to the freedom of being, of resting in the sense of 'I'm alone'. In this context, I mean alone as in 'al-one' or 'all one', the original meaning of the word alone. This is the opposite of feeling lonely and isolated.

Don't use meditation to try to chase certain pleasant experiences. Whatever you experience in meditation is okay – meditation isn't good or bad. The sense of wholeness is your true nature, right here and right now, not just in some exotic meditative experience. Experiences come and go but awareness is always here, whether you want to be aware or not. Identify with that presence and you're immediately reminded of your own sense of wholeness.

Using Mindfulness to Manage Pain

Acute pain is a sharp pain lasting for a short time, sometimes defined as less than 12 weeks. Medicine is quite good at treating acute pain. *Chronic pain* is pain that lasts for over 12 weeks, and doctors have a much harder time treating such a condition. Many consider chronic pain as one of the most underestimated health-care problems in the world today, having a massive effect on both the patient and being a major burden on the health-care system.

The World Health Organisation found that between a half and two-thirds of people with chronic pain struggle to exercise, enjoy normal sleep, perform household chores, attend social activities, drive a car, walk or have sexual relations.

It has repeatedly been found that those who complete an eight-week mindfulness programme find their level of pain reduced. This is surprising because mindfulness asks you to go into the place that hurts and allow the sensation to be there, rather than to fight with the pain itself. The following sections explain how this may work.

Knowing the difference between pain and suffering

Pain is inevitable. Suffering is optional. Pain is a sensation that you're bound to experience from time to time. In fact, pain is often a very useful sensation –

without pain, you'd go round damaging yourself without realising it. If you've ever been anaesthetised in your mouth by your dentist, you know how easy it is to bite the inside of your cheek, even making it bleed, without realising.

Suffering is different. Suffering is something you create yourself, often unknowingly. Say you suffer from arthritis. Each morning, when you wake up, for a split second you just experience the raw sensation – the pain of having arthritis. Then, within a second or so, your mind begins to interpret the experience: 'That stupid disease. Why me? I bet I got it because of the unhealthy food I used to eat. It's not fair. I'm so annoyed! It's all my fault. What will happen in the future?' Unhelpful judgements, interpretations and predictions all lead to suffering.

Pain can be emotional – feelings of sadness, loneliness, grief, anxiety or anger. Suffering is the way you meet those emotions. If you're curious about them, and almost welcome them rather than trying to push them away, fight or block them, you're unlikely to create much suffering. However, if you avoid the emotions through addictions, like drugs or excessive alcohol use, to avoid these feelings, you're likely to increase your own suffering.

Dealing with a headache

As I write, my head is aching. So, what do I do? Mindfulness is about awareness, so I become aware of the sensation in my head. I notice that my shoulders are tensing up due to the pain, so I breathe into them, and the tension seems to melt a little. I also take frequent breaks, and drink lots of water. I remember that I'm not my headache. The headache arises and at some point is going to pass away. The actual experience of pain only exists in this moment. I don't need to 'tolerate' the pain because even if I stop tolerating, the pain is still there. Tolerating is a state of extra unnecessary tension. I can also become aware of the shape, size, colour and texture of the pain sensation in my head.

I breathe into the pain and some resistance eases around the pain. I know that the pain only exists from one moment to the next. I notice and let go of the desire for the headache to go away.

This may give you some idea of the spirit with which to practise mindfulness when coping with painful sensation. The idea is to turn your attention towards the difficulty and become really curious about it – but not to try and get rid of it. I suppose it's a bit like trying to soothe a crying baby: getting angry usually doesn't help. By giving the baby your attention, although it's uncomfortable when she's crying, you're able to meet her needs.

All the avoidant strategies can't make the pain go away, they just numb it for the time being. This can be helpful in the short term to help you to cope, but by avoiding the painful sensations or emotions, you sustain and feed them. Suffering is something you can begin to manage and control by looking more carefully at the thoughts and feelings you're experiencing – the very act of turning towards painful experiences begins to change the level of suffering you have.

Here's a quote from Nisargadatta, a famous Indian spiritual teacher. He experienced the pain of throat cancer in the latter years of his life.

> *Pain is physical, suffering is mental. Beyond the mind there is no suffering. Pain is essential for the survival of the body, but none compels you to suffer. Suffering is due entirely to clinging or resisting; it is a sign of our unwillingness to move on, to flow with life. As a sane life is free of pain, so is a saintly life free from suffering. A saint does not want things to be different from what they are; he knows that, considering all factors, they are unavoidable. He is friendly with the inevitable and, therefore, does not suffer. Pain he may know, but it does not shatter him. If he can, he does the needful to restore the lost balance, or he lets things take their course.*

Being inspired by others

Here are some of the kinds of things my clients with chronic pain conditions say about the effect of mindfulness, which may help you to cope with your pain, and offer you some ways to apply mindfulness.

'I suffer from a chronic pain condition – if I move around for an hour or so on one day, my body is in agony the next day. Mindfulness is pretty much the only thing that has helped relieve the pain I've suffered in the last six years. I can't really move my body and most therapies require some sort of movement. With the body scan, or mindfulness of breathing, I can lie down on the floor and do the meditation, without actually moving. That's a wonderful thing. By the end, I feel really tired, but also as if I've released lots of tension I've been holding for weeks, or even months.'

'I have severe lower back pain. The pain goes shooting down my leg every time I move. I thought the pain was there 24 hours a day, seven days a week. Having done the mindfulness training, the biggest thing I've realised is that there are moments in the day when I have no pain. That's really important for me.'

Coping with pain

Here are a few things to remember about pain when applying mindfulness to the condition:

- Pain can only exist in the present moment. You only need to cope with this moment now. By worrying about the rest of the day, week, month or year you begin to create suffering for yourself.

- Tension increases pain. By becoming aware of the sensation of pain and imaging the breath going into and out of the area of pain, the tension naturally begins to release, thereby reducing the pain. However, if the tension stays, that's okay too – your intention is all you can control here. Become aware of the actual sensation of the pain itself. Notice where the pain is located in the body. Does it have an associated shape, size, texture or colour?

- Trying hard to reduce pain doesn't really work, just like trying to relax can create more tension. By discovering how slowly but surely to acknowledge and accept your pain, your experience may change for the better.

Here's a meditation you can try to help you through your pain:

1. Adopt any position that you feel comfortable in for a few minutes.

2. Feel the sensation of your own breathing. Be aware of your breath with a lightness, a kindness and a sense of gratitude as far as you can.

3. Notice how the pain grabs your attention time and again. Try not to criticise yourself for this. Understand that this is a difficult practice and guide your awareness gently back to the feeling of the in-breath and out-breath around the nose, chest, belly or wherever else you find it most easy to focus on. Continue for a few minutes.

4. Now bring your attention to the sensation of the pain itself. This may feel frightening, or you may be very reluctant to try moving your attention to the pain. However, if you've never done this before, why not give it a go? Imagine your breath going into and out of the centre of the pain, or however close you can comfortably move to the pain.

5. You may find saying the following words to yourself helpful, as you breathe in and out. You may want to make a nice, slow recording of it – perhaps with music in the background if you like – and play the recording back to yourself.

Breathing in, I am aware I am breathing in,

> *Breathing out, I am aware I am breathing out.*

Breathing in, I am aware of pain,

> *Breathing out, I am aware of pain.*

Breathing in, I am aware of pain,

> *Breathing out, I know I am not my pain.*

Breathing in, I am aware of tension,

> *Breathing out, I know I am not my tension.*

Breathing in, I am aware of anger,

> *Breathing out, I know I am not my anger.*

Breathing in, I am aware of sadness,

> *Breathing out, I know I am not my sadness.*

Breathing in, I am aware of anxiety,

> *Breathing out, I know I am not my anxiety.*

Breathing in, I take things moment by moment,

> *Breathing out, this is the only moment.*

Breathing in, I know I am awareness,

> *Breathing out, I know I am free.*

You can change the wording to whatever you feel comfortable with. Feel free to experiment. Practise at least once a day and note its effect.

The butterfly of the mind

The Diving Bell and the Butterfly is the title of a book by Jean-Dominique Bauby that was later made into a film. Bauby, editor of the French *Elle* magazine, wrote the whole book after becoming paralysed, communicating by blinking his left eye when the correct letter of the alphabet was spoken by his companions. He explores the value of the simple things in life, the experience of feeling trapped in his body, like being in a diving bell, while his mind flits around like a butterfly. The book is a reminder of what you have rather than what you don't have – of how precious life is, despite the pain and suffering. As one critic said, 'Read this book and fall back in love with life.'

Using Mindfulness during Ill Health

In the mindfulness-based stress reduction clinic, a popular saying is: 'If you can breathe, there's more right with you than wrong with you.' You don't even have to be able to sit up or to move to benefit from mindfulness. Mindfulness is mind training, and so no matter what the condition of your body, you can still train your mind.

Ultimately, mindfulness is about realising that you're more than just your body, mind and heart. You're more than your fleeting thoughts and fluxing emotions. You're more than your illness. Through the practice of mindfulness, and a natural self-enquiry that arises from meditation, you begin to discover a different dimension of yourself, a dimension in which illness is no longer so big an issue.

You face a myriad of difficulties when you suffer from ill-health. Although the doctors and nurses do all they can to help, they can't help you with everything. Mindfulness offers you a way to support yourself and build some inner resilience so you aren't overwhelmed by all the looming decisions and difficulties you may meet.

The illness may have a physical impact and cause changes to your appearance. Your whole sense of personal identity and self-worth can be questioned when you look different as you gaze at yourself in the mirror. Mindfulness offers a way of connecting with something else other than just your physical body, making you feel more grounded.

Stress increases not only for you but also for family and friends when you all need greater support and calm. Some people even believe that they've brought the disease upon themselves due to stress. This belief leads to further distress. Mindful awareness can help to spot these unhelpful and untrue thoughts, thereby defusing their potency.

Emotional distress is natural following a diagnosis of a disease. This is due to all your ideas about the future, of worries and anxieties about relationships and fear of the physical changes that may take place. Mindfulness can help in this stage to keep you living in the reality of the present moment.

Serious illness puts you face to face with the prospect of death. Facing death may force you to reflect on your priorities, on what is most important in your life. The space offered in mindfulness may help to uncover a direct experience of an understanding through which life and death begin to make sense on some level.

However, illness isn't all negative. Surprisingly, research has shown there are positive effects of terminal illness. Some patients report increased spirituality, and a deeper appreciation and a generally more positive perception of partners and significant others. Some people report greater compassion and willingness to express emotions. Higher levels of spirituality indicate that the patient senses that the illness is part of a bigger picture and is more likely to be at peace amidst such challenging life circumstances.

Mindfulness can reduce the negative impact of a diagnosis, and also encourages spirituality and personal growth, strengthening the sufferer with greater emotional resilience.

Aiding the healing process

When you sit down to meditate, any aches, pains and physical discomfort that you may have managed to ignore during the course of the day become more apparent. The practice of mindfulness is about allowing and managing these uncomfortable feelings rather than totally distracting yourself from them; you use them in a positive way.

Here are some practices you can do to help you to reduce stress and aid the healing process:

✔ **Mindfulness of breath.** Practise focusing your attention on your breathing. If you find focusing on the breath too difficult due to any pain you feel, try counting your breaths, or saying 'in' and 'out' to yourself as you breathe in and out. Allow yourself to become aware of the natural, life-giving energy of your breathing, as it finds its instinctive rhythm. As you breathe, you may become aware of a physical tightness in the body that restricts the breathing process. Allow and accept this, and breathe into the tension. If the tension melts, fine; if the tension doesn't, that's also fine.

✔ **Mindfulness of body.** Being mindful of your body is a particularly important stage if you're unwell. Bring as much kindness as you can to your experience. If you aren't too overwhelmed by the sensation of pain, allow and accept it as far as you can. Feel the sensation of pain in a neutral way, staying with the feeling and doing nothing else. In addition to kindness, bring some curiosity to your experience, as best you can. The more nurturing and gentle you can be in your relationship with your body, the better. Try some yoga, stretching or tai chi if they help to soothe the pain.

✔ **Mindfulness of thoughts and emotions.** In meditation you can welcome your thoughts and emotions rather than resisting them. Be mindfully aware of your thoughts and emotions as they arise and pass away. You may want to use your breath to anchor yourself in the present moment every now and then when you find yourself swept away by thoughts, as happens very often. Notice the nature of your thoughts. Are they catastrophic? Are they always about the illness? Do they focus on the future all the time? What about your emotions? Allow yourself to move into your emotions rather than resist them. Notice in what part of the body they manifest and use your breath to soothe them. Trust in your own capacity to heal, to make whole.

✔ **Mindfulness of being.** Become aware of your own sense of identity – be aware of the sense of 'I am'. Let go of your awareness of your body, your mind, your emotions, your health and illness, your desires and fears. Keep coming back to the sense of being, the sense of 'I am'. Rest in this state of 'beingness'. If you find yourself getting lost in thoughts, remember that your thoughts are simply dancing on top of your awareness. Remember your thoughts and feelings are like waves in an ocean of being, which is you. Expect thoughts to arrive rather than resisting or fighting them. Just as clouds aren't distractions for the sky, so thoughts aren't distractions for your meditation. Just be.

Chapter 15

Coaching Children in Mindfulness

*O*nce you've begun to develop your own mindfulness practice, you can consider how to coach your children in mindfulness too. Mindfulness can help children to become calmer and more focused. Mindfulness is a very natural process and can be practised by children from a young age. In this chapter you can find lots of fun exercises to train your child in mindfulness, as well as some mindful parenting tips to help keep your family smiling in the challenging but rewarding art of bringing up children.

Children and Mindfulness: A Natural Combination

Young children are experts at mindfulness if they're fortunate enough to be brought up with love and care. Babies are like mini Zen masters! Since they haven't learnt language, they see things as they are. A set of keys, a light bulb, or the eyes of another human being are awe-inspiring for them. All actions they take are spontaneous. One moment they can be crying, and the next moment they completely let go of the past, and laugh. They eat when they're hungry, sleep when they're tired and walk when they want to walk. Their minds are full of curiosity – they can't help but explore. They're naturally full of love and affection, which you can see beaming out of their eyes. Babies are often happy just to 'be'. They can look around, and shake their legs and arms, and that's enough. They love to play and don't take things too seriously. Babies don't see themselves as separate individuals; they simply do what they do and go with the flow. Many of these qualities are the essence of mindfulness.

As babies grow up and begin to develop individuality, they begin to lose the sense of focused calm and can end up going from one thing to another, looking for a source of entertainment but lacking the attention to stay with it. From age five upwards, you can begin to teach some very simple mindfulness exercises to help give your child some relief from his overactive mind, helping him to find out how to calm himself down. Often, children enjoy becoming calm and may even ask for the mindfulness exercise if feeling agitated.

As children approach their teenage years, they battle with a huge influx of hormones and struggle with the demands made upon them by the world. They become more serious, as individuality takes a firm hold and begins to suppress emotions. In this challenging transition into adulthood, the innocence of being a baby seems distant and almost a dream. Some simple mindfulness exercises, like mindful breathing for a few minutes, can offer a method to focus the mind inwards without him spiralling out of control each time something doesn't go his way.

Teaching Mindfulness to Children

Before you attempt to teach your children the art of mindfulness, consider how they learn. By adopting the right attitude to this important and challenging endeavour, you're more likely to avoid unnecessary frustration. Follow these tips when teaching mindfulness:

- ✔ **Be light-hearted.** Children don't like taking things too seriously, so bringing an element of play and fun is important. At the same time, be clear in your mind what the purpose of the mindfulness exercises are, and explain them to your children (see the next section for ideas for exercises).

- ✔ **Keep the sessions short.** Children's attention spans just aren't as long as those of adults. You need to adjust the length of the session as appropriate for the child.

- ✔ **Reduce talk and increase action.** Avoid talking about how much meditation helps you and how wonderful it is. You're better off practising more meditation and letting your child learn from what you do rather than what you say.

- ✔ **Remember that some days will be better than others.** Children don't do meditation, the meditation comes to them. Some days you may feel as if nothing works – then suddenly, your child may sit quietly without distraction, for no apparent reason.

- ✔ **Avoid using force.** If your child doesn't want to meditate, you can't force him. This just creates a negative idea about meditation. Meditation isn't like learning the piano, or maths. Mindfulness requires a desire to practise with a sense of curiosity, and using force can't generate the right attitude. Instead, be creative and try something completely different (see the later exercises in this chapter for ideas).

Setting an example

Children learn far more from what you *do* than from what you *say*. Children love copying others, especially people they respect. If a child sees you meditating, he's likely to be curious about what you're doing and why you're doing it. In this way you draw your child towards meditation, rather than forcing meditation upon him.

If you practise very little mindfulness, but think that your child would benefit from the practice, you may have a hard time convincing him of the benefits. He may have seen you react to your stress in unhelpful ways, getting unnecessarily angry and becoming frustrated over small things. Your child may pick up on these reactions and unconsciously begin copying them instead.

If you practise mindfulness on a regular basis, and genuinely put in the time, effort and energy to develop it in your life, your child is going to pick up on this too. He'll notice how you try to calm down when you become upset, how you take mini meditations when things become overwhelming for you, how you're firm when you need to be firm, and light-hearted at other times. If your child sees you making genuine efforts to cultivate mindfulness, he's likely to pick up on this. Even if he doesn't show calm and controlled behaviour at the moment, the memory of his positive perceptions of mindfulness will stay with him, and is likely to flower as he gets older.

Taking baby steps

Don't expect to start with a 30-minute, mindful-breathing exercise with your child the first time you teach him. You may not even be able to do the eating meditation with a raisin or any other food (see Chapter 6 for eating meditation). If your child feels bored, he's likely to give up immediately and do something more interesting instead. You'd probably have a hard time trying to convince him to explore the boredom, or to get interested in the cause of boredom!

If you have high expectations about your child practising mindfulness, you may be disappointed. Keep your expectations reasonably low and be happy with any small progress. Ultimately, meditation is about being in the present moment, so any time at all is very valuable and better than nothing.

Playing Mindfulness Games and Exercises

Children love games. Games help to focus your child's mind and at the same time have an element of fun. Then, in this more focused state of mind, you can do a short, guided imagery for a minute or so, and with young children, that's enough. I know a couple of schools who do this, and the children really look forward to doing the meditations – they enjoy both the fun and the release of any anxieties and stresses in their systems.

Use your intuition to decide which games to use, but be brave too, and try some that you initially doubt. You never know what will happen until you try! Some can be adapted for older children – just use more appropriate props, more adult language and extend the length of the meditations slightly.

You can do these games with one child or more.

Memory game

This game helps to train attention and memory and focuses the mind before a meditation.

1. Put about 20 random items such as pens, scissors, socks and toys onto a tray.

2. Tell the child he has one minute to try to remember as many items as he can. He gets one point for each item he remembers.

3. Cover up the tray with a towel and ask your child to recall the items.

4. Praise your child for however many he gets correct, and challenge him to see if he can remember one more next time you play.

Teddy bear

This exercise helps to encourage belly breathing, and also to focus the attention on the breathing.

1. Ask your child to lie down on the floor, mat or bed.

2. Place a teddy bear on your child's belly and ask him to become aware of the teddy bear as it rises and falls.

3. Encourage your child to be curious about how often the teddy bear goes up and down. Can he make it go up and down a little more slowly? How does that make him feel inside?

Paper windmill spinning

This game is a way of focusing your child's attention on his breathing. The visual cue of a colourful paper windmill is far more interesting than just feeling his breath alone.

1. Give your child a colourful paper windmill (pinwheel). Let him play with it for a while, and then tell him you're going to practise being curious together.

2. Ask him to blow as softly as he can, and to observe what happens. Ask him to see how slowly he can make the paper windmill turn. How does this make him feel?

3. Ask him to blow as hard as possible, and see how fast the paper windmill turns. What happens to all the colours? How does this make him feel?

4. Ask him to experiment with a long or short breath, and notice how long the paper windmill turns for.

5. Ask him to breathe normally, and to watch what happens to the paper windmill. Again, ask him how he feels.

6. Finally, ask him to put the paper windmill down and feel his breath without it. Ask him if he can feel calm and relaxed even without the paper windmill, just by feeling his own breath.

Curious mind

This works if you have several children sitting in a circle. The game feels a bit like playing 'pass the parcel', a popular party game. Although children are naturally curious, this exercise helps them to become aware of the sense of curiosity itself.

1. Find a beautiful, shiny object, wrap it up in layers of newspaper and place it in a box.

2. Now ask the children to try to guess what may be inside. They can shake the box, but nothing else. Let everyone have a guess.

3. Now ask them what it feels like to 'not know' or to be curious. Ask them to look at the faces of the other children – their eyes may be wide open, and there may be smiles around. Encourage curiosity about curiosity!

4. Begin to slowly unwrap the object. Explain how mindfulness is about being curious about everyday experience and in this way reveals the unknown. Tell them that eventually they'll discover a jewel or other beautiful object inside themselves, and they'll enjoy looking inside every day.

Loving-kindness meditation

This is a powerful exercise to practise with your children. If your children really like the exercise, they may be happy to do the meditation everyday before going to sleep. They may find they sleep more deeply and feel calmer and refreshed the next day. Pause after giving each instruction to give your child plenty of time to experience the meditation.

1. Ask your child to find a comfortable, relaxed sitting or lying down posture with his eyes closed, if that feels okay for him.

2. Ask him to remember something that makes him feel happy. He may recall a game he played with a friend, a favourite hobby or much loved cuddly toy. Adjust according to the age of your child.

3. Ask him to place both his hands over his chest and imagine the feeling of warmth, peace and happiness grow from there to all over his body and even the room around.

4. Tell him to imagine this happiness and loving-kindness spreading to everyone in his family, then to all of his friends, all of the children in his class, his school and his town, even those he doesn't get on with very well. Then to all people on the planet, living in all the different countries. Then to all animals and plants on earth including those that live high up in the air and down in the deepest oceans.

Some children may find difficulty in wishing happiness to people or animals they don't like, such as spiders or certain students. Explain that loving kindness includes every living thing, and just as they want to be happy, so do others want to be happy too.

Bubble meditation

I've tried this meditation with children from age ten upwards and they all seemed to like it. You can also try the meditation for younger children too – just simplify the language a little.

1. Ask your child to sit or lie down in a comfortable position. Allow him to use pillows and blankets to make himself cosy. You don't need to ask him to sit up straight for this meditation. He can close his eyes if he is okay with that.

2. Say to him, 'Imagine you have a small, shiny bubble in your hand, that can't be burst. Imagine dropping that bubble on the floor in front of you, and watching it gently expand until it's so big you can step inside it. In fact, the bubble is the size of a large, spacious room. Then, step

inside the bubble. Now, imagine you can instantly decorate the inside of this bubble in any way you like. You can cover it with blankets of your favourite colour or paint the walls and ceiling just as you like. You can have games machines, expensive televisions, and your favourite music playing in the background – whatever you want. Your favourite food is available whenever you need it. Consider all the sights, sounds, smells, tastes being just how you like them to be inside your bubble. You feel really relaxed, comfortable and safe inside this bubble of yours.' Allow him time to really enjoy his own personal bubble that he's created for himself. Children often like imagining what to put inside their bubble and so you can extend this for more than five minutes.

3. Say to your child, 'Now you've created and enjoyed your own personal bubble, you're ready to keep this personal bubble of yours for later on. You step out of your bubble and see the bubble shrinking so you can hold the bubble in your hand once again. Now imagine the bubble becomes so small it can move inside your hand and up your arm. Allow the bubble to go into the centre of your chest, where your heart is. You can keep your bubble here for safety, and any time you feel you need to go back into your bubble, you can.

4. Bring the meditation to a close by asking him to gently open his eyes and then discuss how the practice went.

Drawing meditation

This meditation trains your child to be mindful of shape, colour, light and shade. This is particularly helpful for children who are resistant to traditional meditation with eyes closed, as drawing doesn't feel like meditation at all, and yet they are training their attention for detail with a sense of curiosity.

1. Ask your child to draw an object in the room. He can look at the object as he draws.

2. When he's finished, you can both compare the picture with the actual object. Which bits are close to the reality and which bits aren't quite right? Emphasise this isn't a competition, more of an experiment to see what happens.

3. If the child wants, you can repeat the exercise and see how much better the second drawing is through paying attention.

Body meditation

Children are far more likely to give their attention to the world around them rather than their own bodies. This meditation helps to bring their attention back to their physical body, training their attention to focus on one part at a time, and they also discover to move their attention from one part of the body to another. This capacity to hold and move attention can then be used in their daily lives.

1. Ask your child to lie down in a quiet and relaxing place. He can close his eyes if he wants.

2. Ask him to name each part of his body, beginning with his toes and moving up to his head. After naming each part, ask him to tell you how that part of the body feels. After naming that part of the body, he can move it – this changes the feeling and brings a bit of fun to the exercise too.

3. When you get to the top of his head, gently ring a bell and ask him to put his hand up when he can no longer hear the bell at all. The bell is a way of expanding the attention from a sharp focused one, to a wider, more expansive and open awareness. By asking him to identify when the sound turns into silence, he is drawn naturally into the peaceful silence, and can feel more calm and refreshed.

Mindful Parenting

I think that parenting is the most difficult, stressful, important and probably most fulfilling responsibility in the world. A good parent needs not only to nurture the child with food, shelter and clothing, but to develop the child's mind too. Your behaviour as a parent often reflects what your own parents were like even if you want to change and improve upon certain areas. However, parents often end up repeating the cycle in subtle ways, passing on unhelpful behaviours. Fortunately, mindful parenting can help to break the cycle.

Being present for your children

How can mindfulness help with parenting? Mindful parents are aware and awake to their actions and the actions of their children. This is very important in bringing up a child. Children crave attention. For children, attention is like love. If they don't receive sufficient attention, they misbehave until they get that attention – even being told off is preferable to being ignored.

Attention is a fundamental need for a child. How can you give that attention if you're not attentive yourself? Mindfulness offers ways to hone your attention skills to help bring up a child in a more harmonious and peaceful way.

Here are the benefits of parenting in the present moment:

✔ **You can meet your child's needs.** By living in the present moment, you're more able to meet your child's needs as necessary. You notice if your child needs to eat or sleep or just play. You notice if actually all that he needs is a hug. Each moment is different and fresh and what worked yesterday may not work today. Your child is one day older and different – living moment by moment helps you to see this.

✔ **You can meet your own needs.** By being aware and awake to the present sensations in your own body, and noticing the way you react to situations, you're also better able to look after yourself. Parenting is very tiring, and when you're over-tired you can end up making decisions that just create more difficulties rather than solutions. Awareness of your own reactions helps you to sense when this is happening, and to take whatever appropriate action is necessary.

✔ **You cultivate gratefulness.** Living in the present moment helps you to be grateful for what you have, rather than ungrateful for what you don't. You may notice how much work you have to do, or how frustrated you are by your children's behaviour, but thinking about what isn't going according to plan is draining. Living in the present enables you to see what's going well and what you do have. You may have healthy children and a nice home; you may be having a spell of good weather; or you may have a supportive partner or friend.

✔ **You see things afresh.** One of the other key aspects of mindfully living in the present is adopting an attitude of 'beginner's mind' (for more on seeing things afresh, jump to Chapter 4). This involves seeing things freshly, as if for the first time. If you have a baby, you're able to see how he's always living in beginner's mind. Babies look around the room or area with wonder. By living with this same attitude, you're more able to meet the ever-changing challenge of parenting in the present moment.

✔ **You free yourself from worries.** Living and parenting moment by moment means you can let go of regrets about the past and worries about the future. Neither of them exist in the present moment. Are there any problems at all, right now, if you don't think about them? All worries, concerns, fears and anxieties arise from leaving the here and now, the present moment. All you need to do is take things one day at a time, or better still, one second at a time. You may be worrying about how your children will be tomorrow, or next week, month or year. All you can possibly do is your best, right here and now, and let go of what has happened or may happen.

Trying out tips for mindful parenting

Here are a few tips for practising mindful parenting:

- ✔ **Be present for your child.** The greatest present you can give your child is your presence. Live in the moment and as if everything in front of you is your teacher. Your child will observe and copy this on some level.

- ✔ **Find the balance between love and discipline.** If you're too lenient, your children become spoilt, but if you're too harsh your children become overly cold and closed. Set clear boundaries, but ensure that you praise good behaviour and attitudes, and don't just criticise their errors.

- ✔ **Trust your intuition.** Your sense of the best thing to do is more intelligent than logical thinking – your intuition has access to all your unconscious learning that has operated in humanity for thousands of years. Use a combination of your head and heart in your decisions.

- ✔ **Look for a balance in situations.** You can't get your own way all the time, and neither can your child. But perhaps a place in between satisfies you both to a certain extent and feels right.

- ✔ **Imagine things from your child's perspective.** What's it like to be dominated by adults most of the time? How does your child feel if adults' seemingly silly desires are all they can think about? If you were your child, how would you want your parents to act towards you?

- ✔ **Take some time to meditate every day, even if for a short period of time.** Don't force your child to do the same, but answer his questions about meditation honestly and simply, and play mindful games with him when you can.

- ✔ **Practise mindful listening.** Listen to your child as if you're listening to a piece of music or the sounds of nature. Listen with a gentle attentiveness and respond as necessary. Listening to your child can be like a mindfulness meditation.

- ✔ **Observe your own behaviour as much as you observe your child's behaviour.** See how you like to do what you like doing, just as your child likes to do what *he* likes doing.

- ✔ **Look after yourself.** Ensure that you eat properly, sleep enough (I know this can be difficult), and take exercise. You may need to be really creative to fit some of these things into your daily schedule.

- ✔ **Be light-hearted.** You don't need to take things too seriously. If you made a mistake in your parenting, don't beat yourself up about the fault – instead see if you can laugh or at least smile about it. You're human after all, and so is your child.

Mulla Nasruddin stories

Children love stories of Nasruddin, known throughout the Middle East. The stories seem to suggest that Nasruddin was foolish, but they all contain gems of hidden wisdom within. Here are a few examples:

- Nasruddin was on his hands and knees one dark evening, under the light of a street lamp. A neighbour came out to ask what the problem was. Nasruddin said he had dropped his keys and so was looking for them. The neighbour helped him search but couldn't find the keys. In the end the neighbour asked, 'Where exactly did you drop them?' Nasruddin said, 'Over there,' pointing to his front door. The neighbour retorted, 'Then why are you looking under the lamp?!' Nasruddin replied, 'Because there's light here.'

- One day Nasruddin went into his favourite coffee shop and said, 'The moon is more useful than the sun.' An old man asked, 'Why?' Nasruddin replied, 'We need the light more during the night than during the day.'

- A friend asked Nasruddin, 'How old are you?' 'Fifty,' he replied. 'But you said the same thing two years ago!' 'Yes,' replied Nasruddin, 'I always stand by what I've said.'

- 'When I was in the desert,' said Nasruddin to his friend, 'I caused an entire tribe of horrible and bloodthirsty people to run.' 'How did you do it?' 'Easy. I just ran, and they ran after me.'

- Nasruddin, who wasn't used to public speaking, arose in confusion and said nervously: 'M-m-my f-f-friends, when I c-c-c-came here tonight only God and I knew what I was about to say to you. Now, only God knows!'

- Nasruddin was sitting chatting with a neighbour when his son came up the road holding a chicken. 'Where did you get that chicken?' Nasruddin asked. 'I stole it,' said his son. Nasruddin turned to his neighbour and said proudly, 'There's my boy. He may steal, but he won't lie.'

You can find more stories in full at www. nasruddin.org

Part V
The Part of Tens

"Being mindful means noticing the beauty of nature, like these pretty little shells."

In this part . . .

You have a neat summary of mindfulness in tasty, bite-size chunks. You'll find 10 tips to live in a mindful way every day, find out 10 different ways that practising mindfulness can really help you, 10 common ideas about mindfulness that just aren't true, and 10 different resources including books, CDs and websites. There are even some retreats for you to browse through as well.

Chapter 16

Ten Top Tips for Mindful Living

In This Chapter

▶ Knowing the essence of mindfulness

▶ Discovering practical mindfulness exercises

▶ Exploring tips for applying mindfulness in daily life

Mindfulness is very simple – it's about letting go rather than doing anything else – but the difficulty is in practising mindfulness consistently. This chapter gives you a series of short, easy ways of integrating the principles of mindfulness into your everyday life. Don't underestimate their value – they may take relatively little time and seem overly simplistic, but many of these tips have been proven to be effective. Try them out for yourself and hold back your judgement until you've given the tools a try for at least a few weeks.

Spending Some Quiet Time Every Day

Having some quiet time every day is the most important tip I can give you. I can't emphasise enough the importance of connecting with some form of mindfulness practice on a daily basis, preferably for ten minutes or more. By deliberately practising mindfulness every day, you strengthen your mind's ability to be more aware and awake.

If you want to be more mindful, you need daily training, just as when you want to become fitter, you need to exercise your body on a daily basis. If you only exercised once a week, you wouldn't benefit as much. Your mind goes back to its original state even more quickly than the body.

To practise mindfulness on a daily basis can involve sitting still and feeling the sensation of your breathing, or doing some yoga, or simply sitting out in your garden and looking at the trees and birds with a warm drink before starting work.

Here are some ways to ensure that you remember to be mindful everyday:

✔ Practise at the same time and place every day. This way the mindfulness discipline becomes a routine like brushing your teeth and you don't have to think about it.

✔ Don't push yourself too much. If ten minutes seems too long, just do whatever you can manage. You can gradually build up the time you practise.

✔ Put reminders on your mirror, refrigerator, computer or phone. When you see the reminder, do a little meditation.

Connect with People

In the first instant that you meet someone, within a split second, you judge her. You may think that she's too fat or too thin, you don't like her hairstyle, she reminds you of someone you don't like. Your mind instantly tries to categorise, which is why first impressions are so important in interviews. The moment you make an initial judgement of a person, you begin to look for evidence to support your theory. If she doesn't look you in the eye properly, or fails to say thanks, you take these moments as evidence about her, and your opinion becomes more fixed. Then you create an image in your mind. You think that you know this other person, when all you know are your own judgements of her.

When you meet someone, connect with your senses rather than your ideas. Look the person in the eye in a natural way. Listen to what she has to say, rather than thinking about what you're about to say. Be curious and ask questions rather than imposing your own perceptions so much. See things from the other person's point of view – what would you be like in that person's situation? How would you feel, and what would you want?

Mindfulness is about paying attention with a sense of warmth and kindness, as well as a sense of curiosity and openness. Bring these attitudes to the relationship and see what happens.

Enjoy the Beauty of Nature

Nature has a way of drawing a mindful awareness from you, rather than you forcing yourself to be mindful. Walking amongst old trees with their branches overhanging the path you're treading, smelling the scent of freshly cut grass, listening to the birds sing and the twigs crunching under your feet, you can't help but be aware in the moment. Gardening is also a wonderful way of connecting with nature and experiencing 'flow' (explained in Chapter 5); absorbing yourself in tasks such as weeding and planting and enjoying the fruits of your labours as you see tiny shoots grow into beautiful plants and flowers.

If you have a garden or live near a park or a bit of greenery, realise how fortunate you are. Take time to reconnect with mother nature – make time for doing so. Nature is a miraculous, living being and you're part of that life. As a child you may have loved to play in natural surroundings, jumping in puddles and sliding in mud. With your acute senses, perhaps you were quite happy to explore and observe all day long if permitted. Try reconnecting with a child-like innocence and visit a natural environment, whatever that means to you.

In a famous study in a care home, half the elderly folk were given a plant to look after themselves, and the other half were given a plant but told that the nurses would look after it. Those who had responsibility to water and nurture the plants lived significantly longer than the others. The study concluded that responsibility gave the elderly a sense of control, leading to longer life. The study also suggests that not only looking at nature in a passive way, but also growing plants and ensuring that they thrive as best you can is a healthy and life-enhancing activity to engage in on a regular basis.

Enjoy the Journey

Mindfulness meditation goes way beyond the meditation cushion. You can spend every moment of your day practising mindfulness. Mindful walking, sometimes called *walking meditation*, is a particularly helpful and enjoyable exercise. When I teach mindful walking, I usually take the group to a local park, but you can engage in mindful walking pretty much any time you walk.

Normally, when you're walking, you're probably focusing intently on getting wherever you need to go or you're thinking about something else, which means you're not in the present moment. Walking meditation is about noticing your walking. Feel your feet on the ground as you walk. Try slowing down a little. Notice the rate and depth of your breathing. Be mindful as your arms swing naturally, which is a clever way of ensuring that your body is balanced as you walk. Become aware of your body as a whole as you walk, and the contact of your skin with the wind. Observe the different sounds around you and how your mind categorises them into 'I like' and 'I don't like'. Become aware of your emotions and thoughts, without trying to stop or change them in any way – just observe and absorb. Get a sense of both stepping back from your experience and deepening your connection with your experience at the same time.

Chapter 6 has a more detailed walking meditation.

See the Wonder of the Present Moment

Yesterday is history, tomorrow a mystery, today is a gift, that's why it's called the present.

This moment is the *only moment* you have and you have it right now. Memories of the past come up in the present moment. Ideas of the future are shaped by past experience and projected into an imagined tomorrow. In reality, this present moment is all that's available.

If you're currently going through a difficult time, you probably don't think the present moment is wonderful at all. That's okay. You can remember that you don't have to worry too much about the future, and only need to cope with whatever you're facing here and now. In this sense, being in the present moment is helpful – you don't need to worry about the future.

To really appreciate the present moment, feel your senses. Connect with your sense of sight. Notice the range of different colours in front of you. Reflect on the fact that this experience of colour is partly due to a rapid amount of biochemical reactions turning into electrical impulses going into your brain, leading to this incredible experience called colour. What would it be like to see colour for the first time? How would you describe the experience to someone who'd never seen colour before? Try looking without naming objects or people – just connect with the bare awareness of light itself. Be grateful you have eyes that are able to see in the first place. Look with the effortless gaze of a child.

Another way to really connect with the present is to focus on your breathing. Think these words while breathing in and out, if you find them helpful:

- Breathing in: *I am in the present moment.*
- Breathing out: *This is a wonderful moment.*

Listen to Unpleasant Emotions

How do you see the wonder of the present moment if you feel down, upset or annoyed? In these situations, don't try to impose a different emotion on what you're experiencing. Be in the present moment and open up the emotion as best you can. Remember that all emotions have a beginning and an end – try seeing the feeling as a temporary visitor. Additionally, see yourself as separate from the emotion. The emotion rises and falls but you maintain a sense of stability and greater emotional balance.

Imagine someone turns up at your front door and rings the doorbell. You decide to ignore the sound. The bell rings again and again. You get frustrated and try all sorts of ways of distracting yourself from the sound of the doorbell, but you can't. By simply opening the door and meeting the person ringing the bell, you can stop all your avoidance strategies. You're facing your fears. You're looking towards the unpleasant emotions rather than running away (which is an understandable response).

Moving towards the emotion, without forcing it to go away, often has the effect of dissipating the emotion. The emotion comes in, has a cup of tea or whatever, and off it goes. The emotion just wanted some mindful awareness. The idea is to offer just that – becoming aware of the emotions you spend so much time running away from with a kind, curious, open, non-judgemental awareness, as best you can. Explore and discover what effect this has on negative emotions in the long run, not to get rid of them, but to learn from them.

Chapters 12 and 13 are all about how mindfulness can help you deal with unpleasant emotions.

Remember That Thoughts Aren't Facts

If you had the thought, 'I'm a flying, pink chimpanzee', you obviously wouldn't believe it. That's a crazy idea. Then why do you believe thoughts like 'I'm useless' or 'I'll never get better' or 'I can't go on'? They're thoughts too, that have just popped into your head. Don't believe everything you think. Your mind often makes assumptions and inferences that simply aren't true. 'I'm feeling low at the moment' may be true, but 'I'll always be depressed' is not. 'I find it annoying when she doesn't do her chores' may be true, but 'She never helps me' is unlikely to be true.

As you discover how to observe the nature of your mind in meditation, you realise from experience that thoughts are always arising in your mind, no matter how much meditation you do. Even people who've been practising meditation for years have plenty of thoughts. The thoughts aren't going to stop. You simply need to change your relationship to thoughts. Seeing thoughts as just thoughts rather than facts makes a world of difference. If the thought 'I'm pathetic' comes up and you believe whatever arises in your mind, you're bound to feel low and uneasy. However, if exactly the same thought comes up and you're mindful of it, you see it as just a thought, and not a fact. This takes much of the sting out of the thought and you're free to dismiss it and carry on with whatever you're doing, relatively untouched. This is freedom. Freedom, or peace of mind, isn't about *stopping* your thoughts, but seeing thoughts as just thoughts and not giving them too much attention, and not believing them as reality. Reality is contained in the here and now, beyond ideas and concepts. You're not your mind – you're the observer, the silent witness, always complete, whole and free.

If you practise meditation regularly, you begin naturally to take a step back from your thinking. Normally, if you have a thought, you act on it, especially if you aren't fully conscious of the thought. In meditation, you observe the thought without acting on it. You see your thoughts as a pattern, as energy moving through your mind.

Be Grateful Every Day

Gratitude is the best attitude! Gratitude is when you discover how to want what you have, and not want what you don't have. Usually, people want what they don't have, and don't want what they do have. This is bound to lead to a sense of dissatisfaction. You can practise gratitude right now. Think about this book in your hand at the moment – millions of people in the world don't have a single book. Think about the fact that you can read – another skill inaccessible to millions.

Gratitude is an aspect of mindfulness. Mindfulness doesn't just mean concentrating, but an attention suffused with a warm, kind attitude. To be aware as you're cooking of how fortunate you are to have food available to you is to be mindful.

I find myself practising gratitude when I'm feeling a bit down, which is sometimes a sign that I'm focusing on things that aren't going well. Just reflecting for a moment and trying to think of five things I'm grateful for helps to put things into perspective.

Here are some ways to nurture feelings of gratitude:

- ✔ **Sleep with gratitude.** Before going to sleep, spend a minute or two thinking about five things you're grateful for. They can be very simple things, and you don't have to feel hugely grateful for them. Just go through each one and see what effect that has on your sleep.

- ✔ **Say thank you.** This is a simple act but very powerful. Saying thank you is both an act of gratitude and kindness – you're making clear to the other person that you've recognised her generosity.

✔ **Carry out an action to say thanks.** Send a 'thank you' card, a small gift or do something like making a coffee or helping someone out with her work. As the old saying goes, actions speak louder than words.

✔ **Try being grateful for things you wouldn't be normally.** For example, when things are difficult, you can be grateful for the challenge the difficulty offers. Be grateful for access to running water or your ability to hear. Or try being grateful for being alive in the first place – perhaps this is the greatest miracle.

Here's an extract from a wonderful poem by an unknown author on thanks and gratitude:

Be thankful that you don't already have everything you desire. If you did, what would there be to look forward to?

Be thankful when you don't know something, for it gives you the opportunity to learn.

Be thankful for the difficult times. During those times you grow.

Be thankful for your limitations, because they give you opportunities for improvement.

Be thankful for your mistakes. They will teach you valuable lessons.

Be thankful when you're tired and weary, because it means you've made a difference.

It's easy to be thankful for the good things.

A life of rich fulfilment comes to those who are also thankful for the setbacks.

Find a way to be thankful for your troubles, and they can become your blessings.

Let Go

Constant change is the nature of the universe. Can you think of a single object in the universe that doesn't change? Even stars and galaxies are in a state of change. If everything is changing, then trying to hold on to anything is bound to result in disappointment. The more you hold on to something, the greater the disappointment when it's lost. The antidote to this holding on, this attachment, is to let go.

How do you let go? If you were holding a ball in your hand, and I asked you to let go, you'd just let go. However, if you don't know that the ball is in your hand, that's different. You can't let go of something you're not aware of.

Letting go happens more naturally when you're aware. You may be walking around all day with tension in your shoulders, but if you're not aware of it, the tension will probably stay there. As soon as you become aware of the tension, some of the tightness *may* release. Other tension may stay there, but don't try hard to let go – this only leads to more doing and more tension. You're making letting go into a goal. In this case, just let the tension be there – let it be.

Forgiveness is another way of letting go. When you forgive you're letting go of past hurt and pain. By forgiving others, you're freeing yourself more than anyone else. Forgiveness is for you.

Breathe and Smile!

The muscles in your face link with your feeling of happiness. When you're happy, you smile – you know that of course. But did you know that smiling can make you feel better? Try the process right now, no matter how you feel. Simply hold a subtle, gentle smile as you read these sentences. Continue for a few minutes and note what effect the smiling has. Combine this with feeling your own breathing.

You can apply this technique of feeling your breathing and smiling gently in a systematic way every day for ten minutes, or while you're going about your daily activities. In this way you can be mindful doing whatever you're doing, whether washing the dishes, writing a report or waiting in a queue. Each moment is a opportunity to come back to the here and now, the present moment. You don't need anything extra – your breath and smile are both highly portable!

You may feel reluctant to smile right now because you don't think that it's genuine. You'll smile when you're happy, not now. All I can say is, try it out. Yes, you're bound to feel unnatural at the beginning but that soon goes. Just give it a try, even though it feels strange, and see what happens after a time. As someone said to me once: 'Fake it till you make it!'

Mindfulness is not about forcing your yourself to feel better – it's more about bringing a sense of curiosity to your feelings and thoughts and gaining information from them, whatever you're experiencing. Being aware of thoughts or feelings is far more important than trying to *change* your thoughts or feelings.

Chapter 17

Ten Ways Mindfulness Can Really Help You

. . . .

In This Chapter

▶ Dealing with pain and stress

▶ Improving relationships – including with yourself

▶ Feeling happier and more creative

. . . .

Mindfulness provides a plethora of pleasures that I hope you'll experience for yourself. As soon as you start being mindful on a regular basis you'll find mindfulness quite addictive! In this chapter I give you a snapshot of the benefits of mindfulness, many of which are backed up by scientific research.

Training the Brain

Until fairly recently, scientists thought that the connections and structure of the adult brain were fixed, because changing the brain's connections would be far too complex to do.

Now we know the truth – your brain *can* change! Scientists looked at violinists' brains, and found that the part of the brain responsible for finger dexterity was much bigger compared to non-violinists. They also studied London taxi drivers, who need to know all the complex road networks and 10,000 different streets in London ('the knowledge') . When scientists compared the cabbies' brains to 'normal' brains, they found the part responsible for location was significantly *bigger*. The longer the drivers worked, the more significant the change.

The evidence proves that through training and simple everyday experience, the physical brain actually changes. Repetitive experience changes the brain more than anything else. The discovery that the brain changes in response to experience is now called *neuroplasticity* and it gives everyone tremendous hope – you can *change your brain* through training at any age!

With the help of the Dalai Lama, top neuroscientist Professor Richard Davidson scanned the brains of meditating monks who'd engaged in prolonged meditation for a minimum of 10,000 hours (not all in one go!). The meditation they did was a compassion meditation, similar to the metta meditation described in Chapter 6. The monks' brains totally changed through the practice of this meditation. The front left part of the brain (left prefrontal cortex if you're really curious) associated with positivity was activated – in fact, it went off the scale! No scientist had ever seen so much positive effect in a human being before. The scientists found that the monks' entire brains had been rewired to be more positive. This proves that mindfulness and compassion aren't fixed, but are skills that you can train in.

Okay, monks' brains become more positive because they spend most of their time meditating. But what about you and me? We don't have time to meditate for that long – can short lengths of time meditating mindfully help? Does the brain improve after, say, 30 minutes a day for two weeks?

The incredible answer is yes. Scientists have also looked at short-term mindfulness meditation. People were randomly assigned to two groups. One group trained in cognitive behavioural therapy to show them how to see challenges in their lives with greater positivity. The other group was trained in metta (mindful loving kindness) meditation. Some of those in the metta group had greater activation in the brain region signifying positivity and also reported greater love for themselves, compared to the cognitive behavioural therapy group. Helpful changes did indeed happen within a fortnight of practice.

So mindfulness meditation does change the brain, and the more you practise, the greater the positive change within your brain. One more reason to pop in that CD in this book and start meditating!

Improving Relationships

Several studies show that people's relationships tend to improve when they begin to practise mindfulness meditation. Several reasons indicate why this may be the case.

Mindfulness can switch off stress. When you feel threatened by a nasty remark, or overly challenged at work or home, your body and mind engage in a stress response. You become less understanding and more reactive and judgemental. Obviously, this can have a detrimental effect on personal relationships. You may snap easily when your partner asks what's wrong, or respond emotionally when you come home to realise that dinner hasn't been cooked. Mindfulness makes you more relaxed in your day-to-day life, making you less likely to react unhelpfully.

Mindfulness develops your capacity to accept your experience from moment to moment. This accepting stance translates itself into improved relationships with others. In knowing how to be more accepting of another person's faults (nobody's perfect!), you're more likely to develop greater understanding, and increase the possibility of noticing people's positive qualities.

Being judgemental isn't the greatest relationship booster in the world. However, research shows that meditators are less judgemental and more focused in the moment, even when they're not meditating. This may explain why your relationships improve once you start meditating – you're connecting with what other people say rather than wasting your energy judging them.

Mindfulness leads to higher levels of empathy and compassion for both yourself and others. A more caring attitude naturally leads you to give greater levels of attention and helps you to see from other people's perspective. Ultimately, a feeling of love is at the heart of any meaningful relationship, and, as love grows in meditation, the quality of relationships naturally deepens.

Boosting Creativity

Your creativity depends entirely on your state of mind. You can't expect to have exciting and perceptive ideas if your mind is overworked and jam-packed with opinions and points of view. Creativity requires letting go of the old to make way for the new. Mindfulness meditation is about being aware of your thoughts without judging them; this lack of judgement allows new and unique ways of thinking to arise. In most creativity exercises, the emphasis is always to stop judging ideas and just let them flow – in a mindfulness practice called choiceless awareness, described in Chapter 6, you do exactly the same thing.

Mindfulness, over the long term, leads to a calmer state of mind. When the conscious mind settles down, you begin to access the immense creative capacity and knowledge of the subconscious mind. You normally only access this creativity when sleeping, which is almost totally out of your control. With meditation, the creative ideas that arise are more practical. Most of my good ideas have arisen while meditating. By giving my mind the opportunity and space just to be, I tap into my creativity, accessing idea after idea.

Reducing Depression

Some types of depression are thought to be caused by repetitive negative thinking patterns (rumination) and avoiding uncomfortable thoughts and feelings rather than facing up to them (experiential avoidance). Mindfulness, as part of mindfulness-based cognitive therapy explained in Chapter 13, helps combat depression in several ways. Mindfulness:

✔ **Develops your capacity to stay with, experience and face difficult experiences and emotions instead of avoiding them.** Avoiding difficult emotions has been found to be the key way in which relapsing into depression occurs. You can gradually develop an attitude of acceptance, kindness and curiosity towards experience through regularly practising mindfulness, enabling a healthier approach towards emotions.

✔ **Shifts you towards a 'being mode' of mind.** This being mode (described in full in Chapter 5) enables you to witness your depression as something that rises and falls within you, rather than as a core part of who you are. You can step back from your internal experience in a beneficial way and see things from a bigger perspective. This shift in perspective helps to prevent you from seeing the depression as something that'll never end, changing the idea 'I'm depressed' to 'The feeling of depression is here at the moment, but not forever. All feelings have a beginning and an end.'

✔ **Helps you to understand the patterns of the mind.** Being mindful helps you to see how your mind easily goes into an unaware 'automatic pilot' mode, which leads to negative thinking cycles, leading to further depression. Becoming aware of these habits of mind is the first step to beginning to see them in a different perspective and thereby reducing their potency.

✔ **Develops healthier habits of mind.** Depression is deepened through rumination. Mindfulness disables this negative thinking cycle by encouraging you to connect your attention to the present moment. This focus reduces the inner resources devoted to rumination. As mindfulness develops into a habit, when mild feelings of sadness arise, your likely response is to focus on the sensations in your body, rather than spiralling into major depression.

Turn to Chapter 13 for much more on combating depression with mindfulness.

Reducing Chronic Pain

Incredible as it sounds, mindfulness can actually reduce chronic pain. Participation in Dr Jon Kabat-Zinn's mindfulness-based stress reduction

(MBSR) programme has shown, in several research studies, the benefits of mindfulness for those suffering from chronic pain.

In one study, 90 patients suffering chronic pain were trained in mindfulness meditation for ten weeks. Experts observed a significant reduction in pain, negative body image, negative moods, anxiety and depression. The patients also engaged in more activity, including everyday activity such as preparing food and driving, which they'd struggled with before. The use of pain-reduction drugs decreased and feelings of self-esteem increased. These patients did much better than a group that underwent normal pain-management programmes.

The most exciting aspect was the result of a follow-up four years later. The majority of the chronic pain patients reported that most of their improvements had lasted, or even improved further. This was probably due to the fact that, incredibly, over 90 per cent of the participants continued to practise some form of mindfulness meditation. This is a major achievement, considering they'd trained four years previously.

All these positive benefits may be partly due to the way mindfulness can train you to accept difficult bodily sensations instead of trying to resist them or pretending the discomfort isn't there. Paradoxically, acceptance seems to reduce the pain. You discover how to feel the pain and experience it as a moment-to-moment feeling rather than avoiding it and tensing up your muscles. You can help the muscles around the painful region relax, thereby reducing the pain itself.

Giving Deeper Meaning to Life

Before I started practising meditation, I found life rather hollow and empty. I had friends and family, a comfortable place to live and a good career, but something was definitely missing. Life was a bit of a grind, and lacked zest and vitality. I still remember the first meditation class I attended. The teacher calmly talked about the nature of awareness, and how, through regular practice, you can become more aware. This need for awareness resonated with me – the whole thing made sense. However, I lacked discipline to begin with, and discovered a lack of a regular meditation routine didn't really work. With further practice, many wonderful teachers and good fortune, I was able to deepen my meditation. The practice of meditation itself became a driving force for a more meaningful and authentic life.

When you've touched a sense of deep peace and calmness within yourself, you no longer ask what the meaning or purpose of life is. You're clear in your own mind that peace, kindness, empathy and joy are available to be cultivated in your own being. You know that the suffering, pain and sorrow in the world is partly a reflection of humanity's inability to tap into this inner source of nourishment. You see how your low moods and frustrations are partly due to seeing things from the wrong perspective. Then you know that your purpose is to access your own inner resources as often and as deeply as possible, not just for yourself, but for the sake of everyone around you. Wellbeing is contagious.

Reducing Stress

Mindfulness can reduce stress. One key way is by becoming aware of the underlying thoughts, ideas and attitudes towards a particular situation. In doing so, you create the possibility of naturally changing your response to the stressful situation. Responding to stress appropriately is an important way of reducing stress.

Dr Richard Lazarus, world-famous stress researcher and psychologist, defined stress as 'a particular relationship between the person and the environment that is *appraised* by the person as taxing or exceeding his or her resources and endangering his or her wellbeing'. I like his insight. The definition explains how an event may be stressful for you, but not for someone else – the level of stress experienced depends on whether you see the situation (the stressor) as something you can cope with or not.

Mindfulness reduces stress in many ways and at many different levels. For example, say your boss has a tendency to lose his cool easily and shouts at you often, even though you're doing your best. How would mindfulness help? Well, first of all, by being more mindful you'd notice the fact that you're stressed. You may feel your jaw tightening or your shoulders hunching before you've even got to work, but through your mindful attention you may loosen them. Then when your boss shouts at you, you're more aware of the choices you have. You know what effect saying nothing, reacting with insults, or storming out would have. All these reactions are automatic and sometimes lead to more harm than good. The very fact of being aware of your reactions, changes them. You naturally begin to move from *reacting* to negative events, to *responding* with greater wisdom. You begin to think more creatively, which may include behaving more assertively, or looking to work in a different department or workplace.

Secondly, through regular practice of mindfulness meditation, you give your body and mind a rest. Instead of spending your time doing and achieving this and that, you provide a space for yourself to simply be. This 'being' mode is tremendously nourishing and uplifts your inner resources for relaxing rather than stressing out.

Thirdly, you begin to see things from a different perspective. Although your car isn't starting this morning, at least it gives you a chance for a cup of tea while you wait for a mechanic. Even though there's a big queue at the bank, at least you have enough money to live on, unlike many unfortunate people. You may even use the opportunity to practise mindfulness as you wait in the queue.

Combating Anxiety

Everyone experiences feelings of anxiety in their lives, perhaps before an interview or an exam. However, if you suffer from a generalised anxiety disorder, the feeling becomes a part of your day-to-day existence. Anxiety can significantly disrupt activities you found easy in the past.

Anxiety and worry are based on thinking about the future. You may be concerned about what will happen later, next month, or next year. Your mind drifts into predicting negative future outcomes and thereby generates challenging emotions. Mindfulness counteracts this by encouraging you to live in the here and now, from moment to moment and non-judgementally. You begin to free yourself from your dangerously drifting mind and allow yourself to emerge in the sensory world of the present.

 Mindfulness enables you to step back from the contents of your mind and emotions. You discover how to identify less with the thoughts going through your mind, and realise that they're just thoughts, rather than facts. This enables your thoughts to lose their power, which therefore reduces the anxiety.

Surprisingly, research has found that *trying* to stop worrying increases the worry. Through being more mindful, you change your *relationship* to thoughts, being more compassionate and accepting of them rather than trying to eliminate them. This mindful approach seems to be far more effective than trying to prevent worrying thoughts completely. Read Chapter 13 for more about using mindfulness to combat anxiety.

Regulating Eating Habits

Are you aware of what you eat? Do you taste each mouthful and chew it thoroughly before swallowing? Do you give your attention to what you're eating, or do you distract yourself with television, newspapers or books? Do you use food as a way of coping with unpleasant emotions?

If you feel empty inside, you may eat to help try to fill that space. Or every time you're worried, you may grab a bar of chocolate. Perhaps stress drives you to open the fridge door, or makes you limit your food to feel more in control. Mindfulness offers a different way of regulating and coping with your difficult and uncomfortable emotions rather than by eating, or avoiding eating.

 Mindful eating is about becoming more aware of the process of preparing and eating food, being less judgemental and more accepting of your current eating habits. Mindful eating also includes being aware of the messages your body sends to you, and using that awareness to determine how much or little to eat. Through this increased awareness, you can choose what to eat and what not to eat from a wiser state of mind. You're able to savour the taste of the food, and enjoy the process of eating. With awareness you're more likely to be in touch with physical hunger and able to notice when you've eaten sufficiently. So mindful eating can even help you maintain a healthy weight!

Increasing Your Happiness

Everybody wants to be happy. All your actions can be explained as your personal desire for greater happiness. The question is, what's the best way to increase happiness? It turns out that simply trying to think positive doesn't work – you need to engage in something regularly that uplifts your sense of wellbeing in a more authentic way.

Positive psychologists, scientists that study happiness, think that mindfulness is the answer. Mindfulness seems to train the brain to naturally become more positive, and increases resilience. Resilience is the capacity to cope with stress and catastrophe in a healthy way. It ensures that you bounce back to your happy self sooner rather than later following difficulties. It also strengthens your capacity to cope with difficulties in the future. Regular mindfulness exercises change the very structure of your brain, helping to increase your resilience in difficult times.

Through practising mindfulness on a regular basis, you also begin to discover that happiness is an inside job. You can have all the money and power in the world, but if your thoughts are very negative, and you believe your thoughts to be true, you're not going to be happy. Conversely, you can have very few possessions, but if your mind is naturally open, receptive and positive, having practised mindfulness daily, you're bound to experience a deeper sense of wellbeing.

Chapter 18

Ten Mindfulness Myths to Expose

*W*hen I told a friend of mine that I teach mindfulness, he said, 'I don't think that's for me – my mind's full enough already, buddy!' Mindfulness isn't about filling up the mind of course. Mindfulness isn't just meditation either. If you want to ensure that you've got the right idea about mindfulness, check out this chapter and do some 'mind emptying' – take this opportunity to root out any wrong ideas you may have about the ancient and modern science and art of mindfulness.

Mindfulness Is All about the Mind

You may have heard the quip, 'What is mind? Doesn't matter. What is matter? Never mind!'

As a human being you have the capacity to think. In fact, you can't help but think. Thinking seems to happen whether you like it or not. Thinking is almost like breathing, and probably happens more frequently. Some experts estimate humans think up to 60,000 thoughts a day! Mindfulness isn't all about the mind; it takes a step back from thinking rather than stops thinking.

Mindfulness can more appropriately be called *heartfulness*. In ancient Eastern languages like Sanskrit or Pali, the words for mind and heart are the same, so perhaps the word 'mindfulness' is a little misleading. What does heart-fulness mean? If you have an open, warm heart you may be: kind, gentle, caring, accepting, understanding, patient, trusting, joyful, honest, grateful, light-hearted, loving and humble. Perhaps you're not all of those things, but I share those words to express the spirit of mindfulness with you. The idea is to bring one or more heart qualities to your mindful awareness. Naturally, you can't bring *all* of them in at the same time, but you can get a sense of the kind of attitude to bring to your awareness.

Mindfulness isn't a cold, harsh awareness. A thief needs to be attentive when planning to steal something, but that isn't mindfulness. Mindfulness has a sense of kindness as well as curiosity about it.

If, when you're being mindful, you sense you're being critical, struggling a lot and being unkind to yourself or you think that your attention doesn't have a warmth about it, don't beat yourself up about it. You'll end up frustrated. Simply be aware of whatever you're being mindful of, and in its own time some kindness will naturally grow. You don't need to force things too much – the less you force things, the better.

Some people think that mindfulness means you need to think about whatever you're focusing on. This isn't quite right. If you're being mindful of your breathing, this means you're feeling the sensation of the breathing in your body – you're not trying to think about the breathing.

Mindfulness Is the Latest Fad

Mindfulness is at least 2,500 years old, if not older. Mindfulness was refined mainly in the East, but aspects of it appear in many traditions, religions, cultures and philosophies.

Awareness is a natural aspect of being human. Paying attention is something very natural that you 'do' everyday. Awareness is so normal and natural, you can easily overlook it. Attention is right here, right now, as you read this sentence. Mindfulness is based on just that – paying attention with certain attitudes to help develop the quality of your attention. So, it doesn't really make sense to consider mindfulness as a fad.

Mindfulness is rapidly growing in popularity in the West. Therapists are training in mindfulness, more hospitals are offering mindfulness to their patients, and various schools are beginning to integrate mindfulness to improve the children's sense of wellbeing. If you don't fully understand what mindfulness is, and use mindfulness as a tool here and there, it may appear to be a technique you find helpful until some other idea comes along. But for millions of people all over the world, mindfulness is a way of living and something to be nurtured, developed and deepened throughout their lives.

Mindfulness is fundamental to everyday existence. The greater the level of your awareness, the more you're alive, in a sense. Being unaware from day to day, living on automatic pilot, is almost like being the walking dead – you're not connecting to your senses and what it means to be alive.

A fad is something that works for a short time, and is then given up. Mindfulness has been proven to work over thousands of years and isn't going to die away!

Mindfulness Is Positive Thinking

You can interpret all situations in a positive or negative way but it's helpful to regard situations optimistically rather than always expecting the worst. Through your regular practice of mindfulness you become more aware of your own thought patterns, both negative and positive. When negative thoughts arise, mindfulness helps you to recognise your own habitual reactions. You may try seeing the situation differently, whether positively or more realistically, and see what effect that has. Mindfulness doesn't tie you into any positive thinking rules – you just bring a sense of curiosity to the experience.

I don't recommend fighting with negative thoughts. Battling with your own mind creates a struggle and you can end up increasing the level of negativity in yourself. The more you fight a thought, the stronger the thought becomes.

Ultimately mindfulness takes a step back from all thoughts, both negative and positive. Thoughts are thoughts, not facts. You can't control thought completely – all you can do is watch, take a step back, and stop reacting to your thoughts. The more you can do that, the more you feel in control and the less you feel helpless and stressed. Chapter 5 has more about detaching yourself from thoughts.

Mindfulness Is Only for Buddhists

Buddhists don't have the exclusive rights to mindfulness. Mindfulness, or a mindful awareness, is a universal human attribute and skill, a fundamental quality of being alive, just like eyes, ears and a stomach are part of a human body. To be mindful is to be aware, and awareness is not and cannot be attributed to any one religion.

However, mindfulness *was* investigated and developed by Buddha and followers of Buddha. Therefore, if you want, you can read and study more about mindfulness in Buddhist texts, no matter what your religious beliefs. You can also find out about mindfulness in several other religions and philosophies such as Hinduism, Taoism, Advaita, Sufism and many more. However, you find out far more by just being mindful yourself and exploring and learning through your own experience.

As one modern sage, Nisargadatta, said 'The greatest Guru is your inner self.' Even the Buddha often said, 'Don't simply believe what I am saying – find out for yourself in your own experience.'

Mindfulness isn't a religion or belief system. If anything, mindfulness points towards an approach to living. The mission of the Center for Mindfulness in Massachusetts is simply 'an awakened and compassionate world'. If you really want a goal for your mindfulness practice, I think that to become more awakened and compassionate is a good one.

If you're religious and look deeply into your own faith, you're likely to find some way or system to strengthen the capacity to let go of conceptual thinking and train your quality of attention. So, you don't need to change your religion to find mindfulness a meaningful discipline. To be mindful is to develop the innate human capacity to be aware – you can be of any faith or no faith at all and be mindful.

Mindfulness Is Only for Tough Times

Mindfulness is used to alleviate depression, chronic pain, anxiety, addiction relapse, stress, and high blood pressure, and even to manage the stress and treatment of cancer. Initial results in these areas are very encouraging and the application of mindfulness is sure to develop along with all the other treatments. However, mindfulness isn't only for the hard times. Consider this: you can't just start saving money in a recession. You need to save money in the good times too, so when things are really difficult you have some cash to help you out. In fact, saving money is much easier and more effective when times are good. In the same way, you can benefit by developing your mindfulness discipline when things are going relatively well. When the going gets tough, you can naturally bring your mindfulness skills to the challenge, and dip into your inner resources to help you cope.

When I first began meditation, partly for managing stress, I never understood the far-reaching effect of the practice. For example, I used to struggle if I had to speak to more than a small group of people; now I'm lucky enough to feel confident to be able to deliver lectures to hundreds of people. This isn't so much due to my own courage, but to the power of mindfulness. Although your meditation may be used to fix a problem to start with, if you persevere, the meditation goes on to nurture all sorts of different areas of your life.

As you begin to understand and practise meditation, you notice benefits. At this stage, some people stop practising. Life seems to be going well, you've resolved the issues, and you kind of forget about the meditation . . . until the next disaster strikes! And then you reach out for help again. Coming and going to and from meditation is part of the natural process, but in the end you come to realise that without a daily discipline, your life is a bit of a roller-coaster. The meditation makes the ride that little bit smoother.

Mindfulness Is a Set of Techniques

A technique is usually a quick method of achieving a certain outcome, like counting to ten to help calm you down when you feel angry. You may have a certain technique for hitting a golf ball, or a technique for reducing conflict in a conversation. Techniques are great for achieving certain results, but they have their limitations too. If you get too stuck on one technique, you can't branch out to new ways of doing things. Sometimes you may get defensive about your particular technique and become actively unwilling to try something different – in this way, techniques can stifle development.

Mindfulness isn't a technique because fundamentally mindfulness isn't goal-oriented. This is quite a difficult concept to grasp because you're probably used to doing things to achieve something. Why would you bother doing something to achieve, ultimately, nothing? Mindfulness has benefits but if you practise to achieve a particular outcome, you limit its potency. A good scientist does an experiment without forcing a certain outcome – all the scientist wants to do is find the truth of the situation by observing the outcome. If the scientist is looking for a particular outcome, perhaps if the experiment is sponsored by a drug company, you're wary of the results as they may be biased. In the same way, if you look for a certain outcome with mindfulness, you're being biased and not really trying the mindfulness wholeheartedly.

Mindful awareness is about being aware of your inner and outer experience, *whatever that experience is.*

Paradoxically, mindfulness underlies and enhances the quality of all other techniques. Without awareness you can't use a technique. The less aware you are, the less likely it is that whatever technique you're using will work. For example, if you use a technique to reduce stress by letting go of negative thinking, but you're not really aware of your thoughts, how do you hope to succeed?

This book does contain lots of tips and techniques to encourage mindfulness, but ultimately, mindfulness itself isn't a technique.

Mindfulness is about letting go of doing. It is about simply being as you are. Being yourself, whatever you think of yourself. Being yourself isn't a technique. You can't *do* non-doing. Non-doing means letting go of all techniques with their desired outcomes and just *being*.

Mindfulness Isn't for Me

Some people may not be keen on meditation, perhaps due to misconceptions and stereotypical views about the practice. Mindfulness doesn't even have to be connected with the typical picture of a meditator: someone sitting cross-legged, perhaps burning incense, aimlessly navel-gazing for some future spiritual high. But mindfulness is for anyone interested in becoming more aware, more awake, more alive, more connected. Although meditation is an extremely helpful way of developing greater mindfulness, you can also simply pay a bit more attention every time you go for a walk, or have a chat with your colleagues, or play sport. You may spend a few minutes feeling your breathing as you rest on the sofa before switching on the television. These are simple ways of waking up to your life, and letting go of automatic pilot. I don't know anyone who can't do with a greater dose of awareness.

You may think that you can't do mindfulness because you're too impatient, too stressy, or too anxious. But mindfulness develops your capacity to be patient, kind, attentive, calm and happy, so you may be the perfect person to try mindfulness! To say you're not patient enough to do mindfulness is like saying you're too unfit to exercise. If you don't exercise at all, you'll never be fit. However, take things easy to begin with – try a short, five-minute medita-tion every day and build from there. Or try some mindful walking for a few minutes. Go to Chapter 6 for ways to practise walking meditations.

Some people think that mindfulness is something weird to do with religion, or some cultish idea. Mindfulness is feeling your own breathing, or listening to the sounds around you, or really tasting the food in front of you. Mindfulness is another word for kindly awareness – nothing mysterious in that sense. You can make mindfulness whatever you want – there are no rules in this game. Some people practise mindfulness for spiritual or religious reasons, just as some people burn incense for religious reasons – that doesn't mean incense is for religious people only!

Mindfulness Meditation Is Relaxation

Relaxation exercises are often designed to loosen the muscles in your body, and the aim of relaxation is to become less tense. So relaxation has a clear goal and you have various methods for achieving it.

Mindfulness is ultimately goalless. You can't really say you had a 'good' medi-tation or a 'bad' meditation, because that would presuppose the kind of expe-riences you're supposed to have. Meditation is about experiencing whatever the content of experience is, from moment to moment. Your intention and attitudes behind the meditation are key. Meditation is about understanding and growing in wisdom by looking within.

Relaxation is often, but certainly not always, a very welcome side effect of meditation. However, when you first practise meditation, you may feel more tense by the end. When I first began to meditate, I was trying to do it well and my attention was overly intense. My body became tense trying to focus, as I tried in vain to force thoughts out. This led to more tension, but was part of the learning process.

Meditation can sometimes release deep-seated trapped emotions that your subconscious mind has hidden away and works hard at keeping out. The process can create more tension temporarily as you face your demons. However, the sooner you release the emotion, the better. As the emotion rises into your conscious mind, the feeling can dissolve, sometimes relaxing a part of the body that has been tense for years. (Chapter 10 has more about dealing with mindfulness bringing up painful emotions.)

Mindfulness Can Be Used Instead of Therapy or Medicine

Mindfulness certainly can't be used *instead of* therapy or medicine. If you suffer from a clinical condition, you need to follow your doctor's recommendations. However, *in addition to* medical advice, you can normally develop a mindfulness practice to support your healing process. Mindfulness helps to manage your stress levels, and can reduce your blood pressure and boost your body's immune function.

Doctors can refer patients to a mindfulness-based stress reduction (MBSR) course, empowering patients to take a more proactive part in looking after their own health and wellbeing though the application of mindfulness. This way of developing inner resources and enhancing resilience to stress has been found to be profoundly wholesome. Chapter 9 goes into more detail about MBSR.

Mindfulness Is Complicated and Boring

How you view mindfulness depends on the rules you create in your head about the process: meditation should be relaxing, enlightening; my mind should be blank; I should feel comfortable; I shouldn't feel emotional; if I don't do it every day I've failed; if it feels difficult I must be doing it wrong.

You need to be aware of the kind of rules you've created in your head about meditation. Any 'must', 'should' or 'ought' is the sign of a rigid rule laid down in your mind. As life has the tendency to flow wherever it wants to go, you find time and again your inner rules being broken and frustration and boredom arising.

Mindfulness is simple but not easy. The simple bit is that mindfulness is about being aware and paying attention. The not-so-easy bit is having the discipline to practise regularly and the ability to trust in the process, no matter how wild your mind appears to be.

Mindfulness has a sense of simple flow about it – doing less rather than more; thinking less rather than more; going with the flow of life rather than spending life wrestling with complications created by the mind.

Here's an example of the simplicity yet difficulty of mindfulness. Right now, if you're aware of the weight of this book in your hand, you're being mindful. If you walk out of the room you're in and feel your feet on the ground, you're being mindful. So mindfulness is simple. However, the difficult bit is overcoming your current habitual thought patterns, which have been strengthening for however long you've been on this planet, and are naturally very powerful. When you put this book down and walk off, notice how long it takes before you're lost in an ocean of thoughts, feelings, stories, frustrations and desires.

If you find meditating boring, you have a few choices:

- ✔ Reduce the length of time you meditate.

- ✔ Become curious about boredom.

- ✔ Let the feeling of boredom go, and re-focus on the present moment again and again.

- ✔ Accept the boredom as part and parcel of life and keep meditating – the boredom will soon pass.

Ultimately, no matter how much trouble you have being mindful, and no matter how confused or bored you may be occasionally, you have a deep and powerful aspect of yourself that nothing can ever touch. Awareness is a mysterious aspect of being human that remains beyond the understanding of science. Awareness is always there, at the root of your being, ever shining, ever knowing. Even when you were lost in thought or caught up in the darkest, most frightening emotion or situation, you were aware, at some level, of what was going on, both inside and outside of yourself.

Chapter 19

Ten Paths to Further Study

. . . .

In This Chapter

▶ Tracking down mindfulness courses

▶ Discovering respected mindfulness organisations and books

▶ Finding suitable retreat centres

▶ Exploring useful websites

. . . .

So, you've begun the exciting journey into mindfulness and want to find out more. Well, you're in luck. Mindfulness is a hot topic, and you can find all sorts of different resources to support your mindfulness practice. Browse through this chapter to see if anything catches your eye.

Websites

You can find out just about everything you need to know about mindfulness on the Internet. The problem is there are so many different websites, it's hard to know where to start. Here are a few to help you to begin mindfully exploring.

Learn Mindfulness

I run an organisation called Learn Mindfulness that offers training in mindfulness for individuals, groups and organisations internationally. My mindfulness courses (as well as an eight-week, mindfulness-based stress reduction course developed by Jon Kabat-Zinn, explained in Chapter 9) are offered online, via telephone and in person, and provide ongoing support.

Visit www.learn-mindfulness.com for training and free resources, including:

- ✔ **Online videos** of lectures on mindfulness
- ✔ **Online guided mindfulness meditations**
- ✔ **Monthly email newsletters**

If you're on Facebook, have a look at the online community created to support and inform the readers of this book with quotations, tips, offers and free resources that I put on regularly. You can share your experiences of and insights into mindfulness, ask questions, or simply join up to feel part of a helpful, mindful community. It's a great way to remind yourself to be mindful too. See www.facebook.com/mindfulnessfordummies.

Insight Meditation Society

The website www.dharma.org is home to the Insight Meditation Society that runs two retreat centres in the United States. The website offers an audio introduction to meditation, a large selection of talks on mindfulness, links to many retreat centres all over the world, a suggested reading list and much more.

Books, CDs and Films

I recommend that you continue to nourish your mindfulness practice with a range of different writers to help deepen your understanding of yourself. Here are some resources that I have enjoyed and still do.

Full Catastrophe Living

This book by Jon Kabat-Zinn (published by Piatkus) is an excellent, detailed guide to the eight-week, mindfulness-based stress reduction course that Kabat-Zinn developed (described in Chapter 9).

Kabat-Zinn has taught mindfulness to thousands of people at the University of Massachusetts Medical Center. Because the mind plays such a big role in stress-related illness, the 500 pages of the book cover huge areas often overlooked in other texts.

Grounded in scientific research, Jon Kabat-Zinn explores the connections between mind and body. Ultimately, through reading the book, you come to realise that no obvious division exists between mind and body. The exercises and suggestions he offers are easy to understand. Although the book is aimed at those suffering from chronic illness, everyone can benefit from the advice and live life more fully.

Peace Is Every Step

Thich Nhat Hanh (pronounced Tik N'yat Hawn) is a Vietnamese Zen Buddhist monk, poet, scholar and peace activist. Nhat Hanh has written many books, and I particularly enjoyed reading this one (published by Rider). He begins the book with:

> *Every day, when we wake up, we have twenty-four brand new hours to live. What a precious gift! We have the capacity to live in a way that these twenty-four hours will bring peace, joy and happiness to ourselves and others.*

Thich Nhat Hanh is probably one of the world's most famous teachers of mindfulness. Because of his lifelong commitment and efforts for peace in Vietnam, he was nominated for the Nobel Peace Prize in 1967 by Martin Luther King, Jr.

You can find many gems in this book to help transform your daily life into conscious awareness with gratitude in what you do. The simplicity and poetry of his words are a joy to read. The book is in short sections that you can read in a few minutes and then reflect on. The book is ideal to read before or after meditating to set you up for the day.

Everything is connected

Part of the purpose of mindfulness, according to Thich Nhat Hanh, is to see how you're interconnected with everything else, and not a separate entity that exists in isolation. This *interbeing* leads to a sense of peace and well-being and reduces feelings like anger and frustration. You come to see that if you're angry towards another person, you're in a way being angry towards yourself. If you're hammering a nail into a piece of wood and accidentally hit your left hand with the hammer in your right hand, your left and right hand don't start fighting each other! On the contrary, your right hand would care and soothe the pain in the left hand because the two hands are one. In the same way, if you begin to see how you're interconnected with everything else, you experience a greater compassion (one of the most positive emotions you can have) and respect for things and people around you.

The Mindful Way Through Depression

The Mindful Way Through Depression is written by Mark Williams, John Teasdale, Zindel Segal and Jon Kabat-Zinn – all top scientists in their respective fields. The authors were the first to develop mindfulness-based cognitive therapy, which is now used to prevent depressive relapse and which the National Institute of Health and Clinical Excellence in the UK recommends for those who've suffered from three or more episodes of clinical depression in their lives.

The book is full of techniques for managing depression with mindfulness, as well as core mindfulness meditations as offered on a typical course. The book also contains lots of stories showing the practical application of mindfulness in people's lives. The book includes an excellent accompanying CD with mindfulness meditations. If you suffer from depression, the book is a must. If you suffer from stress or anxiety, you may find the book helpful too.

Mindfulness CDs

If you want to listen to CDs on mindfulness, try these, from the developer of mindfulness in the West, Jon Kabat-Zinn. Visit www.mindfulnesscds.com or www.learnmindfulness.co.uk to purchase them.

You can choose from a good variety of Mindfulness CDs, starting from the core mindfulness practices, such as the body scan and sitting meditation, to mindful visualisations, like the lake and mountain meditations. There is even a selection of extensive mindful yoga practice CDs to help build your strength and flexibility as well as your capacity to be mindful. Getting CDs from different teachers is a good idea, especially if you like to be guided through your mindfulness meditations to help you experience the range of different ways to practise.

Life Is Beautiful DVD

Co-written, directed and starring Roberto Benigni, this Oscar-winning Italian film is a simultaneously hilarious and haunting comedy out of the tragedy of the Holocaust. The film is a poignant tale of a father's sacrifice to save both his son's life and his innocence in the face of one of the most evil acts inflicted by humanity. The film is actually called *La vita é bella* and is one of my favourite movies, but it's not just me – it's the most widely acclaimed foreign film in US history. Its most powerful lesson is how you can somehow turn the most dark and depressing situation into something completely different by changing the perspective. Mindfulness is partly about seeing things from a bigger perspective, and in this way, transforming your experience – this is creatively and cleverly shown by the genius of Benigni.

Retreats and Lectures

You can't deepen your experience of mindfulness unless you attend a retreat.

Gaia House

Set in a rural area in Devon, south-western England, Gaia House offers mostly silent retreats, and mainly in the Buddhist tradition, led by teachers from all over the world. The organisation was founded in 1983, and offers weekend and week-long retreats there throughout the year.

The silence is designed to help deepen the practice of meditation. Although many people find silence intimidating, in practice, most people say that the silence was what they most enjoyed on their first retreat. You don't need to strike up idle conversation, you can focus on whatever you're doing, and the lack of talking helps to calm the mind.

Although the participants are in silence, the teacher isn't. The teacher often explains and guides the meditations, and if you feel overwhelmed by the experience, there are usually ways to speak to someone about it.

Gaia House offers:

- ✔ **Group retreats.** These retreats are teacher-led over fixed dates, including some one-day retreats.

- ✔ **Personal retreats.** These individual retreats last from one week to several months.

- ✔ **Work retreats.** These retreats offer an opportunity to combine periods of daily work, doing things like gardening or cooking, with intensive meditation, if that's what you fancy. Remember, take one step at a time!

I've been on retreat at Gaia House and the teachers were excellent. Book yourself in well in advance – the courses fill up very quickly. Visit www.gaia house.co.uk.

Mind and Life Institute

The Mind and Life Institute in Boulder, Colorado, encourages a collaboration and research partnership between top Buddhist scholars, including the Dalai Lama, and scientists to help deepen understanding of the nature of reality and promote human wellbeing. The Mind and Life Institute works to support contemplative, compassionate and rigorous scientific research into the effect of mindfulness on the brain to help inform medicine, psychology, neuroscience and education.

The Mind and Life Institute believes that in order for meditation and science to have a long-lasting contribution to society, collaborative research needs to be carried out in world-renowned scientific laboratories and the results need to be published in prominent peer-review journals. So far, research has focused on collecting data from highly experienced meditators using the latest brain-imaging techniques and other scientific measures.

You can get involved in the Institute by attending public meetings between the Dalai Lama and scientists, and public conferences designed to stimulate interest, reading the Institute's publications, or perhaps getting involved in collaborative research projects or educational programmes.

Conferences in the last few years include 'Investigating the Body-mind Connection', 'Mindfulness, Compassion and the Treatment of Depression', and 'Altruism and Compassion in Economic Systems'.

Audio recordings available from the website include 'Educating world citizens for the 21st century', 'The science of a compassionate life', and 'The science and clinical applications of meditation'.

Visit www.mindandlife.org for more information.

Plum Village

Plum Village is a Buddhist retreat centre founded by Thich Nhat Hanh in southern France. I attended a retreat there and enjoyed the light-hearted atmosphere, mixed with the incisive and fascinating talks by Thich Nhat Hanh himself every morning. The retreat was partly in silence, especially at meal times. Everyone seems to enjoy the silence. The summer retreats are also family-friendly, so you can bring the kids along too!

Here's a typical schedule:

5:30 a.m.	Rise
6:00 a.m.	Sitting and walking meditations
7:30 a.m.	Breakfast
9:00 a.m.	Lecture by Thich Nhat Hanh
12:30 p.m.	Lunch
2:00 p.m.	Rest
3:00 p.m.	Class/Study time
6:00 p.m.	Dinner
8:00 p.m.	Exercise
9:30 p.m.	Silence begins
10:30 p.m.	Lights out

If that sounds appealing and you like Thich Nhat Hanh, look out for his summer retreat and book yourself in – he won't be able to teach forever! Visit www.plumvillage.org for more details.

Index

• E •

• **G** •

• R •

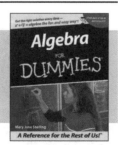

FOR DUMMIES®

A world of resources to help you grow

UK editions

SELF-HELP

978-0-470-74830-5

978-0-470-74764-3

978-0-470-68472-6

Neuro-linguistic Programming
For Dummies
978-0-7645-7028-5

Origami Kit For Dummies
978-0-470-75857-1

Overcoming Depression For Dummies
978-0-470-69430-5

Positive Psychology For Dummies
978-0-470-72136-0

PRINCE2 For Dummies, 2009 Edition
978-0-470-71025-8

Psychometric Tests For Dummies
978-0-470-75366-8

Raising Happy Children
For Dummies
978-0-470-05978-4

Reading the Financial Pages
For Dummies
978-0-470-71432-4

Sage 50 Accounts For Dummies
978-0-470-71558-1

Starting a Business For Dummies,
2nd Edition
978-0-470-51806-9

Study Skills For Dummies
978-0-470-74047-7

Teaching English as a Foreign
Language For Dummies
978-0-470-74576-2

Teaching Skills For Dummies
978-0-470-74084-2

Time Management For Dummies
978-0-470-77765-7

Work-Life Balance For Dummies
978-0-470-71380-8

STUDENTS

978-0-470-74747-6

978-0-470-74711-7

978-0-470-74290-7

HISTORY

978-0-470-99468-9

978-0-470-51015-5

978-0-470-98787-2